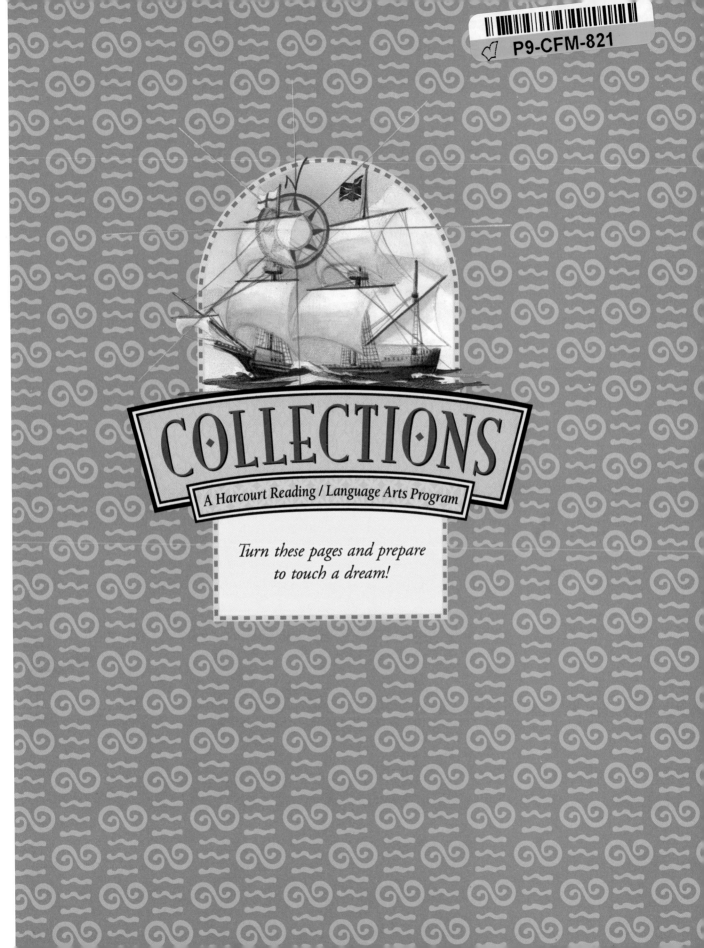

COLLECTIONS

A Harcourt Reading / Language Arts Program

*Turn these pages and prepare
to touch a dream!*

COLLECTIONS
A Harcourt Reading / Language Arts Program

TOUCH A DREAM

SENIOR AUTHORS
Roger C. Farr • Dorothy S. Strickland • Isabel L. Beck

AUTHORS
Richard F. Abrahamson • Alma Flor Ada • Bernice E. Cullinan • Margaret McKeown • Nancy Roser
Patricia Smith • Judy Wallis • Junko Yokota • Hallie Kay Yopp

SENIOR CONSULTANT
Asa G. Hilliard III

CONSULTANTS
Karen S. Kutiper • David A. Monti • Angelina Olivares

Harcourt

Orlando Boston Dallas Chicago San Diego

Visit *The Learning Site!*

www.harcourtschool.com

Printed in the United States of America

ISBN 0-15-312048-7

1 2 3 4 5 6 7 8 9 10   048   2003 2002 2001

Dear Reader,

Everybody has a dream. Some dreams are simple; some are grand. Dreams are those special hopes that we aim for. What's your dream?

In **Touch a Dream,** you will read about people reaching for their biggest goals and making them happen. Some of these people travel to new lands to study rare plants and animals, or to find a new home. Others simply plant a small garden in their city neighborhood. You'll discover some people who help those around them, while others strive to meet their own goals. Every time you read a different story, you will discover a new dream.

Each dream that you read about in this book can teach you a lesson about life. Learn how real people and story characters solve problems or handle changes in their lives. Then use what you learn to help find your own dream.

Now, keep your eyes and your mind wide open, turn the page, and prepare to touch a dream.

Sincerely,

The Authors

The Authors

THEME

YOU CAN DO IT!

CONTENTS

THEME

SIDE BY SIDE

CAR WASH

CONTENTS

THEME MAKE YOURSELF AT HOME

CONTENTS

CREATIVE MINDS

CONTENTS

Community

Contents

Ties

Theme

NEW LANDS

Contents

Using Reading Strategies

A strategy is a plan for doing something well.

You probably already use some strategies as you read. For example, you may **look at the title and illustrations before you begin reading** a story. You may **think about what you want to find out while reading.** Using strategies like these can help you become a better reader.

Look at the list of strategies on page 17. You will learn about and use these strategies as you read the selections in this book. As you read, look back at the list to remind yourself of the **strategies good readers use.**

Strategies Good Readers Use

- Use Prior Knowledge
- Make and Confirm Predictions
- Adjust Reading Rate
- Self-Question
- Create Mental Images
- Use Context to Confirm Meaning

- Use Text Structure and Format
- Use Graphic Aids
- Use Reference Sources
- Read Ahead
- Reread
- Summarize and Paraphrase

Here are some ways to check your own comprehension:

✔ Make a copy of this list on a piece of construction paper shaped like a bookmark.

✔ Have it handy as you read.

✔ After reading, talk with a classmate about which strategies you used and why.

17

THEME YOU CAN DO IT!

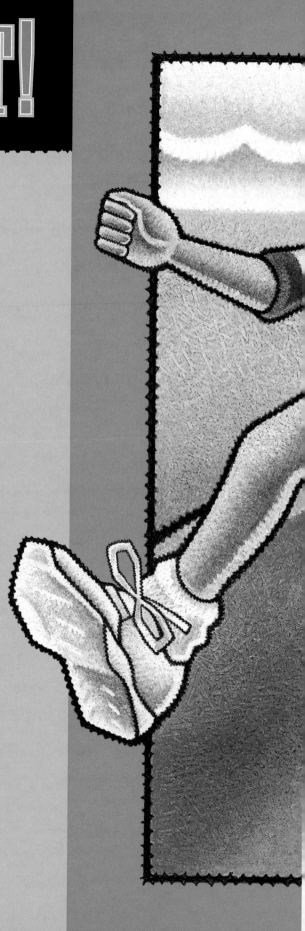

CONTENTS

READER'S CHOICE

Under the Lemon Moon
by Edith Hope Fine

HISPANIC FOLKTALE

Rosalinda's lemon tree stops growing after someone takes all the lemons. In her search for help for her lemon tree, Rosalinda learns a valuable lesson in forgiveness.

READER'S CHOICE LIBRARY

Kate Shelley and the Midnight Express
by Margaret Wetterer

HISTORICAL FICTION

When Kate hears the bridge collapse and the train plunge into the river, she comes to the rescue despite her own fear. Will her heroic actions save the people on the next train?

Notable Social Studies Trade Book
READER'S CHOICE LIBRARY

Granddaddy's Street Songs
by Monalisa DeGross

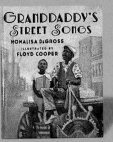

HISTORICAL FICTION

Roddy loves to hear his Granddaddy tell him stories about "the old days" when, as he drove a horse-drawn wagon through the streets, he called out to customers to sell his fruits and vegetables.

Baseball Fever
by Johanna Hurwitz

REALISTIC FICTION

Ezra's scholarly father wants him to develop interests in something other than baseball, but Ezra finds a way to get his father interested in baseball.

Award-Winning Author

Blizzards
by Lorraine Jean Hopping

NONFICTION

Read about some notorious blizzards. Then discover how science uses clues from data to help predict similar storms.

THE
Gardener

Caldecott
Honor Book
ALA Notable Book
Teachers' Choice

by Sarah Stewart

illustrated by David Small

August 27, 1935

Dear Uncle Jim,

Grandma told us after supper that you want me to come to the city and live with you until things get better. Did she tell you that Papa has been out of work for a long time, and no one asks Mama to make dresses anymore?

We all cried, even Papa. But then Mama made us laugh with her stories about your chasing her up trees when you were both little. Did you really do that?

I'm small, but strong, and I'll help you all I can. However, Grandma said to finish my schoolwork before doing anything else.

Your niece,
Lydia Grace Finch

September 3, 1935

Dear Uncle Jim,

    I'm mailing this from the train station. I forgot to tell you in the last letter *three important things* that I'm too shy to say to your face:

    1. I know a lot about gardening, but nothing about baking.

    2. I'm anxious to learn to bake, but is there any place to plant seeds?

    3. I like to be called "Lydia Grace"—just like Grandma.

        Your niece,
        Lydia Grace Finch

On the train
September 4, 1935

Dear Mama,

    I feel so pretty in your dress that you made over for me. I hope you don't miss it too much.

Dear Papa,

    I haven't forgotten what you said about recognizing Uncle Jim: "Just look for Mama's face with a big nose and a mustache!" I promise not to tell him. (Does he have a sense of humor?)

And, dearest Grandma,

    Thank you for the seeds. The train is rocking me to sleep, and every time I doze off, I dream of gardens.

Love to all,
Lydia Grace

September 5, 1935

Dear Mama, Papa, and Grandma,
  I'm so excited!!!
  There are window boxes here! They look as if they've been waiting for me, so now we'll both wait for spring.
  And, Grandma, the sun shines down on the corner where I'll live and work.

Love to all,
Lydia Grace

P. S. Uncle Jim doesn't smile.

December 25, 1935

Dear Mama, Papa, and Grandma,

I adore the seed catalogues you sent for Christmas. And, Grandma, thank you for all the bulbs. I hope you received my drawings.

I wrote a long poem for Uncle Jim. He didn't smile, but I think he liked it. He read it aloud, then put it in his shirt pocket and patted it.

Love to all,
Lydia Grace

February 12, 1936

Dearest Grandma,

Thank you again for those bulbs you sent at Christmas. You should see them now!

I really like Ed and Emma Beech, Uncle Jim's friends who work here. When I first arrived, Emma told me she'd show me how to knead bread if I would teach her the Latin names of all the flowers I know. Now, just half a year later, I'm kneading bread and she's speaking Latin!

More good news: We have a store cat named Otis who at this very moment is sleeping at the foot of *my* bed.

Love to all,
Lydia Grace

P. S. Uncle Jim isn't smiling yet, but I'm hoping for a smile soon.

March 5, 1936

Dear Mama, Papa, and Grandma,

I've discovered a secret place. You can't imagine how wonderful it is. No one else knows about it but Otis.

I have great plans.

Thank you for all the letters. I'll try to write more, but I'm really busy planting all your seeds in cracked teacups and bent cake pans! And, Grandma, you should smell the good dirt I'm bringing home from the vacant lot down the street.

Love to all,
Lydia Grace

April 27, 1936

Dearest Grandma,

 All the seeds and roots are sprouting. I can hear you saying, "April showers bring May flowers."

 Emma and I are sprucing up the bakery and I'm playing a great trick on Uncle Jim. He sees me reading my mail, planting seeds in the window boxes, going to school, doing my homework, sweeping the floor. But he never sees me working in my secret place.

     Love to all,
     Lydia Grace

P. S. I'm planning on a big smile from Uncle Jim in the near future.

May 27, 1936

Dear Mama, Papa, and Grandma,
    You should have heard Emma laugh today when I opened your letter and dirt fell out onto the sidewalk! Thank you for all the baby plants. They survived the trip in the big envelope.
    More about Emma: She's helping me with the secret place. Hurrah!

                    Love to all,
                    Lydia Grace

P. S. I saw Uncle Jim almost smile today. The store was full (well, *almost* full) of customers.

June 27, 1936

Dear Grandma,

Flowers are blooming all over the place. I'm also growing radishes, onions, and three kinds of lettuce in the window boxes.

Some neighbors have brought containers for me to fill with flowers, and a few customers even gave me plants from their gardens this spring! They don't call me "Lydia Grace" anymore. They call me "the gardener."

Love to all,
Lydia Grace

P. S. I'm sure Uncle Jim will smile soon. I'm almost ready to show him the secret place.

July 4, 1936

Dearest Mama, Papa, and Grandma,

    I am bursting with happiness! The entire city seems so beautiful, especially this morning.

    The secret place is ready for Uncle Jim. At noon, the store will close for the holiday, and then we'll bring him up to the roof.

    I've tried to remember everything you ever taught me about beauty.

Love to all,
Lydia Grace

P. S. I can already imagine Uncle Jim's smile.

July 11, 1936

Dear Mama, Papa, and Grandma,

My heart is pounding so hard I'm sure the customers can hear it downstairs!

At lunch today, Uncle Jim put the "Closed" sign on the door and told Ed and Emma and me to go upstairs and wait. He appeared with the most amazing cake I've ever seen— covered in flowers!

I truly believe that cake equals one thousand smiles.

And then he took your letter out of his pocket with the news of Papa's job!

I'M COMING HOME!

Love to all, and see you soon,
Lydia Grace

P. S. Grandma, I've given all of my plants to Emma. I can't wait to help you in your garden again. We gardeners never retire.

Think About It

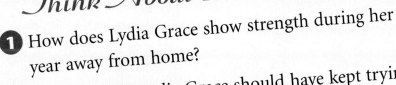

1. How does Lydia Grace show strength during her year away from home?

2. Do you think Lydia Grace should have kept trying to get Uncle Jim to smile? Explain your answer.

3. What information do readers learn from the pictures that Lydia Grace's letters do not tell?

43

NET WT.
200 mg.

SEEDS

$1.⁵⁹

Meet the Author
Sarah Stewart

Sarah Stewart grew up in Texas. As a young girl, she found strength in "safe places" like the library and the garden. She believes both places are full of hope. Books make readers think of all the things they can be and do, and it is inspiring to watch seeds grow into plants. At home today, Ms. Stewart has a library—and five gardens! Ms. Stewart has written poetry and speeches as well as books for children. Her suggestions for writers include studying Latin, reading poems, and taking time to be quiet.

44

David Small grew up in the large city of Detroit, Michigan. He remembers being glad to get away from all the factory buildings when he spent vacations with his grandmother in the country. There was no television, so he played outside a lot when he was there. One day David saw a mural by Diego Rivera in a Detroit museum. It showed something that was part of the real world around him—workers making cars. He decided he wanted to try art himself. Mr. Small has written and illustrated a number of books for children. He is married to Sarah Stewart.

NET WT. 200 mg.

SEEDS

$1.59

Meet the Illustrator David Small

Visit *The Learning Site!*
www.harcourtschool.com

45

Response

Letters and Flowers

MAKE A COLLAGE

It is hard for Lydia Grace to leave her family for a year. Make a collage showing some of the things she does to help herself get through this challenging time. Paste pictures from old magazines and garden catalogs onto a sheet of thick paper. You might also include old letters, used postage stamps, and the names of flowers.

Plant Potting for Beginners

WRITE A HOW-TO PARAGRAPH

Lydia Grace creates a beautiful garden of potted plants. Write a paragraph telling how to pot a plant. In a group, find information in gardening books, on the Internet, or from a plant-store worker or a gardener. In your paragraph, include the materials needed. List the steps in the order they should be done. You could use your paragraph to make an instructional tape or video.

Activities

An Amazing Cake

MAKE A PICTURE

Uncle Jim makes an amazing flower-covered cake to thank Lydia Grace, Ed, and Emma for the garden. Design your own amazing, one-of-a-kind cake for a special event or a special person you know. Draw or paint a picture of your cake. Write a caption telling why the cake is decorated the way it is.

Smile Awhile

WRITE A POEM

Lydia Grace looks for ways to make Uncle Jim smile. As Lydia Grace does, write a poem that will make someone you care about smile. Think about what might make the person feel happy. When you have finished writing the poem, you may want to give it to that person.

Narrative Elements

T he most important narrative elements, or story parts, are **character**, **setting**, and **plot**. To write "The Gardener," the author had to decide

- who the people in the story would be (characters)
- where and when the story would take place (setting)
- what would happen (plot)

This story map gives information about the narrative elements of "The Gardener."

> The plot usually involves a problem faced by the main character. The plot shows how the character solves the problem.

Characters
Lydia Grace, Uncle Jim, Papa, Mama, Grandma, Ed and Emma Beech

Setting
a city in the United States, 1935–1936

PLOT

Problem
Lydia Grace has to go to the city to stay with her Uncle Jim, a baker. Uncle Jim never smiles.

Solution
Lydia Grace plants seeds and baby plants wherever she can. She turns the roof into an outdoor garden as a surprise for Uncle Jim. He bakes a flower-covered cake to show he is pleased.

Every story has the three narrative elements of character, setting, and plot. You can learn about the characters by what they say and do and by what others say about them.

Sometimes you must use clues to figure out the time and place of the setting.

Read the paragraph below. Look for clues about the characters, the setting, and the plot. Use a story map like the one on page 48 to record what you learn.

Sam looked up at the stars from his aunt's attic room. "It's so quiet out here in the country," he thought, but he knew he'd soon get used to the farm and have fun. Tomorrow his cousin Alicia would take him horseback riding!

WHAT HAVE YOU LEARNED?

1. Who are the main characters in "The Gardener"? How do you learn about them?

2. How important to the plot is the setting of "The Gardener"? Could the story take place somewhere else? Explain.

Visit *The Learning Site!*
www.harcourtschool.com

TRY THIS ● TRY THIS ● TRY THIS

Plan a story of your own. It can be set in the past, the present, or the future, here or far away. The characters can be like you and your friends, or they can be different. The plot should show the characters working out some problem. Make a story map and fill in details about your story.

Donavan's Word Jar

by **Monalisa DeGross**
illustrated by **Antonio Cangemi**

DONAVAN'S WORD JAR

DEGROSS DONAVAN'S WORD JAR

MONALISA DEGROSS

All of Donavan Allen's friends like to collect things. For example, his friend Pooh collects buttons. Donavan's collection is different. He collects words. Soon Donavan's word jar is full. He wants to keep collecting words, but he has no more room! Donavan decides to go see Grandma, hoping she can help him solve his problem. His little sister, Nikki, has a cold, and before he goes, Donavan shows her some of his words to help her feel better.

Donavan was reading when he heard his father's footsteps in the hall. He got up from his chair and tiptoed across the room. He didn't want Nikki to wake up. They had played with his words until she picked the word LULLABY. To give her a hint, Donavan sang her a song. Nikki was so tired from playing that she fell asleep.

Donavan's father opened the door and peeped into Nikki's room. Donavan put his finger to his lips to keep his father from speaking. He picked up his jar and followed his father down the stairs and into the kitchen.

"How are you doing, partner?" his father asked.

"Fine, and Nikki's feeling a lot better," Donavan said quickly. Before his father could ask another question, Donavan rushed on. "Can I go over to Grandma's and visit? It's really important." Donavan didn't want to waste another minute. He had had fun keeping Nikki company, but now he wanted to get his problem solved.

"Okay, but you watch yourself crossing the streets in the rain," his dad said. "And Donavan, why don't you ask your grandma if she's free to come to dinner tonight? Tell her I'm doing the cooking," he added.

"I will," Donavan called over his shoulder. He was already pulling on his shiny green slicker, rain hat and yellow rubber boots. He tucked his word jar in the crook of his arm. He thought if his grandma could see his problem, it might help her to come up with a great idea. Donavan opened the kitchen door and stepped out into the steady drizzle.

Donavan pushed open the heavy glass doors to the Mellow View Apartments. He smiled at Mr. Bill Gut, the security guard, as he signed his name in the guest book. Donavan pushed the button and got onto the elevator. His grandma lived on the fourth floor. Donavan didn't like where Grandma lived now. Everyone there seemed so gloomy. He wondered if all senior citizens' apartment buildings were like that. He missed the big house that Grandma used to live in, with its front porch and large backyard. Grandma had decided that her old house was too large after Grandpop died, so she sold it and moved. Now Grandma lived in the senior citizens' building just a few blocks from where Donavan lived. He could see her anytime he wanted, and that was the best thing about her new apartment.

Donavan knocked on the apartment door and waited. When his grandma opened the door and saw him, she smiled.

"Donnie! What a pleasant surprise," Grandma said, opening the door wider. "It's nice to see you. Come in."

Donavan went inside and began to take off his coat. He looked around Grandma's apartment. His grandma was a collector, too. She collected anything given to her by her family and friends. Donavan thought this was a silly idea the first time she explained it to him. But then he decided that he liked the way Grandma's different collections blended together. Her apartment reminded him of a patchwork quilt—colorful, warm, and cozy. Old-fashioned dolls in lace-trimmed dresses were propped against an assortment of pretty teapots. Strange seashells of different shapes and sizes surrounded potted philodendron, ivy, and African violets in small clay pots. Tin cans with faded labels from long, long ago shared a shelf with tiny ceramic animals. Grandma also collected fancy old hats. She had a large felt hat with lots of peacock feathers. Another hat was box-shaped and covered with a veil. The veil was sprinkled with lots of glittery stars. In the bands of some of her hats, Grandma had stuck postcards friends had sent her from faraway places. One postcard invited her to "Sunny, funny Acapulco." Another postcard said that things were just "Dandy in Dixieland."

Donavan's favorite place in Grandma's apartment was her picture wall. Here she displayed photographs of people she knew and liked. Grandma said that if she had not seen a person for a long time, she would visit her wall. So whenever he missed his grandpop, Donavan would go to the wall and visit him.

"Donnie," Grandma called from the kitchen, "would you like to have some lunch?"

"Is it soup?" Donavan loved Grandma's soup.

"Yes, it's your favorite, and I have plenty of crackers," Grandma answered. "Did you call your dad and let him know that you got here safely?" Grandma asked.

"Not yet, I'm getting ready to do it now. I'll tell Dad I'm staying for lunch," Donavan said. He wondered which of his favorite soups Grandma had fixed, he had so many.

After lunch, Donavan set his jar on the dining room table and explained his problem to his grandma. When he finished talking, he sat back in his chair and waited for her solution.

Grandma reached over and plucked a few slips of paper from Donavan's jar. She looked at a slip of paper and laughed.

"Donnie," Grandma said, "do you remember when Pooh traded your ice-cream cone for a broken kite?"

"I won't ever forget that," Donavan said, frowning. Grandma showed him the word BAMBOOZLE, and they both laughed. "And this word EMPORIUM," Grandma said shaking her head slowly. "It makes me think of long ago, when I was a young girl. I used to buy licorice at Mr. McCready's store." She selected another word from the jar. "Donnie, where did you get this word?" she asked. She was surprised to see

KALEIDOSCOPE written on the slip of paper. "I haven't seen one of those in years. I wonder if kids still play with them."

"I have never seen a kaleidoscope, Grandma, but I saw a picture of one in an old catalog. That's where I found the word," Donavan answered.

Grandma read several more words before she looked at Donavan over the rims of her wire glasses.

"Donnie," she said, "you sure have got yourself a treasure here. This is a wonderful collection of words." Donavan smiled and sat up a little straighter.

Grandma's praise made him feel good, but Donavan still needed a solution to his problem.

"Do you see my problem, Grandma?" he asked. "I thought of getting a larger jar, but that would only get full, too."

"Well, honey, what do other collectors do when their collections grow too large?" she asked.

"I dunno," Donavan said. He thought about it for a minute. "Well, Pooh collects buttons, but he never gets too many because he trades them for other things."

"Like what?" Grandma asked.

"Sometimes he trades for a poster, or for a few comics. Once he traded three buttons for a T-shirt," Donavan explained.

"You think you could do that?" Grandma asked.

"No, Grandma, I can't think of anything I could get worth my words," he said. "And I really don't want to give any of my words away," he added.

Grandma settled back in her chair. She didn't say anything for a long while, and Donavan began to feel a little uneasy. Maybe, just maybe, his grandma didn't have a solution.

She dipped her hand back into the word jar and pulled out a few more words.

"There are some words in this jar that I know folks living here could use," she said. Donavan slipped to the edge of his chair and wondered what his grandma was going to say. She continued.

"Now, I like the word PERSNICKETY. That word fits Miz Marylou to a T. That woman has to have everything she does just right." Grandma slipped another word from the jar. "CANTANKEROUS—that's a perfect word for our guard, Bill Gut. I'll bet he argues with flies."

Grandma laughed and Donavan joined in. He loved the sound of his grandma's laughter. After they caught their breaths, Grandma said, "I enjoyed your words, Donnie. I'm sure a lot of people would." She smiled at him and waited to see if he had something to say.

"Grandma, I'd be glad to let any of your friends see my words. But they couldn't keep them—I'd have to have them back for my collection." Donavan's voice was firm.

"Well, I am sorry if I didn't help you."

"Oh, Grandma, that's okay," Donavan answered, trying hard not to show his disappointment. He did not want to hurt his grandma's feelings. "Besides," he said getting up from the table, "if we don't have a solution today, maybe you'll think of something tomorrow."

Grandma helped him with his boots, hat, and coat. Donavan picked up his word jar and tucked it firmly under his arm. Grandma walked with him to the door.

"Take care of yourself, 'Wordgatherer,'" she said, hugging him close.

In the elevator, Donavan thought about his word jar. It had taken months, weeks, days, and hours to fill it. Deciding which words to keep was hard. Then Donavan checked the spelling and made sure he understood what each new word meant. What had his grandma been thinking of? It seemed like she wanted him to just give his words away. He loved his word collection. But he had to think of a way to handle it, now that it was growing so large.

The elevator doors opened, and Donavan stepped into the lounge. He saw three of Grandma's neighbors sitting around the television set. They didn't seem to care much what was on. And there was Mr. Perkins, sitting by the window, looking at the raindrops hitting the windowpane. Miss Millie had a magazine opened on her lap, but she wasn't reading it. Mr. Crawford, the mailman, was sitting on a hassock rubbing his feet. He looked as if he couldn't take another step. No one in the room was talking to or looking at each other, except Miz Marylou and Mr. Bill Gut.

They were standing at the security guard's desk arguing very loudly. No one else was paying any attention to them. As Donavan walked closer he could hear every word they said.

"Miz Marylou, this lounge will open or close when I say so," Mr. Bill Gut said in a gruff voice.

"Well, I am telling you, Bill, that's a mistake. That should be decided by the people who live here," she answered back.

"I'm the guard, and I say what goes on in this lounge," Mr. Bill Gut bellowed.

"Well, I live here and I say that people who live here should set the time," Miz Marylou said almost as loudly.

Donavan looked from one to the other. They both began to shout at the same time, since neither one was listening to what the other was saying. Donavan set his word jar on the corner of the desk and dug around inside the jar until he found a certain word. He tugged Miz Marylou's sleeve and then Mr. Bill's jacket. They both looked down, surprised to see Donavan standing there.

"I think you two need this word," Donavan said in a stern voice.

They both looked at the yellow slip of paper in Donavan's hand. Miz Marylou giggled, and Mr. Bill Gut smiled.

"Well, Marylou, what time do you think is a good time to open?" Mr. Bill Gut asked, scratching his head.

"Bill, I checked with a couple of people and they suggested ten o'clock. What do you think of that?" Miz Marylou asked, smiling at Mr. Bill Gut.

Donavan let out a loud sigh of relief. He had come at just the right time—they needed the word COMPROMISE. Miz Marylou and Mr. Bill weren't shouting anymore. They were talking to each other quietly; they were coming to an agreement. That sure made Donavan feel good. His word had been just what they needed.

Donavan suddenly remembered that his father had asked him to invite Grandma to dinner. He ran back to the elevator and pushed the UP button.

"Back so soon?" Grandma asked, opening the door. "I thought you had gone home."

"I forgot to invite you to dinner tonight. Dad is going to cook. Do you want to come around?" Donavan asked.

compromise

It didn't take Grandma long to make up her mind. She loved Donavan's father's cooking.

"Well, I certainly do—in fact, why don't I just get my coat and walk with you?" Grandma suggested. "Maybe we could talk about your word jar a little bit more," she said.

Donavan waited while Grandma got her coat and locked her apartment door. She was carrying a big brown paper sack, and he wondered what was in it. As they walked down the hall, Donavan began to tell Grandma about how he had helped Miz Marylou and Mr. Bill Gut.

When Grandma and Donavan got to the lounge, Donavan could not believe what he saw. Grandma's neighbors were up and around, laughing and talking. They all seemed excited. He looked around to see what was going on. Donavan saw that they were waving little yellow slips of paper in their hands.

"MY WORDS! THEY HAVE MY WORDS!" Donavan shouted.

Some people had one slip of paper in their hands, others had two. Mr. Avery was no longer slumped in front of the TV. He was tacking one of Donavan's words up on the bulletin board. Miss Millie was looking up the word on her slip of paper in a pocket dictionary. Donavan looked over at the desk and saw Mrs. Agnes digging into his word jar. There were people in a line behind her laughing and talking. They were waiting to get a word from his jar.

"WHAT'S GOING ON?" Donavan asked, as loud as he could. "GRANDMA! STOP THEM. THEY ARE TAKING MY WORDS!" He turned to his grandma, but she looked just as surprised as he felt.

"Donnie, calm down. They didn't know. You left the jar on the desk," she said in a quiet voice.

"I AM GOING TO GET MY WORD JAR," Donavan said firmly. "EXCUSE ME," he shouted. "EXCUSE ME, MAY I GET PAST?" he yelled, moving through the crowd. He pushed a little, he even shoved a bit. It was no use. Donavan couldn't stop what was happening.

Mr. Crawford, the mailman, passed Donavan and waved his word over his head. "PERSEVERANCE," he called out. "That's just the word I need. Some days I get so tired, I can

hardly make it. I'm going to try just a little harder to keep going," he said, tucking the word in his shirt pocket.

Donavan stopped pushing and stood still.

"Wow! One of my words made Mr. Crawford feel better," Donavan said. He looked around and saw Miss Millie talking to Mr. Foote. Donavan was surprised.

"BOISTEROUS," he heard Miss Millie say in her soft voice. Grandma always told Donavan that Miss Millie was so shy that she hardly ever spoke to anyone.

Mr. Foote, on the other hand, spoke to everyone. "Well, I'll be darned," Mr. Foote said in surprise. "My word is TIMID!"

"Perhaps we should exchange words," Miss Millie suggested.

"Oh, no. Maybe I need to quiet down some. Sometimes I am a bit loud," Mr. Foote said softly.

"You're right, I think I'll keep my word too. I am going to start speaking to people more. I am going to change my ways." Miss Millie's voice sounded like she meant it.

"Did my words do that, make them want to change?" Donavan asked himself in surprise.

All around him, Grandma's neighbors were laughing and talking to each other. They had never acted so lively before.

"Nikki was right. Words can make people feel better," Donavan said quietly.

"Donavan!" Miz Marylou called out, as she walked over and stood next to him. "Your words are wonderful. I just couldn't help myself, after you gave Bill and me a word, I . . . I . . . well, I got carried away. I just gave Mr. Kincaid the word LEISURE. That man works entirely too hard," she said smiling. "And Donavan, people just started coming up and asking for words, and if they didn't get one they wanted, they just traded it." She looked so pleased, it was hard for Donavan not to smile.

Mr. Bill Gut came over and pinched Donavan's cheeks. Mr. Perkins patted his shoulders. Everyone wanted to thank him for sharing his words. Donavan felt as if the sun had come out inside him. Mr. Bill Gut pointed to the empty jar on the desk and said, "Looks like we cleaned you out, young fellow."

When Grandma pushed through the crowd, she looked worried.

"Donnie, are all of your words gone?" she asked. "Honey, I am so sorry, I know you didn't want to give your words away. Maybe you could ask for them back?" she said.

Donavan looked up at her and smiled.

"Grandma, they love my words. The words made them talk to each other. Look," he said, pointing to Mr. Foote and Miss Millie. "They are talking to each other." Donavan was so excited. "And Grandma, Mr. Crawford the mailman doesn't look so tired anymore." Grandma looked around the room and smiled.

"Donnie, you know Mr. Mike got the word CHORTLE, and I actually heard him giggle," she said laughing. "But, Donnie, they didn't give you anything for your words." Grandma was still worried.

"Yes, they did. They made me feel like a magician. My words changed them." The sunshine Donavan felt inside was shining all over his face.

Think About It

1. What does Donavan discover about the words he has collected? How does he make this discovery?

2. Do you think Donavan shows strength or weakness when he finds that the neighbors are taking his words? Tell why you think as you do.

3. What idea do you think the author wants readers to get from this story?

Meet the Author

Monalisa DeGross

How did you become interested in writing?
When I was younger I was always trying to create something. As an adult, I found that when I created stories in my head and wrote them down, I was creating stories for picture and chapter books.

You wrote about Donavan's relationship with his grandmother. Your new book is Grandaddy's Street Songs. *Is there a message in that?*
Yes. I want kids to understand the wonderful and powerful relationship that can be found from knowing and interacting with someone from another generation. It's an excellent way to find out how things were long ago.

Visit *The Learning Site!*
www.harcourtschool.com

Monalisa De Gross

69

I Love the Look of Words

Popcorn leaps, popping from the floor
of a hot black skillet
and into my mouth.
Black words leap,
snapping from the white
page. Rushing into my eyes. Sliding
into my brain which gobbles them
the way my tongue and teeth
chomp the buttered popcorn.

When I have stopped reading,
ideas from the words stay stuck
in my mind, like the sweet
smell of butter perfuming my
fingers long after the popcorn
is finished.

I love the book and the look of words
the weight of ideas that popped into my mind
I love the tracks
of new thinking in my mind.

by Maya Angelou
illustrated by Tom Feelings

TOM FEELINGS
SOUL LOOKS BACK
IN WONDER

ALA Notable
Book
Coretta Scott
King Award

71

Collectors All

CONDUCT A SURVEY

Donavan collects words, and his grandma collects hats, photos, and many other items. Find out what a few of your classmates collect. Ask how and why they began collecting. Show your findings in a chart. For each classmate, include this information: name, kind of collection, and reasons for collecting.

Response Activities

Making Connections

WRITE A POEM

In "I Love the Look of Words," the poet uses words to form pictures in the reader's mind. Donavan uses words to express ideas. Choose one of Donavan's words and write a poem about it. Have your poem express the meaning of the word.

On the Scene

CONDUCT INTERVIEWS

Imagine that a TV news reporter was on the scene when Grandma's neighbors chose words from Donavan's jar. With some classmates, role-play interviews between the reporter and the neighbors. The reporter should ask which word each person chose and how the word helped him or her.

Persnickety Snake, Cantankerous Kangaroo

DRAW A CARTOON CHARACTER

Donavan collected some very descriptive adjectives, such as *persnickety* and *cantankerous*. Find an adjective of your own that could be used to describe a cartoon character you make up. Be sure you understand exactly what your adjective means. Then draw your character. Write a caption that includes the adjective.

My Name Is María Isabel

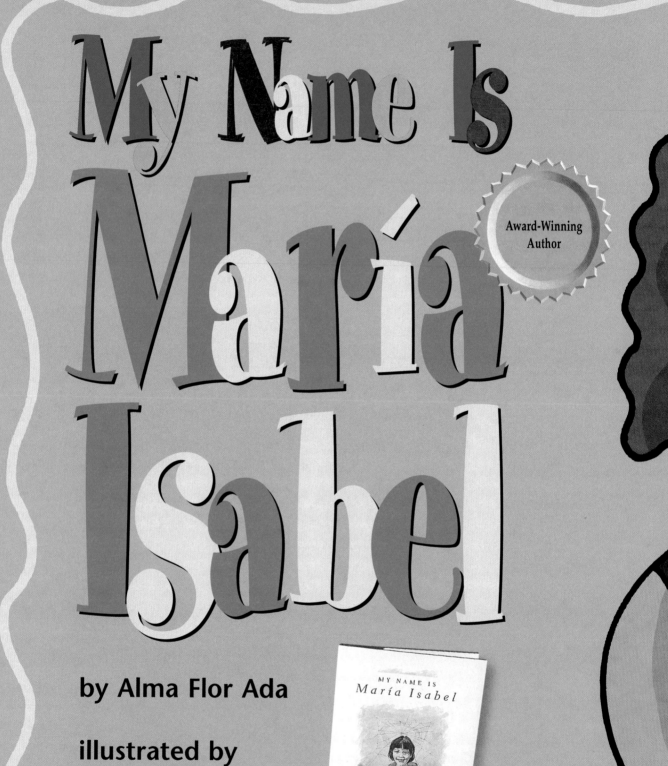

by Alma Flor Ada

illustrated by
José Ortega

María Isabel Salazar López is proud of being named for her Puerto Rican grandmothers. She has a problem, though. Her teacher calls her Mary López because there are two other Marías in the class. María Isabel sometimes doesn't recognize her new name. She does not have a part in the play *Amahl and the Night Visitors* because the teacher called on Mary López when she assigned parts, and María Isabel didn't respond. The play is the main part of the school's Winter Pageant. Every day, the pageant draws closer, and María Isabel knows her parents are eager to see her in the show.

Everything at school now revolved around plans for the Winter Pageant. The class was making wreaths and lanterns. The teacher explained to the class that Christmas is celebrated differently in different countries, and that many people don't celebrate Christmas at all. They talked about Santa Claus, and how he is called Saint Nicholas in some countries and Father Christmas in others. The class also talked about the Jewish feast of Hanukkah that celebrates the rededication of the Temple of Jerusalem, and about the special meaning of the nine candles of the Hanukkah menorah.

The teacher had asked everyone to bring in pictures or other things having to do with the holidays. A lot of kids brought in photographs of their families by their Christmas trees. Mayra brought in pictures of New Year's Day in Santo Domingo. Michelle brought in a picture of herself sitting on Santa's lap when she was little. Gabriel brought in photos of the Three Kings' Day parade in Miami, Florida. He had been there last year, when he went to visit his Cuban grandmother. Marcos brought in a piñata shaped like a green parrot that his uncle had brought back from Mexico. Emmanuel showed everyone a photo album of his family's trip to Israel, and Esther brought in cards her grandfather had sent her from Jerusalem.

One day, Suni Paz came to the school. She sang Christmas songs from different countries and taught the class to sing a Hanukkah song, "The Candles of Hanukkah."

María Isabel went home humming softly "Hanukkah . . . Hanukkah . . . Let us celebrate." The bus trip seemed a lot shorter as the song ran through her head. It almost felt as if she had traveled to all those different countries and had celebrated all those different holidays.

María Isabel was still singing while she made dinner and set the table:

"With our menorah,
Fine potato latkes,
Our clay trumpets,
Let us celebrate."

Her voice filled the empty kitchen. María Isabel was so pleased she promised herself that she'd make a snowman the next time it snowed. And she'd get it finished before the garbage men picked up the trash and dirtied up the snow.

But after Suni Paz's visit to the school, the days seemed to drag by more and more slowly. María Isabel didn't have anything to do during rehearsals, since she didn't have a part in *Amahl*.

The teacher decided that after the play the actors would sing some holiday songs, including María Isabel's favorite about the Hanukkah candles. Since she didn't have a part, María Isabel wouldn't be asked to sing either.

It didn't seem to matter much to Tony and Jonathan, the other two kids who weren't in the play. They spent rehearsal time reading comics or whispering to each other. Neither boy spoke to María Isabel, and she was too shy to say anything to them.

The only fun she had was reading her library book. Somehow her problems seemed so small compared to Wilbur the pig's. He was in danger of becoming the holiday dinner. María Isabel felt the only difference was that the characters in books always seemed to find answers to their problems, while she couldn't figure out what to do about her own.

As she cut out bells and stars for decorations, María Isabel daydreamed about being a famous singer. Someday she would sing in front of a large audience, and her teacher would feel guilty that she had not let María Isabel sing in the Winter Pageant.

But later María Isabel thought, My teacher isn't so bad. It's all a big misunderstanding. . . . If only there was some way I could let her know. Even if I'm not a great singer someday, it doesn't matter. All I really want is to be myself and not make the teacher angry all the time. I just want to be in the play and to be called María Isabel Salazar López.

"I've asked my boss if I can leave work early the day of the school pageant," María Isabel's mother said one evening as she served the soup. "Papá is also going to leave work early. That way we'll be able to bring the rice and beans."

"And best of all, we can hear María Isabel sing," her father added.

María Isabel looked down at her soup. She had not told her parents anything. She knew they were going to be very disappointed when they saw the other kids in her class taking part in the play. She could just hear her mother asking, "Why didn't you sing? Doesn't the teacher know what a lovely voice you have?" María Isabel ate her soup in silence. What could she say?

"Don't you have anything to say, Chabelita?" asked her father. "Aren't you glad we're coming?"

"Sure, Papá, sure I am," said María Isabel, and she got up to take her empty bowl to the sink.

After helping her mother with the dishes, María Isabel went straight to her room. She put on her pajamas and got into bed. But she couldn't sleep, so she turned the light on and continued reading *Charlotte's Web*. María Isabel felt that she was caught in a sticky, troublesome spider's web of her own, and the more she tried to break loose, the more trapped she became.

When the librarian had told her that she would like the book, María Isabel had felt that they were sharing a secret. Now as she turned the pages, she thought that maybe the secret was that *everyone* has problems. She felt close to poor little Wilbur, being fattened up for Christmas dinner without even knowing it. He was a little like her parents, who were so eager to go to the pageant, not knowing what was waiting for them.

"It just isn't fair that this can't be a happy time for all of us!" María Isabel said out loud. She sighed. Then she turned off the light, snuggled under her blanket, and fell asleep trying to figure out a way to save Wilbur from becoming Christmas dinner.

Two days were left until the pageant. The morning was cloudy and gray. On the way to school, María Isabel wondered if it was going to snow. Maybe she would be able to make that snowman. But shortly after she got to school, it started to drizzle.

Since they couldn't go outside, the students spent their time rehearsing. No one made a mistake. Melchior didn't forget what he had to say to Amahl's mother. Amahl dropped his crutch only once. Best of all, though, the shepherds remembered when they were supposed to enter, without bumping into the Three Kings.

Even Tony and Jonathan seemed interested in the play. They volunteered to help carry the manger and the shepherds' baskets on- and offstage.

Satisfied with the final rehearsal, the teacher decided there was time for one last class exercise before vacation. "It's been a couple of days since we've done some writing," she said when the students returned to class. "The new year is a time for wishes. Sometimes wishes come true; sometimes they don't. But it's important to have wishes and, most of all, to know what you really want. I'd like you all to take out some paper and write an essay titled 'My Greatest Wish.'"

María Isabel sighed and put away *Charlotte's Web*. Charlotte had just died, and María Isabel wondered what was going to happen to the sack of eggs that Wilbur had saved, and when Charlotte's babies would be born. But María Isabel would have to wait to find out. She bit down on her pencil and wrote: "My greatest wish . . ."

This shouldn't be so hard, María Isabel thought. If I finish writing early, I can probably finish my book. She started to write: "My greatest wish is to make a snowman. . . ."

María Isabel read over what she had just written, and realized that it wasn't what she really wanted. She put the paper aside, took out a new sheet, and wrote down the title again. "My greatest wish is to have a part in *Amahl*. . . ."

María Isabel stopped writing again. She thought, Would Charlotte have said that her greatest wish was to save Wilbur? Or would she have wished for something impossible, like living until the next spring and getting to know her children? The teacher just said that wishes don't always come true. If I'm going to wish for something, it should be something really worth wishing for.

María Isabel took out a third sheet of paper and wrote down the title again. This time, she didn't stop writing until she got to the bottom of the page.

My Greatest Wish

When I started to write I thought my greatest wish was to make a snowman. Then I thought my greatest wish was to have a part in the Winter Pageant. But I think my greatest wish is to be called María Isabel Salazar López. When that was my name, I felt proud of being named María like my papá's mother, and Isabel, like my grandmother Chabela. She is saving money so that I can study and not have to spend my whole life in a kitchen like her. I was Salazar like my papá and my grandpa Antonio, and López, like my grandfather Manuel. I never knew him but he could really tell stories. I know because my mother told me.

If I was called María Isabel Salazar López, I could listen better in class because it's easier to hear than Mary López. Then I could have said that I wanted a part in the play. And when the rest of the kids sing, my mother and father wouldn't have to ask me why I didn't sing, even though I like the song about the Hanukkah candles so much.

The rest of the class had already handed in their essays and were cleaning out their desks to go home when María Isabel got up. She quietly went to the front of the room and put her essay on the teacher's desk. María Isabel didn't look up at the teacher, so she didn't see the woman smiling at her. She hurried back to her desk to get her things and leave.

Holiday spirit was everywhere at school the next day. The paper wreaths and lanterns the class had made were hung up all over the room. The teacher had put the "greatest wish" essays up on the bulletin board, next to the cutouts of Santa Claus, the Three Kings, and a menorah.

All the students were restless. Marta Pérez smiled when María Isabel sat down next to her. "Look at the pretty Christmas card I got from my cousin in Santo Domingo," she said excitedly. María Isabel looked at the tropical Christmas scene, all trimmed in flowers. But she couldn't answer Marta because the teacher had started to speak.

"We're going to do one last rehearsal because there's a small change in the program."

The rest of the kids listened attentively, but María Isabel just kept looking down at her desk. After all, she had nothing to do with the pageant.

Then she heard the teacher say, "María Isabel, María Isabel Salazar López . . ." María Isabel looked up in amazement.

"Wouldn't you like to lead the song about the Hanukkah candles?" the teacher said with a wide grin. "Why don't you start by yourself, and then everyone else can join in. Go ahead and start when you're ready."

María Isabel walked nervously up to the front of the room and stood next to the teacher, who was strumming her guitar. Then she took a deep breath and began to sing her favorite holiday song.

While her mother was getting the rice and beans ready that night, Mr. Salazar called María Isabel over to him. "Since you can't wear makeup yet, Chabelita, I've brought you something else that I think you'll like." In the palm of his hand were two barrettes for her hair. They were shaped like butterflies and gleamed with tiny stones.

"Oh, Papá. They're so pretty! Thank you!" María Isabel exclaimed. She hugged her father and ran to her room to put them on.

At school the next day, María Isabel stood in the center of the stage. She was wearing her special yellow dress, a pair of new shoes, and the shining butterflies. She spoke clearly to the audience. "My name is María Isabel Salazar López. I'm going to sing a song about the Jewish feast of Hanukkah, that celebrates the rededication of the Temple in Jerusalem." The music started, and María Isabel began to sing.

The Candles of Hanukkah

One little candle,
Two little candles,
Three little candles,
Let us celebrate.
Four little candles,
Five little candles,
Six little candles,
Let us celebrate.
Hanukkah, Hanukkah,
Let us celebrate.
Seven little candles,
Eight little candles,
Nine little candles,
Let us celebrate.
Hanukkah, Hanukkah,
Let us celebrate.
With our menorah,
Fine potato latkes,
Our clay trumpets,
Let us celebrate.
With our family,
With our friends,
With our presents,
Let us celebrate.

And the butterflies in María Isabel's hair
sparkled under the stage lights so much that it
seemed that they might just take off and fly.

Think About It

1 What is the challenge María Isabel faces? How does she solve her problem?

2 Would you have chosen María Isabel's way of telling her teacher what she wanted, or a different way? Tell why.

3 How does the author show that the teacher did not hurt María Isabel's feelings on purpose, and that she felt sorry about her mistake?

Meet the Author
Alma Flor Ada

Alma Flor Ada (signature)

Alma Flor Ada was born in Cuba and lived in Spain and Peru before coming to the United States. She is a college professor and has had many children's books published in several countries. In this interview, she tells about being a writer.

Question: *When did you become interested in writing?*

Alma Flor Ada: When I was a child in Cuba, in the fourth grade, I thought the textbooks we used were very ugly. So I told myself that when I grew up, I would write books that were fun to look at. Then, as an adult, I went to college and graduate school and did scholarly writing. One day when my daughter was about five, she said, "I am making a book. Do you know why?" I replied, "No, why?" And she said, "Because the books you make are so ugly!" That brought everything back to me. I decided to collect the poems and stories of my childhood, and that was my first project. When I began, I thought of myself as a collector of stories. I didn't know that I was also a writer, but that is what I became.

Question: *Was there anything about your childhood that prepared you to become a writer?*

Ada: My grandmother was a wonderful storyteller. She could make her stories so real that I felt I was actually there. My father loved to tell stories, too. Every night he invented a new story to explain something, such as how fire was used for the first time or how someone thought of making shoes. My father was a professor and my mother was a teacher, so we always had books in our home. I liked poetry and fairy-tale books when I was very young. Later I liked to read about real people just like me.

Question: *How did you get the idea for* My Name Is María Isabel*?*

Ada: I wrote the story about María Isabel because I observed a teacher who kept saying a child's name wrong. The child would not correct the teacher out of courtesy and respect, but I knew it hurt. Our name is important to all of us.

Question: *Do you write in both Spanish and English?*

Ada: Yes, I do. Most of my early books were in Spanish. I wrote *My Name Is María Isabel* in Spanish first. I am happy that most of my books are published both in English and in Spanish.

**Visit *The Learning Site!*
www.harcourtschool.com**

Response Activities

Talk It Over

WRITE A CONVERSATION

In the weeks before the Winter Pageant, María Isabel reads *Charlotte's Web*. She tries to think of a way to solve Wilbur the pig's problem. Imagine that Wilbur and María Isabel discuss their problems. With a partner, write what they might say to each other. Read your conversation to classmates.

What Is Courage?

WRITE A PARAGRAPH

María Isabel finds that she needs courage to solve her problem. Think about a time when you needed courage to do something. Then write a paragraph telling what courage is and why it is important. Use examples from your own experience and the experience of María Isabel.

Calendar Hunt

RESEARCH HOLIDAYS

María Isabel learns about many kinds of winter holidays. With a partner, look through a calendar that shows holidays. Make two lists. In the first, write names of holidays you know about. In the second, write names of holidays you've never heard of. Choose one holiday from the second list. See what you can find out about it in the reference section of your school library, and write a brief report.

A Song of Celebration

LEARN A SONG

María Isabel learns to sing a song about Hanukkah. Learn a song that celebrates one of your favorite holidays. Write the words on paper, or type them on a computer and print them out. Decorate the borders with pictures that give a feeling for the holiday. If you like, teach your song to some classmates.

Prefixes and Suffixes

Notice the underlined words in these sentences from "My Name Is María Isabel."

1. It's all a big <u>mis</u>understanding.
2. María Isabel walked <u>nervously</u> up to the front of the room and stood next to the teacher, who was strumming her guitar.

Each underlined word contains a prefix or a suffix. A **prefix** is a word part added to the beginning of a word. A **suffix** is a word part added to the end of a word.

Story Word	Meaning of Prefix or Suffix	Meaning of Word
<u>mis</u>understanding	wrong, badly	wrong understanding, a failure to understand
nervous<u>ly</u>	in a way that is	in a way that is nervous

Did you notice the word *rededication* in the story? It has both a prefix and a suffix.

Prefix		Base Word		Suffix		
re- (again)	+	dedicate	+	-ion (the act of)	=	rededication (the act of dedicating again)

You see prefixes and suffixes almost every time you read. If you know what they mean, you can figure out the meanings of many new words. Read the paragraph below. Identify prefixes and suffixes in the underlined words. Tell how each one changes the meaning of the base word.

Mr. Kraft asked Valerie to <u>rewrite</u> the school play. She accepted the task <u>eagerly</u>. First, she added a <u>narrator</u>, but Mr. Kraft was still <u>dissatisfied</u>. Then, Valerie wrote ten new speaking roles. Finally, she wrote a new song for the play. "This is wonderful!" Mr. Kraft said. "It will be our best holiday <u>performance</u> ever."

WHAT HAVE YOU LEARNED?

1. What other words with prefixes or suffixes can you find in the paragraph above? Tell what the words mean.

2. The prefixes *un-, im-,* and *in-* mean "not." Add one of these prefixes to each of the following words to make it mean the opposite: *like, happy, possible, complete.*

TRY THIS • TRY THIS • TRY THIS

Make as many words as you can by adding prefixes and suffixes to these base words: *act, decorate.* Write the words in a web.

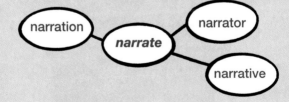

Visit *The Learning Site!*
www.harcourtschool.com

95

LOU
GEHRIG

**THE
LUCKIEST
MAN**

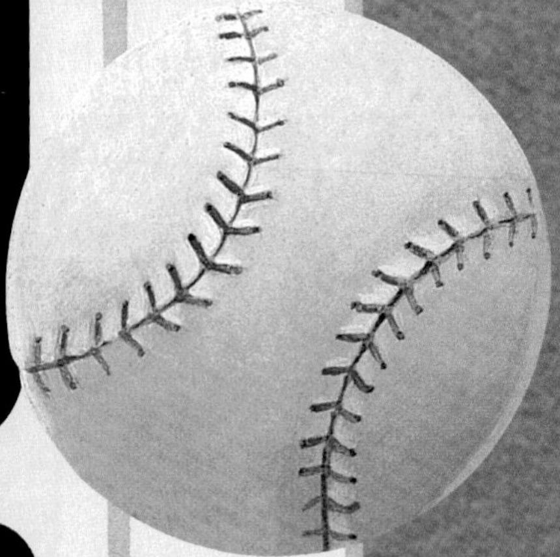

BY
David A. Adler

ILLUSTRATED BY
Terry Widener

ALA Notable
Book

*Boston Globe-
Horn Book Honor*

1903 was a year of great beginnings. Henry Ford sold his first automobile and the Wright Brothers made the first successful flight in an airplane. In baseball, the first World Series was played. The team later known as the Yankees moved from Baltimore to New York. And on June 19, 1903, Henry Louis Gehrig was born. He would become one of the greatest players in baseball history.

Lou Gehrig was born in the Yorkville section of New York City. It was an area populated with poor immigrants like his parents, Heinrich and Christina Gehrig, who had come to the United States from Germany.

Christina Gehrig had great hopes for her son Lou. She dreamed that he would attend college and become an accountant or an engineer. She insisted that he study hard. Through eight years of grade school, Lou didn't miss a single day.

Lou's mother thought games and sports were a waste of time. But Lou loved sports. He got up early to play the games he loved—baseball, soccer, and football. He played until it was time to go to school. In high school Lou was a star on his school's baseball team.

After high school Lou Gehrig went to Columbia University. He was on the baseball team there, too, and on April 26, 1923, a scout for the New York Yankees watched him play. Lou hit two long home runs in that game. Soon after that he was signed to play for the Yankees.

The Yankees offered Lou a $1,500 bonus to sign plus a good salary. His family needed the money. Lou quit college and joined the Yankees. Lou's mother was furious. She was convinced that he was ruining his life.

On June 1, 1925, the Yankee manager sent Lou to bat for the shortstop. The next day Lou played in place of first baseman Wally Pipp. Those were the first two games in

what would become an amazing record: For the next fourteen years Lou Gehrig played in 2,130 consecutive Yankee games. The boy who never missed a day of grade school became a man who never missed a game.

Lou Gehrig played despite stomachaches, fevers, a sore arm, back pains, and broken fingers. Lou's constant play earned him the nickname Iron Horse. All he would say about his amazing record was, "That's the way I am."

Lou was shy and modest, but people who watched him knew just how good he was.

101

In 1927 Lou's teammate Babe Ruth hit sixty home runs, the most hit up to that time in one season. But it was Lou Gehrig who was selected that year by the baseball writers as the American League's Most Valuable Player. He was selected again as the league's MVP in 1936.

Then, during the 1938 baseball season—and for no apparent reason—Lou Gehrig stopped hitting. One newspaper reported that Lou was swinging as hard as he could, but when he hit the ball it didn't go anywhere.

Lou exercised. He took extra batting practice. He even tried changing the way he stood and held his bat. He worked hard during the winter of 1938 and watched his diet.

But the following spring Lou's playing was worse. Time after time he swung at the ball and missed. He had trouble fielding. And he even had problems off the field. In the clubhouse he fell down while he was getting dressed.

Some people said Yankee manager Joe McCarthy should take Lou out of the lineup. But McCarthy refused. He had great respect for Lou and said, "Gehrig plays as long as he wants to play." But Lou wasn't selfish. On May 2, 1939, he told Joe McCarthy, "I'm benching myself . . . for the good of the team."

When reporters asked why he took himself out, Lou didn't say he felt weak or how hard it was for him to run. Lou made no excuses. He just said that he couldn't hit and he couldn't field.

On June 13, 1939, Lou went to the Mayo Clinic in Rochester, Minnesota, to be examined by specialists. On June 19, his thirty-sixth birthday, they told Lou's wife, Eleanor, what was wrong. He was suffering from amyotrophic lateral sclerosis, a deadly disease that affects the central nervous system.

Lou stayed with the team, but he didn't play. He was losing weight. His hair was turning gray. He didn't have to

be told he was dying. He knew it. "I don't have long to go," he told a teammate.

Lou loved going to the games, being in the clubhouse, and sitting with his teammates. Before each game Lou brought the Yankee lineup card to the umpire at home plate. A teammate or coach walked with him, to make sure he didn't fall. Whenever Lou came onto the field, the fans stood up and cheered for brave Lou Gehrig.

But Yankee fans and the team wanted to do more. They wanted Lou to know how deeply they felt about him. So they made July 4, 1939, Lou Gehrig Appreciation Day at Yankee Stadium.

Many of the players from the 1927 Yankees—perhaps the best baseball team ever—came to honor their former teammate. There was a marching band and gifts. Many people spoke, too. Fiorello La Guardia, the mayor of New York City, told

Lou, "You are the greatest prototype of good sportsmanship and citizenship."

When the time came for Lou to thank everyone, he was too moved to speak. But the fans wanted to hear him and chanted, "We want Gehrig! We want Gehrig!"

Dressed in his Yankee uniform, Lou Gehrig walked slowly to the array of microphones. He wiped his eyes, and with his baseball cap in his hands, his head down, he slowly spoke.

"Fans," he said, "for the past two weeks you have been reading about a bad break I got. Yet today I consider myself the luckiest man on the face of the earth."

It was a courageous speech. Lou didn't complain about his terrible illness. Instead he spoke of his many blessings and of the future. "Sure, I'm lucky," he said when he spoke of his years in baseball. "Sure, I'm lucky," he said again when he spoke of his fans and family.

Lou spoke about how good people had been to him. He praised his teammates. He thanked his parents and his wife, whom he called a tower of strength.

The more than sixty thousand fans in Yankee Stadium stood to honor Lou Gehrig. His last words to them—and to the many thousands more sitting by their radios and listening— were, "So I close in saying that I might have had a bad break, but I have an awful lot to live for. Thank you."

Lou stepped back from the microphones and wiped his eyes. The stadium crowd let out a tremendous roar, and Babe Ruth did what many people must have wanted to do that day. He threw his arms around Lou Gehrig and gave him a great warm hug.

The band played the song "I Love You Truly," and the fans chanted, "We love you, Lou."

When Lou Gehrig left the stadium later that afternoon, he told a teammate, "I'm going to remember this day for a long time."

In December 1939 Lou Gehrig was voted into the Baseball Hall of Fame. And the Yankees retired his uniform. No one else on the team would ever wear the number four. It was the first time a major-league baseball team did that to honor one of its players.

Mayor Fiorello La Guardia thought Lou's courage might inspire some of the city's troubled youths to be courageous, too. He offered Lou a job working with former prisoners as a member of the New York City Parole Commission. Lou had many opportunities to earn more money, but he believed this job would enable him to do something for the city that had given him so much.

Within little more than a year, Lou had to leave his job. He was too weak to keep working. He stayed at home, unable to do the simplest task.

Lou had many visitors. He didn't speak to them of his illness or of dying. When he saw one friend visibly upset by the way he looked, Lou told him not to worry. "I'll gradually get better," he said. In cards to his friends Lou wrote, "We have much to be thankful for."

By the middle of May 1941, Lou hardly left his bed. Then on Monday, June 2, 1941, just after ten o'clock at night, Lou Gehrig died. He was thirty-seven years old.

On June 4 the Yankee game was canceled because of rain. Some people thought it was fitting that the Yankees did not play; this was the day of Lou Gehrig's funeral.

At the funeral the minister announced that there would be no speeches. "We need none," he said, "because you all knew him." That seemed fitting, too, for modest Lou Gehrig.

Think About It

1. Why did thousands of people love and respect Lou Gehrig?

2. Do you think Lou Gehrig was lucky, as he said he was? Explain your response.

3. The author included some real quotations from various people. Why do you think he included them?

Meet the Author
David A. Adler

Team: New York Writers
Position: Third base and right (write) field

Bats right-handed. Throws right-handed. Writes right-handed.

Hits (books published): 142

David A. Adler loves baseball, and he loves to write. He is married and has three sons. One son loves baseball. Two sons love to write. All three sons love to read.

David A. Adler

Meet the Illustrator
Terry Widener

Team: Texas Illustrators

Position: Drawing Board

Bats right-handed. Throws right-handed. Paints right-handed.

Hits (featured illustrations): magazines (*Esquire, Harper's, Sports Illustrated, Time*) and books

Terry Widener loves to watch baseball, coach soccer, and play golf. He is married and has three children. His oldest daughter plays golf. His youngest daughter and son play soccer.

Wings of Hope

by Marianne J. Dyson

Eleven-year-old Kimberly Renaud was a little scared. She was about to take her very first flight—not in a big jet, but in a plane so small that passengers seated inside could touch both sides with arms outstretched. But what was really different about this flight was that both the pilot and the passenger rode to the plane in wheelchairs.

The pilot was Theron Wright. An accident left Theron paralyzed from the waist down. He was in college at the time, and had just received his pilot's license. After the accident, Theron thought he'd never fly again. That all changed when he met Rick Amber.

Rick had been a fighter pilot for the U.S. Navy during the Vietnam War. In 1971, his jet crashed, and Lieutenant Amber lost the use of his legs.

In 1993, he founded Challenge Air. This nonprofit group offers free flights to disabled and seriously ill children. The pilots (who call themselves

"disAbled pilots") want kids to know that anyone can overcome a physical or mental obstacle. The group's motto is, "All it takes is desire, and truly the sky is the limit." The pilots have flown more than 6,000 children and their friends in seventeen states across the country.

Theron Wright learned to fly again using Rick Amber's plane. It had been set up to be flown using hand controls alone. "Rick taught me not to quit and to continue striving to achieve my goals in aviation," says Theron.

Kimberly Renaud smiled as Challenge Air volunteers helped her into the back seat of Theron's plane. To protect her ears from engine noise, she was given a headset to wear. A pillow served as a booster to help her see out of the window. With safety belts snug, Theron taxied the plane down the runway at Houston's Hobby Airport, then roared off into a blue sky.

From high above the city, Kimberly saw downtown skyscrapers and the hospital where she goes for treatment. "We saw houses, and I saw the city and little cars. Everything looked small from up there," she remarked. After landing, Kimberly received her gold aviator's wings (a special Challenge Air pin).

Kimberly loves math and wants to work with computers when she grows up. Challenge Air has shown her that there really is no limit—not even the sky—to what you can achieve when you believe in yourself.

Think About It

How do Challenge Air volunteers teach children about meeting challenges?

Response

A Day to Remember

WRITE A NEWS STORY

Imagine you are a sportswriter who was at Yankee Stadium on July 4, 1939, the day Lou Gehrig was honored. Write a news story about this event. Tell when, where, and why the event took place, who was at the stadium, and what happened. Be sure to include a headline.

You might want to tape yourself reading your story as a news reporter would.

Record Makers, Record Breakers

MAKE A BAR GRAPH

In 1995 Cal Ripken, Jr., broke Lou Gehrig's record of playing in 2,130 games in a row. With a partner, look in a sports almanac. Find five baseball players who hold the top five records in one category. For example, you could find the five players who hit the most home runs in a single season. Make a bar graph to show your findings.

Activities

Let's Trade

DESIGN A TRADING CARD

Design a trading card to honor Lou Gehrig or another athlete you admire. On one side of an index card, draw or paste a picture of the athlete. On the other side, write some information about the person.

Making Connections

WRITE A CHARACTER SKETCH

Even though they had bad breaks, Lou Gehrig and Theron Wright were able to make the best of life. Write a character sketch that describes another person who has or had great troubles but a great attitude. You can write about a famous person or about someone you know. If you need help thinking of descriptive words, use a thesaurus.

Newbery
Honor

LAURA INGALLS WILDER

On the Banks of
Plum Creek

ILLUSTRATED BY GARTH WILLIAMS

ON THE BANKS OF Plum Creek

Laura and her family are pioneer settlers in Minnesota. The family includes Ma and Pa, sisters Mary, Laura, and Carrie, and a dog named Jack. In the months after Pa builds the family a house, they face great challenges. First, a plague of grasshoppers destroys the wheat crop. Next, there is a terrible rainstorm, and then a prairie fire almost destroys the haystacks. At the beginning of winter, Pa and Ma plan a trip to town. Before they go, Pa gets a supply of firewood ready in case of a blizzard.

By Laura Ingalls Wilder   *Illustrated by Garth Williams*

Embroidery by Nancy Freeman

Now in the daytimes Pa was driving the wagon up and down Plum Creek, and bringing load after load of logs to the pile by the door. He cut down old plum trees and old willows and cottonwoods, leaving the little ones to grow. He hauled them and stacked them, and chopped and split them into stove wood, till he had a big woodpile.

With his short-handled ax in his belt, his traps on his arm, and his gun against his shoulder, he walked far up Plum Creek, setting traps for muskrat and mink and otter and fox.

One evening at supper Pa said he had found a beaver meadow. But he did not set traps there because so few beavers were left. He had seen a fox and shot at it, but missed.

"I am all out of practice hunting," he said. "It's a fine place we have here, but there isn't much game. Makes a fellow think of places out west where —"

"Where there are no schools for the children, Charles," said Ma.

"You're right, Caroline. You usually are," Pa said. "Listen to that wind. We'll have a storm tomorrow."

But the next day was mild as spring. The air was soft and warm and the sun shone brightly. In the middle of the morning Pa came to the house.

"Let's have an early dinner and take a walk to town this afternoon," he said to Ma. "This is too nice a day for you to stay indoors. Time enough for that when winter really comes."

"But the children," said Ma. "We can't take Carrie and walk so far."

"Shucks!" Pa laughed at her. "Mary and Laura are great girls now. They can take care of Carrie for one afternoon."

"Of course we can, Ma," said Mary; and Laura said, "Of course we can!"

They watched Pa and Ma starting gaily away. Ma was so pretty, in her brown-and-red Christmas shawl, with her brown knit hood tied under her chin, and she stepped so quickly and looked up at Pa so merrily that Laura thought she was like a bird.

The next day was mild as spring.

Then Laura swept the floor while Mary cleared the table. Mary washed the dishes and Laura wiped them and put them in the cupboard. They put the red-checked cloth on the table. Now the whole long afternoon was before them and they could do as they pleased.

First, they decided to play school. Mary said she must be Teacher, because she was older and besides she knew more. Laura knew that was true. So Mary was Teacher and she liked it, but Laura was soon tired of that play.

"I know," Laura said. "Let's both teach Carrie her letters."

They sat Carrie on a bench and held the book before her, and both did their best. But Carrie did not like it. She would not learn the letters, so they had to stop that.

"Well," said Laura, "let's play keeping house."

"We *are* keeping house," said Mary. "What is the use of playing it?"

The house was empty and still, with Ma gone. Ma was so quiet and gentle that she never made any noise, but now the whole house was listening for her.

Laura went outdoors for a while by herself, but she came back. The afternoon grew longer and longer. There was nothing at all to do. Even Jack walked up and down restlessly.

The afternoon grew longer and longer.

He asked to go out, but when Laura opened the door he would not go. He lay down and got up, and walked around and around the room. He came to Laura and looked at her earnestly.

"What is it, Jack?" Laura asked him. He stared hard at her, but she could not understand, and he almost howled.

"Don't, Jack!" Laura told him, quickly. "You scare me."

"Is it something outdoors?" Mary wondered. Laura ran out, but on the doorstep Jack took hold of her dress and pulled her back. Outdoors was bitter cold. Laura shut the door.

"Look," she said. "The sunshine's dark. Are the grasshoppers coming back?"

"Not in the winter-time, goosie," said Mary. "Maybe it's rain."

"Goosie yourself!" Laura said back. "It doesn't rain in the winter-time."

"Well, snow, then! What's the difference?" Mary was angry and so was Laura. They would have gone on quarreling, but suddenly there was no sunshine. They ran to look through the bedroom window.

A dark cloud with a fleecy white under-side was rolling fast from the northwest.

Mary and Laura looked out the front window. Surely it was time for Pa and Ma to come, but they were nowhere in sight.

"Maybe it's a blizzard," said Mary.

"Like Pa told us about," said Laura.

They looked at each other through the gray air. They were thinking of those children who froze stark stiff.

"The woodbox is empty," said Laura.

Mary grabbed her. "You can't!" said Mary. "Ma told us to stay in the house if it stormed." Laura jerked away and Mary said, "Besides, Jack won't let you."

"We've got to bring in wood before the storm gets here," Laura told her. "Hurry!"

They could hear a strange sound in the wind, like a far-away screaming. They put on their shawls and pinned them under their chins with their large shawl-pins. They put on their mittens.

Laura was ready first. She told Jack, "We've got to bring in wood, Jack." He seemed to understand. He went out with her and stayed close at her heels. The wind was colder than icicles. Laura ran to the woodpile, piled up a big armful of wood, and ran back, with Jack behind her. She could not open the door while she held the wood. Mary opened it for her.

Then they did not know what to do. The cloud was coming swiftly, and they must both bring in wood before the storm got there. They could not open the door when their arms were full of wood. They could not leave the door open and let the cold come in.

"I tan open the door," said Carrie.

"You can't," Mary said.

"I tan, too!" said Carrie, and she reached up both hands and turned the door knob. She could do it! Carrie was big enough to open the door.

Laura and Mary hurried fast, bringing in wood. Carrie opened the door when they came to it, and shut it behind them. Mary could carry larger armfuls, but Laura was quicker.

They filled the woodbox before it began to snow. The snow came suddenly with a whirling blast, and it was small hard grains like sand. It stung Laura's face where it struck. When Carrie opened the door, it swirled into the house in a white cloud.

Laura and Mary forgot that Ma had told them to stay in the house when it stormed. They forgot everything but bringing in wood. They ran frantically back and forth, bringing each time all the wood they could stagger under.

They piled wood around the woodbox and around the stove. They piled it against the wall. They made the piles higher, and bigger.

Bang! they banged the door. They ran to the woodpile. Clop-clop-clop they stacked the wood on their arms. They ran to the door. Bump! it went open, and bang! they back-bumped it shut, and thumpity-thud-thump! they flung down the wood and ran back, out-doors, to the woodpile, and panting back again.

They forgot everything but bringing in wood.

They could hardly see the woodpile in the swirling whiteness. Snow was driven all in among the wood. They could hardly see the house, and Jack was a dark blob hurrying beside them. The hard snow scoured their faces. Laura's arms ached and her chest panted and all the time she thought, "Oh, where is Pa? Where is Ma?" and she felt "Hurry! Hurry!" and she heard the wind screeching.

The woodpile was gone. Mary took a few sticks and Laura took a few sticks and there were no more. They ran to the door together, and Laura opened it and Jack bounded in. Carrie was at the front window, clapping her hands and squealing. Laura dropped her sticks of wood and turned just in time to see Pa and Ma burst, running, out of the whirling whiteness of snow.

Pa was holding Ma's hand and pulling to help her run. They burst into the house and slammed the door and stood panting, covered with snow. No one said anything while Pa and Ma looked at Laura and Mary, who stood all snowy in shawls and mittens.

At last Mary said in a small voice, "We did go out in the storm, Ma. We forgot."

Laura's head bowed down and she said, "We didn't want to burn up the furniture, Pa, and freeze stark stiff."

"Well, I'll be!" said Pa. "If they didn't move the whole woodpile in. All the wood I cut to last a couple of weeks."

There, piled up in the house, was the whole woodpile. Melted snow was leaking out of it and spreading in puddles. A wet path went to the door, where snow lay unmelted.

Then Pa's great laugh rang out, and Ma's gentle smile shone warm on Mary and Laura. They knew they were forgiven for disobeying, because they had been wise to bring in wood, though perhaps not quite so much wood.

Sometime soon they would be old enough not to make any mistakes, and then they could always decide what to do. They would not have to obey Pa and Ma any more.

"We did go out in the storm, Ma. We forgot."

They bustled to take off Ma's shawl and hood and brush the snow from them and hang them up to dry. Pa hurried to the stable to do the chores before

the storm grew worse. Then while Ma rested, they stacked the wood neatly as she told them, and they swept and mopped the floor.

The house was neat and cosy again. The tea-kettle hummed, the fire shone brightly from the draughts above the stove hearth. Snow swished against the windows.

Pa came in. "Here is the little milk I could get here with. The wind blew it up out of the pail. Caroline, this is a terrible storm. I couldn't see an inch, and the wind comes from all directions at once. I thought I was on the path, but I couldn't see the house, and—well, I just barely bumped against the corner. Another foot to the left and I never would have got in."

"*Charles!*" Ma said.

"Nothing to be scared about now," said Pa. "But if we hadn't run all the way from town and beat this storm here—" Then his eyes twinkled, he rumpled Mary's hair and pulled Laura's ear. "I'm glad all this wood is in the house, too," he said.

The house was neat and cosy again.

Think About It

1 What decision do Laura and Mary have to make when they see the storm coming? Why is this decision difficult?

2 Do you think the sisters handle the emergency well? Explain.

3 What do you think each member of the family learns from this experience?

About the Author
Laura Ingalls Wilder

Laura Ingalls Wilder faced many challenges growing up as one of the early settlers of wild frontier land. Here are some things she wrote about her stories and her life.

I was born in the "Little House in the Big Woods" of Wisconsin on February 7 in the year 1867. I lived everything that happened in my books . . . I wanted children now to understand more about the beginning of things, to know what is behind the things they see — what it is that made America as they know it. Today so many things have made living and learning easier. But the real things haven't changed. It is still best to be honest and truthful; to make the most of what we have; to be happy with simple pleasures and have courage when things go wrong.

**Visit *The Learning Site!*
www.harcourtschool.com**

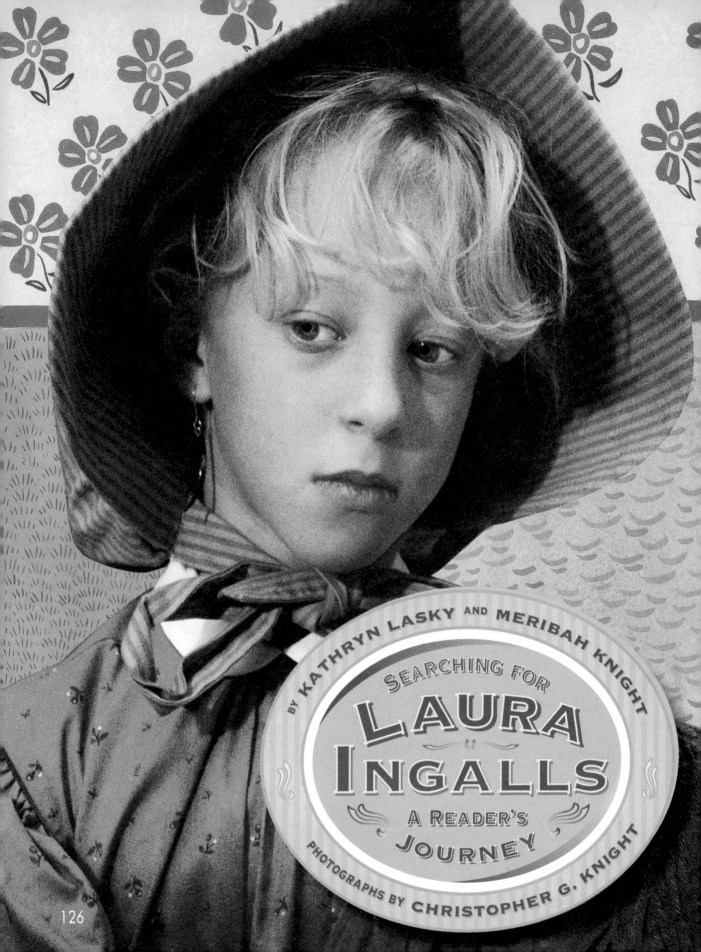

BY **KATHRYN LASKY** AND **MERIBAH KNIGHT**

SEARCHING FOR

LAURA INGALLS

A READER'S
JOURNEY

PHOTOGRAPHS BY **CHRISTOPHER G. KNIGHT**

In 1873 the Ingalls family sold their farm in Wisconsin and set out in their covered wagon to the western prairie of Minnesota. Laura was six and Mary was eight. They first lived in a dugout house on the banks of Plum Creek, two miles north of Walnut Grove.

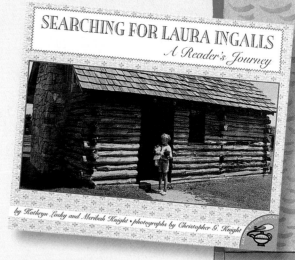

SEARCHING FOR LAURA INGALLS
A Reader's Journey
by Kathryn Lasky and Meribah Knight • photographs by Christopher G. Knight

The creek was Laura's whole world. It was her playground, her favorite place to be. It was where she tested herself and dared herself to do things that were unimaginable and sometimes naughty. It was at the creek that she nearly drowned one day when she disobeyed Pa and went by herself to the footbridge. She had gone there just to dip her feet in the water from the bridge. But the water was high and the current was stronger than she thought. It grabbed at her and nearly pulled her into the roaring creek. And she didn't know how to swim! She might have drowned.

Her father had taken her once to the deep, cool pool in the shade of the tall willows. They had waded into the water with all their clothes on. Her father had helped her and held her up in the water. She had always wanted to go back, but it was strictly forbidden. So for the most part Laura had to content herself with wading in the creek when the water was low and the current not too strong.

But Meribah could swim, and if there was one thing she wanted to do more than anything else, ever since she had read *On the Banks of Plum Creek*, the fourth book in the series, it was to swim in that very same creek where

127

Laura had waded. And to do it in her clothes. She had even picked out the skirt. It was the special one that she had packed, pink calico with a matching blouse. She had it all planned out.

But before they got to the creek there was another museum, with a replica of a covered wagon just like the one the Ingallses traveled in, and a schoolhouse just like the one where Laura and Mary went to school.

The creek looks almost the same as it did when Laura played on its banks, but there are beautiful cornfields as far as you can see all around. The dugout house caved in long ago and is now just an indentation in the bank.

I finally had my dream come true, but it was almost a bad dream, a nightmare. I got to go wading and swimming in Plum Creek.

It was warm and the current in the creek was going really fast. When I waded into the water I fell, but I got used to it and started to swim. When I stood up my clothes were heavy and wet. I felt like stones were hanging on my skirt. I climbed trees that were sticking out over the creek.

I remembered in the book how Laura went to look under branches and rocks for the old crab, the one she used to scare Nellie Oleson, the stuck-up girl in the book. I looked for it, too. I couldn't find it, so I swam along some more and hung from branches.

But guess what? When I came out of Plum Creek I saw this thing that looked like a glob of mud on my foot, and then I thought, It's a black slug, but then I thought, Slugs aren't black. Then I remembered. It came back all awful. It was a leech just like the ones Laura got on her. I had forgotten this whole part of the book, the part about the leeches. My stomach flip-flopped, my brain went crazy, and I started to scream. Of course my dad just had to take a picture before he pulled it off me.

THINK ABOUT IT

How were Meribah's experiences at Plum Creek similar to Laura's?

Response Activities

Facing the Challenge

WRITE A PARAGRAPH

When they see the blizzard coming, Laura and Mary act fast. Because they do, their family will stay warm through the long storm. What do Laura and Mary learn about themselves from this experience? Write a paragraph to answer this question.

Be Prepared

MAKE A LIST

The blizzard catches the Ingalls family by surprise. What natural disaster could happen where you live? In a group, make a list of things to keep in an emergency kit in case of a natural disaster. For ideas, you could look at Internet safety sites. Organize your list so it is easy to use. You might share the list with your family.

Snowflake Art

CREATE SCIENTIFIC DRAWINGS

To Laura, the swirling snowflakes feel like grains of sand. Find out what a snowflake really is. Look in an encyclopedia or a science book to find out how snowflakes form and what they look like up close. Draw some snowflakes. Display your drawings, and tell classmates what you have learned.

Making Connections

DESIGN TIME CAPSULES

What if Meribah could travel back in time to meet Laura? What if Laura could travel to the future to meet Meribah? For each girl, draw a time capsule she could take with her on her trip. In each girl's capsule, draw five things that show what life is like in her time. Use information from the story and from a social studies book. Tell your classmates why you included each thing.

Try, Try Again

WRITE SPEECHES Choose two characters from this theme who tried hard to do something. Imagine that they are going to speak to a group of students at your school. What advice might they give about facing a problem or challenge? Write a short speech for each one to give.

Character Words

FIND DESCRIBING WORDS Look back through the selections in this theme for words that describe people. Make a chart and list ten of these words. Beside each word, write the name of the character the word describes. Also list other characters in this theme that these words could describe.

Describing Word	Character Described	Other Characters

All Kinds of Challenges

DISCUSS CHALLENGES Talk with a small group of classmates about the problems and challenges that the main characters in the selections faced. You may use these questions to guide your discussion:

- Which character do you think faced the greatest problem or challenge?

- Did any characters need help in solving their problems or meeting their challenges?

- Which characters shared something with others as they met the challenges in their own lives?

- Which characters learned something about themselves?

- What did you learn about how to face problems and challenges in your own life?

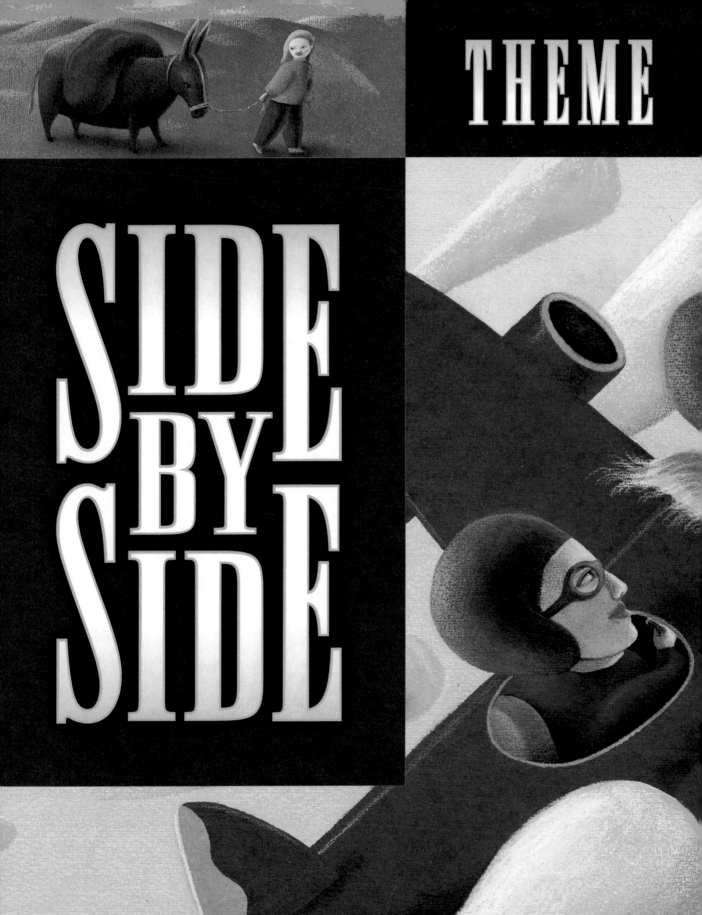

THEME

SIDE
BY
SIDE

CONTENTS

135

READER'S

Can We Be Friends? Nature's Partners
by Alexandra Wright

NONFICTION

Why would a bird put itself in danger inside a crocodile's mouth? Discover how the crocodile uses the plover bird as a toothbrush and how the bird uses the crocodile for its next meal.

READER'S CHOICE LIBRARY

Andy and Tamika
by David A. Adler

REALISTIC FICTION

Andy is very busy. He is hoping that the new baby will be a boy, and he is trying to come up with a name. He is preparing his gerbils as prizes for the school carnival. And he is preparing a celebration to welcome Tamika into his home.

Award-Winning Author
READER'S CHOICE LIBRARY

CHOICE

Rikki-Tikki-Tavi
by Rudyard Kipling

TALE

This timeless tale taken from *The Jungle Book* tells how Rikki-Tikki-Tavi, a mongoose, is adopted by a family in India. In this thrilling story, Rikki-Tikki-Tavi protects the family from deadly cobras that invade their house and garden.

Notable Social Studies Trade Book

Booklist Editor's Choice

Antonio's Rain Forest
adapted by Anna Lewington

NONFICTION

Antonio José lives in the Amazon rain forest, where his family makes rubber from the sap of rubber trees. The rubber tappers develop a community plan to save their way of life.

Outstanding Science Trade Book

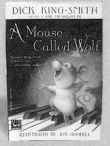

A Mouse Called Wolf
by Dick King-Smith

FANTASY

Wolfgang Amadeus Mouse (Wolf, for short) discovers that he has a gift for singing as he listens to Mrs. Honeybee play the piano. His voice really is music to her ears when he uses it to call for help after Mrs. Honeybee takes an unfortunate fall.

Award-Winning Author

137

The Seven

by Linda and Clay Goss

illustrated by Greg Tucker

Children

A Fable About Unity

A farmer and his wife had seven children. Now, folks from neighboring farms were always telling them how well-blessed they were to have such fine, healthy children.

But sometimes the farmer and his wife didn't feel quite so lucky because the seven children constantly argued and fought with each other. They yelled and screamed at the top of their voices. They threw stools and bowls across the room. Sounds of screams and things crashing into walls could be heard all day and sometimes even all night. At suppertime, when the family gathered at the table, the seven children made faces at one another and kicked at each other's feet. There was no peace in the farmer's home.

One evening, for supper, the farmer's wife cooked everyone's favorite meal—chicken and dumpling stew. She placed the big pot of stew in the middle of the long table and announced, "It's time to eat."

The farmer and the seven children rushed to the table as they always did, and blessed the food. Slowly, the mother served the farmer his bowl of stew. The farmer served a bowl of stew to his wife. None of the seven children could wait their turn for a bowl of stew. They grabbed the pot, yanked it this way and that, and flung it to the wall. All the delicious-looking chicken and dumplings spilled out onto the floor.

The farmer pounded on the table and shouted, "Enough is enough! Clean up the mess you have made and go to bed." The seven children began to cry and blame one another.

Later that night, the farmer and his wife couldn't sleep. "I'm worried about our children," said the wife.

"They are certainly a wild bunch, but I believe buried in their hearts is kindness," said the farmer.

"You are right, my dear husband, but we need a way to dig up that treasure buried beneath their hearts," said the wife.

Early the next morning, the farmer woke up each of the seven children. "Hurry and do your chores, children, for we are going on a journey through the woods," said the farmer.

The seven children were full of anticipation. They loved walking through the woods. Quickly, they did their chores and ran to the table to eat their morning meal.

But, instead of finding seven bowls of hot rice, they saw seven neatly tied bundles lying on the table. "Where is our food?" asked the seven children.

"It's time to go on our journey," said the father. "We will eat fruits and berries along the way."

"Oh, goody," shouted the children.

"And take these bundles with you," said their mother. "Don't open them now, for you will need them later." She gave each of the seven children a bundle and a hug. And so, off they went.

The farmer led his seven children through a part of the forest that was unfamiliar to them. There were no clear-cut walkways. They saw one fruit tree, but it bore very little fruit. They saw only one sweet berry bush, but it was surrounded by a thicket of thorns. Mosquitoes buzzed around their ears. Snakes glided across their path. They walked all day long.

When they came to a clearing, the farmer and the seven children stopped to rest. The farmer said to them, "My dear children, I must return home at once. There is something out here your mother and I want all of you to find. When you have it, you will be able to return home."

"But, Father," said one of the seven children, "the sun is going down."

The farmer said no more and walked away.

"What shall we do now?" said one of the seven children.

"I will decide, because I am the oldest," said the oldest child.

"But I am the smartest. I should decide what we should do," said the child next to the oldest one.

"I'm hungry," said the child before the child in the middle.

"I'm thirsty," said the child in the middle.

"I'm scared," said the child after the child in the middle.

"My legs hurt," said the child next to the youngest child.

"I want to go home," said the youngest child, and he cried as loudly as he could.

The seven children began arguing over which direction to take and what should be done next and who should be doing it!

One of the seven children claimed that he knew what their mother and father wanted them to find, but he wasn't going to tell any of them.

Each of the seven children was curious about what was in the others' bundles, but no one wanted to share the contents with anyone else. Finally each of the seven children ran off into the woods in a different direction, hoping to get as far away from the others as possible.

When she was safely away, the oldest child opened up her bundle and found two flint stones. The child next to the oldest child opened up his bundle and found kindling, bits and pieces of dry sticks and twigs. One of the seven children found a net made of tiny

strings in his bundle. Another one of the children unfolded a large quilted blanket that was inside her bundle. The middle child discovered a canteen of water in her bundle. The child next to the youngest child had a bundle wrapped within a bundle within a bundle. Inside the last bundle she saw a loaf of banana bread. The youngest child was very confused because he had found a piece of cloth inside his bundle. Something was drawn on the cloth but he could not tell what it was because the woods had become dark and strange animal sounds could be heard. The youngest child screamed out in terror. The other children, fearing that their brother was in danger, ran through the woods to help him. Then he showed them what he had found in his bundle.

"We will need to make a fire with my flint stones so we can see what is on the piece of cloth," said the oldest child.

"I will help you, my sister. I have some kindling," said the child next to the oldest child.

After they had made the fire, they set the net up like a tent so the mosquitoes wouldn't bite them. They passed the canteen around so each of them could drink some water. The child next to the youngest child gave each of her brothers and sisters a piece of banana bread. They looked at the piece of cloth and realized that it was a map showing them how to get back home.

Feeling somewhat better, they lay under the blanket and went to sleep. The next morning, the seven children woke up. They felt strong and happy. They were glad they had stayed together and were able to make it through the night without harm coming to any of them.

The seven children followed the directions on the map and returned home through the woods safely. The farmer and his wife were pleased to see their children. Holding hands, the family formed a circle and gave thanks to their

HOME SWEET HOME

creator. Then the children told their mother and father how each one of their brothers and sisters had shared what was in the bundles.

"Oh, children, did you find the thing your dear mother and I wanted you to find?"

"Yes, Father," said the oldest of the seven children. "Together we used what we had been given and found our way out of the forest. We found unity."

The youngest of the seven children spoke up. "Yes, but we also found Mother's delicious banana bread!"

The father, mother, and all the children laughed. The father looked around at his family enjoying each other and feeling happy that they were together again. He said, "We are together as a family; this is our strength. Together we have found unity."

Think About It

1 Why do you think the authors included the description of dinner?

2 How do the children's parents help them find the kindness "buried in their hearts"?

3 Do you think this story is a good way of teaching about unity? Explain your answer.

Meet the Authors
Linda and Clay Goss

Linda Goss grew up in a Tennessee town where it seemed that everyone was a storyteller. Her ability to combine drama with storytelling has led her to be named the official storyteller for the city of Philadelphia, where she lives with her husband, Clay Goss, and their children.

Clay Goss also works in the arts. In addition to writing plays and television scripts, he has written books with his wife.

In the spirit of unity, the whole Goss family contributed ideas for this book.

Linda Goss

Clay Goss

Response Activities

Award Ceremony

WRITE ABOUT A CHARACTER

The seven children work together to accomplish a goal: returning home safely. Make an award for one of the children. Write a sentence on the award, telling what the child did to deserve it. Illustrate the award with a picture of how that child showed kindness and helped to create unity in the family.

Helping Each Other

ACT OUT A SCENE

In a group, act out the parts of the seven children on the night they open their bundles and share what is in them. You may want to make or collect props such as the quilted blanket, the banana bread, and the cloth map.

Good Lessons

READ A FABLE

"The Seven Children" teaches an important lesson. Find another fable that teaches a lesson about getting along or working together. Read the fable to classmates, or record it and play the tape. Compare it with "The Seven Children."

Words to Remember

WRITE A SAYING

The farm family's motto might be "We are together as a family; this is our strength." Another saying about working together is "United we stand. Divided we fall." Find a saying about teamwork and cooperation, or make up your own. Write your saying in fancy lettering, and decorate a frame for it.

Predict Outcomes

As you read "The Seven Children," did you think about what the parents wanted their children to find on the journey? Maybe you thought of one of these ideas:

- The parents wanted the children to find a special place.
- The parents wanted them to find courage.
- The parents wanted them to find a way to work together to solve problems.

When you think about what will happen next in a story, you are **making predictions**. As a reader, you make predictions all the time. You read what's in the story, you add that to what you already know, and you quickly make a prediction. You may want to record your predictions for a story in a chart like this one.

PREDICTION CHART

What I Predict Will Happen	What Actually Happens
The children will use the net to catch fish for dinner.	The children use the net to keep mosquitoes away.

To make predictions, you use what you know about the type of selection you are reading. In a fable, for example, you know the characters will probably learn a lesson. In a nonfiction book about Kwanzaa, you would expect to find information about the holiday.

When you make predictions, you are being an active reader. This helps you really think about what you are reading. It makes reading fun, too!

Look at the two book covers below. Make predictions about what might happen or what you might learn in each book.

To make a prediction, you use what you see or read and what you already know.

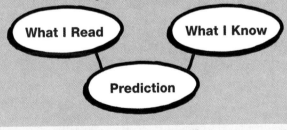

WHAT HAVE YOU LEARNED?

1. How did the title and subtitle of "The Seven Children: A Fable About Unity" help you make predictions about the story? Explain.

2. Imagine that your teacher says your class can do anything as long as it involves math, reading, science, history, or art. Make a prediction about what will happen.

TRY THIS • TRY THIS • TRY THIS

Choose a story. Then draw a web that shows a prediction you made and how you made it.

What I Read   What I Know

Prediction

Visit *The Learning Site!*
www.harcourtschool.com

The Garden of Happiness

by Erika Tamar
illustrated by Barbara Lambase

Notable
Social Studies
Trade Book

On Marisol's block near East Houston Street, there was an empty lot that was filled with garbage and broken, tired things. It had a funky smell that made Marisol wrinkle her nose whenever she passed by.

One April morning, Marisol was surprised to see many grown-ups busy in the lot. Mr. Ortiz carried a rusty refrigerator door. Mrs. Willie Mae Washington picked up newspapers. Mr. Singh rolled a tire away.

The next afternoon, Marisol saw people digging up stones. Mr. Ortiz worked with a pickax.

"¿Qué pasa?" Marisol asked.

Mrs. Willie Mae Washington leaned on her shovel and wiped her forehead. "I'm gonna grow black-eyed peas and greens and sweet potatoes, too," she said. "Like on my daddy's farm in Alabama. No more store-bought collard greens for me."

"We will call it The Garden of Happiness," Mr. Singh said. "I am planting *valore*—such a beautiful vine of lavender and red. Yes, everyone is happy when they see this bean from Bangladesh."

On another day, Marisol watched Mr. Castro preparing the ground. Mrs. Rodriguez rolled a wheelbarrow full of peat moss. Marisol inhaled the fresh-soil smell of spring.

"Oh, I want to plant something in The Garden of Happiness!" Marisol said.

"Too late, *niña*," Mr. Ortiz said. "All the plots are already taken."

Marisol looked everywhere for a leftover spot, but the ground was crisscrossed by markers of sticks and string. She looked and looked. Just outside the chain-link fence, she found a bit of earth where the sidewalk had cracked.

"¡Mira! Here's my patch!" Marisol called. It was no bigger than her hand, but it was her very own. She picked out the pebbles and scraped the soil with a stick.

Marisol noticed a crowd of teenagers across the street from the lot. They were staring at a brick wall. It was sad and closed

up, without windows for eyes. Marisol crossed over to ask
what they were doing.

"City Arts is giving us paint to make a mural on the
wall," a girl told her.

"What will it be?" Marisol asked.

"Don't know yet," one of the big boys said. "We haven't
decided."

"I'm making a garden," Marisol said. "I haven't decided,
either, about what to plant."

In The Garden of Happiness, the ground had become soft and dark. Mr. Castro talked to his seedlings as he placed them in straight rows. "Come on now, little baby things, grow nice and big for me."

Marisol had no seedlings or even small cuttings or roots. *What can I do*, she thought, *where can I find something to plant?*

She went to the corner where old Mrs. Garcia was feeding the pigeons. Marisol helped herself to a big flat seed. The birds fluttered about angrily. "Only one," she told them, "for my garden."

Marisol skipped back to her patch. She poked a hole with her finger, dropped in the seed, and patted the soil all around. And every single day that spring, Marisol carried a watering can to the lot and gave her seed a cool drink.

Before long, a green shoot broke through in Marisol's patch. Even on rainy days, she hurried to the lot to see. Soon there were two leaves on a strong, straight stalk, and then there were four. It became as high as Marisol's knee!

Green things were growing all around in The Garden of Happiness. Mr. Castro's tiny seedlings became big bushy things with ripe tomatoes shining like rubies.

"What's *my* plant?" Marisol asked. Now it reached to her shoulder. "What's it going to be?"

"Dunno," Mrs. Willie Mae Washington answered. "But it sure is *somethin'*!"

Marisol pulled out the weeds in the late afternoons, when it wasn't so summer-hot.

Sometimes she watched the teenagers across the street. They measured the wall. They talked and argued about what they would paint.

Often Marisol saw Mr. Ortiz in his plot, resting in a chair.

"I come back from the factory and breathe the fresh air," he said. "And I sit among my *habichuelas*, my little piece of Puerto Rico."

"Is *my* plant from Puerto Rico? Do you know what it is?" Marisol asked.

Mr. Ortiz shook his head and laughed. "*¡Muy grande!* Maybe it's Jack's beanstalk from the fairy tale."

By the end of July, Marisol's plant had grown way over her head. And then, at the very top, Marisol saw a bud! It became fatter every day. She couldn't wait for it to open.

"Now don't be lookin' so hard," Mrs. Willie Mae Washington chuckled. "It's gonna open up behind your back, just when you're thinkin' about somethin' else."

One morning, Marisol saw an amazing sight from halfway down the block. She ran the rest of the way. Standing higher than all the plants and vines in the garden was a flower as big as a plate! Her bud had turned into petals of yellow and gold.

"A sunflower!" Mrs. Anderson exclaimed as she pushed her shopping cart by. "Reminds me of when I was a girl in Kansas."

Mrs. Majewska was rushing on her way to the subway, but she skidded to a stop. "Ah, *słoneczniki!* So pretty in the fields of Poland!"

Old Mrs. Garcia shook her head. "No, no, *los girasoles* from Mexico, where they bring joy to the roadside."

"I guess sunflowers make themselves right at home in every sun-kissed place on earth," Mrs. Willie Mae Washington said.

"Even right here in New York City," Marisol said proudly.

The flower was a glowing circle, brighter than a yellow taxi. *A flower of sunshine*, Marisol thought, *the happiest plant in The Garden of Happiness.*

All summer long, it made the people on the street stop and smile.

Soon the air became cool and crisp with autumn. Mr. Castro picked the last of his tomatoes. Mr. Singh carried away a basket full of beans. Mrs. Rodriguez picked her *tomatillos*. "To dry and cut up for *salsa*," she said.

Mrs. Willie Mae Washington dug up orange potatoes. "I can almost smell my sweet potato pie." She winked at Marisol. "I'm gonna save an extra big slice for a good little gardener I know."

But something terrible was happening to Marisol's flower. Its leaves were turning brown and dry.

Marisol watered and watered until a stream ran down the sidewalk. But her flower's leaves began to fall.

"Please get well again," Marisol whispered.

Every day, more golden petals curled and faded.

"My flower of sunshine is sick," Marisol cried. "What should I do?"

"Oh, child," Mrs. Willie Mae Washington said. "Its season is over. There's a time to bloom and a time to die."

"No! I don't want my flower to die!"

"*Mi cariño*, don't cry," Mrs. Rodriguez said. "That's the way of a garden. You must save the seeds and plant again next spring."

Marisol's flower drooped to the ground. The Garden of Happiness wasn't happy for her anymore. The vines had tumbled down. The bushy green plants were gone. She

collected the seeds and put them in her pocket, but spring was much too far away.

Marisol was too sad to go to the empty lot anymore. For a whole week, she couldn't even look down the block where her beautiful flower used to be.

Then one day she heard people calling her name.

"Marisol! Come quick!"

"Marisol! *¡Apúrate!* Hurry!"

A golden haze shone on the street. There was a big crowd, like on a holiday. Music from the *bodega* was loud and bright. And what she saw made Marisol laugh and dance and clap her hands.

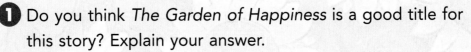

THINK ABOUT IT

1 Do you think *The Garden of Happiness* is a good title for this story? Explain your answer.

2 At the end of the story, what information do you get from a picture, not from words? Why do you think the author chose to end the story this way?

3 How do Marisol and the other gardeners show how much they care about their garden?

Erika Tamar

Erika Tamar says, "I think I always wanted to be a writer—except for the period when I wanted to be a movie star." After studying creative writing, she started working in film production. Later, the books her children brought home gave her the idea to try a different kind of storytelling.

Erika Tamar likes to base her stories on things and people she has known. In New York City, where she lives, she was inspired by the murals and gardens people made to brighten up their neighborhoods. She admired their creativity in turning plain-looking buildings and empty lots into beautiful places and decided to write about it.

Erika Tamar

Meet the Illustrator

Barbara Lambase

Barbara Lambase loves gardens and thinks they are a perfect way of bringing people together. She wanted to illustrate *The Garden of Happiness* because it showed people from different cultures working together and caring about their neighborhood. From her parents, Barbara Lambase learned to respect all cultures. She enjoys visiting other countries and tries not to miss a museum.

Barbara Lambase has won many awards for her artwork. When she is not painting or thinking about painting, she enjoys animals, gardening, good conversation, reading, and the radio. Her dog, her cat, and the radio are her painting companions. She lives in California.

Barbara Lambase

 **Visit *The Learning Site!*
www.harcourtschool.com**

165

I do not plant my garden,
but every year it appears.
On summer days I go out hunting
for those ripe wild raspberries
that glow so red against the leafy green
along the forest's edge. And then I watch as
catbirds! thrushes! bluebirds!
gobble berries, too.
On summer days I go out
hunting the tart and sweet blueberries
that lie hidden under clusters of leaves
down low, or high, in trees. And then I watch
as cedar waxwings eat the ones I've left.
This garden is for all of us—
for me and for the birds,
for all the hunters and the gatherers,
for the turtles, the chipmunks, and the slugs,
for the bees, the butterflies,
and the bugs.

written and illustrated by Lynne Cherry

Award-Winning
Author

The City

If flowers want to grow
right out of the concrete sidewalk cracks
I'm going to bend down to smell them.

written by David Ignatow
illustrated by Erika LeBarre

Response Activities

Sunflower Focus

WRITE A REPORT

Sunflowers are an important farm crop. In a group, learn more about these plants. Find out where sunflowers grow and how many seeds each plant produces. If possible, read the label on a package of shelled sunflower seeds for information about their food value. Write a short report about what you learn.

Garden Plan

MAKE A DIAGRAM

Imagine that you can have a plot in a community garden. List your favorite flowers, vegetables, and fruits. Figure out which ones grow where you live, and find out which ones need the most space to grow. Decide on the size and shape of your plot. Make a diagram that shows where you could put each plant. Draw symbols that show each item clearly. Use art software if possible.

MAKE A COMPARISON CHART

Look back at Erika Tamar's story and Lynne Cherry's poem, and compare the two gardens. For each garden, list where it is, how it got there, and what grows in it. Also note who benefits from each garden.

Gardener's Feast

PLAN A MEAL

Make a list of all the foods Marisol's fellow gardeners grew. Think about the special dishes they planned to make. Then create a dinner menu that includes these foods. Add some of your favorite dishes to make the meal complete. If possible, use a computer to type your menu.

169

NIGHTS
of the
PUFFLINGS

WRITTEN AND PHOTO-ILLUSTRATED
BY BRUCE MCMILLAN

ALA
Notable Book

Outstanding Science
Trade Book

SLJ Best Book

171

Halla *(HATTL•lah)* searches the sky every day. As she watches from high on a cliff overlooking the sea, she spots her first puffin of the season. She whispers to herself, "Lundi" *(LOON•dah)*, which means "puffin" in Icelandic.

Soon the sky is speckled with them—puffins, puffins everywhere. Millions of these birds are returning from their winter at sea. They are coming back to Halla's island and the nearby uninhabited islands to lay eggs and raise puffin chicks. It's the only time they come ashore.

While Halla and her friends are at school in the village beneath the cliffs, the puffins continue to land. These "clowns

of the sea" return to the same burrows year after year. Once back, they busy themselves getting their underground nests ready. Halla and all the children of Heimaey *(HAY•mah•ay)* can only wait and dream of the nights of the pufflings yet to come.

173

On the weekends, Halla and her friends climb over the cliffs to watch the birds. They see puffin pairs *tap-tap-tap* their beaks together. Each pair they see will soon tend an egg. Deep inside the cliffs that egg will hatch a chick. That chick will grow into a young puffling. That puffling will take its first flight. The nights of the pufflings will come.

In the summer, while Halla splashes in the cold ocean water, the puffins also splash. The sea below the cliffs is dotted with puffins bobbing on the waves. Like Halla, many puffins that ride the waves close to shore are young. The older birds usually fly further out to sea where the fishing is better. The grown-up puffins have to catch lots of fish, because now that it's summer they are feeding more than just themselves.

Halla's friend, Arnar Ingi (ATT•*nar* ING•*ee*), spies a puffin overhead. "Fisk" (FIHSK), he whispers as he gazes at the returning puffin's bill full of fish. The puffin eggs have hatched, and the parents are bringing home fish to feed their chicks.

The nights of the pufflings are still long weeks away, but Arnar Ingi thinks about getting some cardboard boxes ready.

174

Halla and her friends never see the chicks—only the chicks' parents see them. The baby puffins never come out. They stay safely hidden in the long dark tunnels of their burrows. But Halla and her friends hear them calling out for food. "*Peep-peep-peep.*" The growing chicks are hungry. Their parents have to feed them—sometimes ten times a day—and carry many fish in their bills.

All summer long the adult puffins fish and tend to their feathers. By August, flowering baldusbrá (BAL•durs•broh) blanket the burrows. With the baldusbrá in full bloom, Halla knows that the wait is over. The hidden chicks have grown into young pufflings. The pufflings are ready to fly and will at last venture out into the night. Now it's time.

It's time for Halla and her friends to get out their boxes and flashlights for the nights of the pufflings. Starting tonight, and for the next two weeks, the pufflings will be leaving for their winter at sea. Halla and her friends will spend each night searching for stranded pufflings that don't

make it to the water. But the village cats and dogs will be searching, too. It will be a race to see who finds the stray pufflings first. By ten o'clock the streets of Heimaey are alive with roaming children.

In the darkness of night, the pufflings leave their burrows for their first flight. It's a short, wing-flapping trip from the high cliffs. Most of the birds splash-land safely in the sea below. But some get confused by the village lights—perhaps they think the lights are moonbeams reflecting on the water. Hundreds of the pufflings crash-land in the village every night. Unable to take off from flat ground, they run around and try to hide.

Dangers await. Even if the cats and dogs don't get them, the pufflings might get run over by cars or trucks.

Halla and her friends race to the rescue. Armed with their flashlights, they wander through the village. They search dark places. Halla yells out "puffling" in Icelandic. "Lundi pysja!" *(LOON•dah PEESH•yar)*. She has spotted one. When the puffling runs down the street, she races after it, grabs it, and nestles it in her arms. Arnar Ingi catches one, too. No sooner are the pufflings safe in the cardboard boxes than more of them land nearby. "Lundi pysja! Lundi pysja!"

For two weeks all the children of Heimaey sleep late in the day so they can stay out at night. They rescue thousands of pufflings. There are pufflings, pufflings everywhere, and helping hands too—even though the pufflings instinctively nip at helping fingers. Every night Halla and her friends take the rescued pufflings home. The next day they send their guests on their way. Halla meets her friends and, with the boxes full of pufflings, they hike down to the beach.

It's time to set the pufflings free. Halla releases one first. She holds it up so that it will get used to flapping its wings.

Then, with the puffling held snugly in her hands, she counts "Einn–tveir–ÞRÍR!" (*EYN • TVAIR • THEER*) as she swings the puffling three times between her legs. The last swing is the highest, launching the bird up in the air and out over the water beyond the surf. It's only the second time this puffling has flown, so it flutters just a short distance before safely splash-landing.

Day after day Halla's pufflings paddle away, until the nights of the pufflings are over for the year. As she watches the last of the pufflings and adult puffins leave for their winter at sea, Halla bids them farewell until next spring. She wishes them a safe journey as she calls out "goodbye, goodbye" in Icelandic. "Bless, bless!"

Think About It

1 What signs tell the children that the young pufflings' first flight is getting closer?

2 What is your favorite photograph in this selection? Describe it and tell what you like about it.

3 How does the author make readers feel what it is like to help the pufflings?

Photo-illustrator Highlights Iceland
Bruce McMillan

Author and photographer Bruce McMillan says he loves happy endings.

NEWS

Meet the Author

REYKJAVIK, ICELAND — Children's book author Bruce McMillan has traveled all over, from Alaska to the Caribbean, to create his popular books. Three of his recent works, *Nights of the Pufflings*, *Gletta the Foal*, and *My Horse of the North*, are set in Iceland.

McMillan has been taking photographs all his life, but he did not start writing until he spent two years living on an island off the coast of Maine. While he was there, he wrote a book about lobstering and took photographs for it. He decided to make it a children's book because he noticed not many children's books had photographs.

McMillan gets most of his ideas from his own interesting experiences and things happening around him. For example, he tells about growing apples and making sneakers. He does more than just give information, though. He likes to tell a story with his books. "I love a happy ending," he says.

Bruce McMillan likes speaking to groups about his work—and they can tell that he likes being an author. His readers hope he will create many more colorful books to enjoy.

Visit *The Learning Site!*
www.harcourtschool.com

181

RESPONSE

Calling All Citizens!

MAKE A PERSUASIVE POSTER
Imagine you are on Heimaey Island, Iceland, a few weeks before the puffins arrive. The mayor has asked you to make a poster announcing the nights of the pufflings. On your poster, tell why the pufflings need the community's help. Also describe how people can help them. Make your poster so convincing that every person on Heimaey Island will want to take part.

Puffin Trivia Quiz

WRITE QUESTIONS
Puffins spend only part of the year on land. Where do they spend the rest of their time? Where else besides Iceland do puffins nest? Find the answers to these and other questions about puffins. (There are even several Web sites about puffins!) Use what you learn to hold a "Puffin Trivia Quiz." Write your questions and answers on cards. Then use them to quiz your classmates.

ACTIVITIES

Puffins and Pelicans

MAKE A BOOKLET

Work in a group to create an illustrated booklet about sea birds, including puffins and pelicans. On each page, show a sea bird and write a paragraph that describes it. Make a cover and a table of contents for the booklet.

A Team Effort

PROPOSE A PROJECT

Think of an activity that would make a good project for a group of student volunteers. Write a short proposal for the project. Tell why you think it would be a good project, how many people would be needed, what equipment or supplies might be needed, and what the main steps in the project would be.

FOCUS SKILL Cause and Effect

Why do the baby puffins in "Nights of the Pufflings" need to be rescued? Read this passage.

Most of the birds splash-land safely in the sea below. But some get confused by the village lights — perhaps they think the lights are moon-beams reflecting on the water. Hundreds of the pufflings crash-land in the village every night.

When one event makes another event happen, it is a **cause**. The **effect** is what happens. You can use a diagram like this to show cause and effect:

Cause
The pufflings get confused by the village lights.

Effect
The pufflings land in the village instead of in the sea.

Understanding cause and effect helps readers better understand what they read.

184

A single cause may have a single effect—for example, a plant may die if you do not water it. Often, however, several causes work together to produce an effect.

In this paragraph, the effect is underlined. Find the causes.

Puffins are not the only animals that have to make it to the ocean to live. Sea turtles lay their eggs in the sand. Poachers collect the eggs and sell them. Predators dig them up and eat them. Even after they hatch, baby sea turtles are not safe. They have to crawl to the sea. Along the way, they may be eaten by birds. <u>Even though thousands of eggs are laid in the sand, only a few baby turtles survive.</u>

WHAT HAVE YOU LEARNED?

1 What would happen if the children did not rescue the pufflings?

2 Human actions have an effect on wildlife. What might you do that would have a good effect on a kind of wildlife?

Visit *The Learning Site!* www.harcourtschool.com

TRY THIS • TRY THIS • TRY THIS

Make a plan for helping wild birds in your neighborhood. Use a chart to show what you will do.

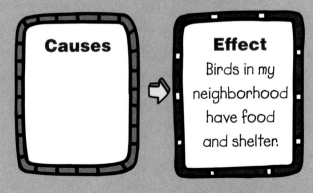

Causes

Effect
Birds in my neighborhood have food and shelter.

Charlotte's Web

a play by Joseph Robinette
based on the book by E. B. **WHITE**
illustrated by Tom Saecker

As a newborn piglet on the Arables' farm, Wilbur becomes Fern Arable's pet. No one believes Fern when she says that Wilbur can talk. After several weeks, Fern's father sells the growing pig to her uncle, Homer Zuckerman, who lives down the road. This part of the play takes place in the Zuckerman's barn. On his first morning there, Wilbur is so lonely he can't even eat. He hears the voice of someone offering to be his friend. He wonders where the voice is coming from. Then he sees Charlotte.

Characters

Fern Arable:
A young girl

Avery Arable:
Her brother

Homer Zuckerman:
Her uncle

Lurvy:
A hired hand

Wilbur:
A pig

Templeton:
A rat

Charlotte:
A spider

Goose

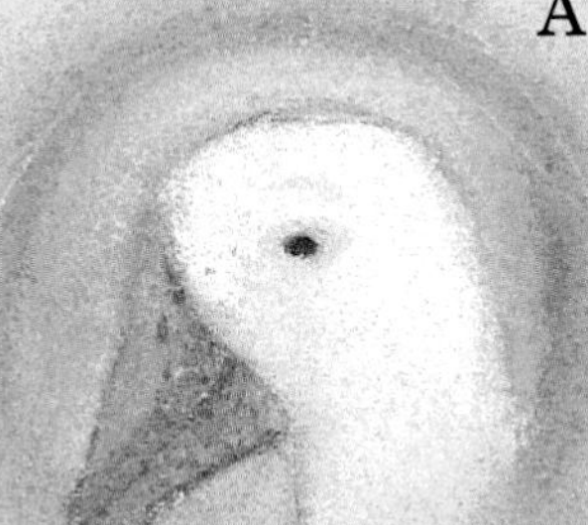

Gander

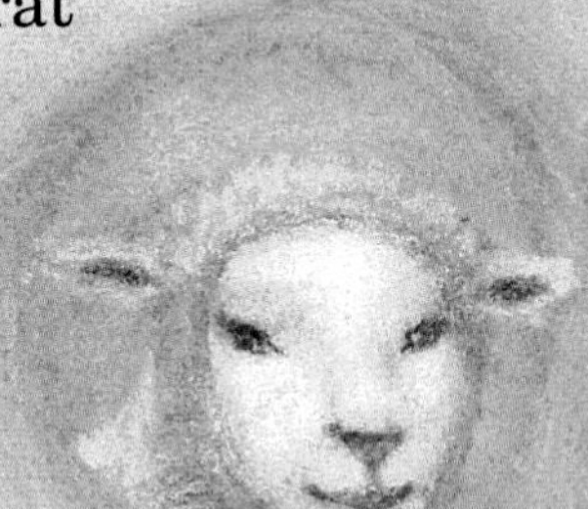

Sheep

Narrator

187

CHARLOTTE: *(Entering.)* Salutations.

WILBUR: *(Excitedly.)* Oh, hello. What are salutations?

CHARLOTTE: It's a fancy way of saying "hello."

WILBUR: Oh. And salutations to you, too. Very pleased to meet you. What is your name, please? May I have your name?

CHARLOTTE: My name is Charlotte.

WILBUR: Charlotte what?

CHARLOTTE: Charlotte A. Cavatica. I'm a spider.

WILBUR: I think you're beautiful.

CHARLOTTE: Thank you.

WILBUR: And your web is beautiful, too.

CHARLOTTE: It's my home. I know it looks fragile. But it's really very strong. It protects me. And I trap my food in it.

WILBUR: I'm so happy you'll be my friend. In fact, it restores my appetite. *(He begins to eat from the trough.)* Will you join me?

CHARLOTTE: No, thank you. My breakfast is waiting for me on the other side of my web.

WILBUR: Oh. What are you having?

CHARLOTTE: A fly. I caught it this morning.

WILBUR: *(Choking.)* You eat . . . flies?

CHARLOTTE: And bugs.

WILBUR: Ugh!

CHARLOTTE: That's the way I'm made. I can't help it. Anyway, if I didn't catch insects and eat them, there would soon be so many, they'd destroy the earth, wipe out everything.

WILBUR: Really? I wouldn't want *that* to happen. Perhaps your web is a good thing after all.

CHARLOTTE: Now, if you'll excuse me. I'm going to have my breakfast. *(She exits behind the web.)*

WILBUR: *(With uncertainty.)* Well, I've got a new friend, all right. But Charlotte is . . . brutal, I think. How can I learn to like her, even though she is pretty, and very clever, it seems. *(He glances back at the web, then slowly lies down. The Narrator enters.)*

NARRATOR: Wilbur was suffering the doubts and fears that often go with finding a new friend. But as the days passed by, he slowly discovered that Charlotte had a kind heart and that she was loyal and true. *(A pause.)* Spring soon became summer. The early summer days on a farm are the happiest and fairest of the year. Lilacs and apple blossoms bloom. The days grow warm and soft. And now that school was over, Fern could visit the barn almost every day. *(He exits as Fern enters. The Sheep, Templeton and Charlotte enter and greet her with animal sounds which soon give way to clear voices.)*

FERN: Hi, everybody! *(She sits on a stool.)* Wilbur, here's a little piece of pineapple-upside-down cake for you. *(He applauds, takes it and begins to eat.)*

CHARLOTTE: *(On a perch near the web, looking offstage.)* Attention, everyone. I have an announcement. After four weeks of unremitting effort on the part of our friend, the Goose, the goslings have arrived. *(All applaud as the Goslings chirp offstage.)* We're very happy for the mother. And the father is to be congratulated, too.

GANDER'S VOICE: *(Offstage.)* Thank you. Thank you. Thank you. We're as pleased as can be, be, be.

WILBUR: What a wonderful day. Brand-new goslings and pineapple-upside-down cake.

TEMPLETON: By the way, Wilbur, I overheard the Zuckermans talking about all the weight you're putting on. They're very happy.

WILBUR: Good.

SHEEP: You know why they're happy, don't you?

WILBUR: You asked me that once before, but you didn't tell me why.

CHARLOTTE: Now, now, old sheep.

SHEEP: He has to know sometime.

WILBUR: Know what?

SHEEP: Wilbur, I don't like to spread bad news. But they're fattening you up because they're going to kill you.

WILBUR: *(Dismayed.)* They're going to *what*? *(Fern is rigid on her stool.)*

SHEEP: Kill you. Turn you into smoked bacon and ham. It'll happen when the weather turns cold. It's a regular conspiracy.

WILBUR: Stop! I don't want to die. I want to stay with all my friends. I want to breathe the beautiful air and lie in the beautiful sun.

SHEEP: You're certainly making a beautiful noise. If you don't mind, I think I'll go outside where it's quieter. *(He exits.)*

WILBUR: But I don't want to die.

CHARLOTTE: Wilbur, quiet down. *(A pause as Wilbur tries to control himself.)* You shall not die.

WILBUR: What? Who's going to save me?

CHARLOTTE: I am.

WILBUR: How?

CHARLOTTE: That remains to be seen. *(The Gander enters.)*

GANDER: Excuse me, excuse me, excuse me. But all this noise is keeping the goslings awake.

CHARLOTTE: We'll try to keep it down. By the way, how many goslings are there?

GANDER: Seven.

TEMPLETON: I thought there were eight eggs. What happened to the other egg?

GANDER: It didn't hatch. It was a dud, I guess.

TEMPLETON: Can I have it?

GANDER: Certainly, -ertainly, -ertainly. Add it to your nasty collection. *(Templeton exits.)* Imagine wanting a junky, -unky, -unky old rotten egg.

CHARLOTTE: *(Laughing lightly.)* A rat is a rat. But, my friends, let's hope that egg never breaks. A rotten egg is a regular stink bomb. *(Templeton enters with the egg.)*

TEMPLETON: Don't worry. I won't break it. I handle stuff like this all the time.

AVERY'S VOICE: *(Offstage.)* Fern!

FERN: In here, Avery. *(Templeton sets the egg down by the trough and exits hurriedly.)*

AVERY: *(Entering.)* Mother sent me to get you. You're going to miss supper.

FERN: Coming. Bye, everybody. And thank you, Charlotte, for whatever it is you're going to do to save Wilbur.

AVERY: Who's Charlotte?

FERN: The spider over there.

AVERY: It's tremendous! *(He picks up a stick.)*

FERN: Leave it alone.

AVERY: That's a fine spider, and I'm going to capture it. *(He advances toward Charlotte.)*

FERN: You stop it, Avery.

AVERY: I want that spider. *(She grabs the stick.)* Let go of my stick, Fern!

FERN: Stop it! Stop it, I say! *(Avery runs after Fern and stumbles against the trough. The trough falls over onto the goose egg. The Gander exits.)*

AVERY: Help!

FERN: *(Wrinkling her nose.)* What's that smell?

AVERY: I think we broke a rotten egg. Goodnight, what a stink! Let's get out of here. *(He and Fern quickly exit.)*

TEMPLETON: *(Emerging from his hiding place.)* My beloved egg. *(He gathers the pieces and exits crying.)*

CHARLOTTE: I'm glad that's over. I hope the smell will go away soon. *(A pause.)*

WILBUR: Charlotte?

CHARLOTTE: Yes.

WILBUR: Were you serious when you promised you would keep them from killing me?

CHARLOTTE: I've never been more serious in my life.

WILBUR: How are you going to save me?

CHARLOTTE: Well, I really don't know. But I want you to get plenty of sleep and stop worrying. And I want you in bed without delay. *(He stretches out on the straw as the lights begin to dim.)*

WILBUR: Okay. Goodnight, Charlotte.

CHARLOTTE: Goodnight, Wilbur. *(A pause.)*

WILBUR: Thank you, Charlotte.

CHARLOTTE: Goodnight. *(The barn is now in shadows. Wilbur falls asleep.)* What to do. What to do. I promised to save his life, and I am determined to keep that promise. But how? *(A pause.)* Wait a minute. The way to save Wilbur is to play a trick on Zuckerman. If I can fool a bug, I can surely fool a man. People are not as smart as bugs. *(A pause.)* Of course. That's it. This will not be easy, but it must be done. *(She turns her back to the audience.)* First, I tear a section out of the web and leave an open space in the middle. Now, I shall weave new threads to take the place of the ones I removed. *(She chants slightly.)*

> **Swing spinnerets.**
> **Let out the thread.**
> **The longer it gets,**
> **The better it's read.**

(She begins to "write" with elaborate movements, though her actions are deliberately indistinguishable.) Attach, girl. Attach. Payout line. Descend. Complete the curve. Easy now. That's it. Back up. Take your time. Now tie it off. Good.

(She chants.)

The message is spun.
I've come to the end.
The job that I've done
Is all for my friend.

(She steps aside as a special light reveals the words "Some Pig" written in the web. (She reads aloud.) "Some Pig." *(She smiles.)* Not bad, old girl, for the first time around. But it *was* quite exhausting. I'd better catch a little nap before daybreak. *(She exits behind the web. The lights begin to brighten as a rooster crows. Wilbur begins to stir. He is having a bad dream.)*

WILBUR: No, no. Please don't. Stop! *(He wakes up.)* Oh, my goodness. That was a terrible dream. There were men with guns and knives coming out here to take me away. *(Lurvy enters carrying a bucket. Wilbur retreats slightly.)*

LURVY: Here you go, pig. Breakfast. Lots of good leftovers today. *(He sets down the bucket.)* Absolutely de—de— *(He sees the writing in the web.)* What's that? I'm seeing things. *(Calling offstage.)* Mr. Zuckerman! Mr. Zuckerman! I think you'd better come out to the pig pen quick! *(He exits hurriedly.)*

WILBUR: *(Unaware of the writing in the web.)* What did he see? There's nothing here but me. *(He feels himself.)* That's it. He saw me! He saw that I'm big and healthy and—and ready to be made into . . . ham. They're coming out here right now with guns and knives. I just know it. What can I do! *(A pause.)* Wait! The fence that Lurvy patched up. Maybe it's loose again. I have to get out. I have no choice. It's either freedom . . . or the frying pan. *(He sees the bucket.)* But first, a little sustenance. *(He drinks from the bucket.)* Now, I'm ready. I'm breaking out of this prison. They'll never take me alive! *(A beat.)* They'll never take me dead, either. *(Another beat.)* What am I saying? I've got to get out of here. *(He starts to rush offstage.)* Chaaarrrge! *(He exits running. A crash is heard offstage.)*

CHARLOTTE: *(Entering, yawning.)* What was that? Wilbur, where are you?

WILBUR'S VOICE: *(Offstage.)* I'm free.

HOMER'S VOICE: *(Offstage.)* Now, Lurvy, what could be so important that you had to drag me out here before I've finished—

LURVY'S VOICE: *(Offstage.)* You'll see, Mr. Zuckerman. You'll see. *(They enter.)*

HOMER: All I can see is—the pig's not here!

LURVY: What?

HOMER: Look out there in the chicken yard. *(He points offstage.)* He's escaped. Let's go!

LURVY: But . . . look at the spider web, Mr. Zuckerman.

HOMER: No time right now. Gotta catch that pig.
(They exit.)

HOMER'S VOICE: *(Offstage.)* Head him into the corner, Lurvy. Run him back this way!

CHARLOTTE: Oh, no. *(The Goose and Gander enter.)*

GANDER: What—what—what's all the fuss?

GOOSE: There's so much noise, noise, noise—

GANDER: The goslings can't sleep. *(Offstage noises are heard. Wilbur enters before Homer and Lurvy.)*

GOOSE AND GANDER: *(Cheering Wilbur.)* Go, go, go, Wilbur! Don't let them catch you! Run, run, run! *(Wilbur does a U-turn and exits again, eluding Homer and Lurvy, who also exit.)*

CHARLOTTE: Now stop this! Don't encourage him. If Wilbur does escape, he'll never stand a chance in the outside world. So, if he runs through here again, we've got to stop him. *(The chase is heard coming closer.)* Get set! Here he comes.

WILBUR: *(As he enters running.)* I'll make it this time! I saw an open gate that leads to the woods. Thank you, everybody, for all your—*(The Goose and Gander catch him and hold him down.)* What is this? Even my friends have turned against me! *(Homer and Lurvy are heard offstage. Wilbur squirms as he is held down.)* I'll not go down without a fight! I'll struggle all the way to the butcher block! I won't be bacon for anybody! *(Homer and Lurvy enter breathlessly. The Goose and Gander quickly let go of Wilbur, whose bravado quickly disappears as he cowers.)*

HOMER: Well, you certainly gave us a run for our—

LURVY: Mr. Zuckerman. Mr. Zuckerman. Look! This is what I wanted to show you. *(He points to the web. They ALL stare at it for a moment. Wilbur, the Goose and Gander see it, too.)*

HOMER: *(Amazed.)* A miracle has happened on this farm.

LURVY: A miracle.

HOMER: "Some Pig." I don't believe it. *(Wilbur begins to regain his confidence.)* You'd better hurry and take care of the chores, Lurvy.

LURVY: Sure thing, Mr. Zuckerman. *(He exits.)*

HOMER: I'm sure we'll have lots of visitors today when word of this leaks out. I've got to call the minister right away and tell him about this miracle. Then I'll call the Arables. But first, I've got to tell Edith. She'll never believe this. Edith! Edith! *(He exits. Wilbur, the Goose and Gander applaud and congratulate Charlotte.)*

WILBUR: *(Himself again.)* Oh, Charlotte. Thank you, thank you, thank you.

CHARLOTTE: It seems to have worked. At least for the present. But if we are to save Wilbur's life, I will have to write more words in the web. And I need new ideas. Any suggestions?

GANDER: How, how, how about "Pig Supreme"?

CHARLOTTE: No good. It sound like a rich dessert.

GOOSE: How about "terrific, terrific, terrific"?

CHARLOTTE: Cut that down to one "terrific" and it will do very nicely. I think it might impress Zuckerman. How do you spell "terrific"?

GANDER: I think it's tee, double ee, double rr, double eye, double ff, double eye, double see, see, see, see, see.

CHARLOTTE: What kind of acrobat do you think I am?

GANDER: Sorry, sorry, sorry.

CHARLOTTE: I'll spell the word the best way I can. *(The Goslings are heard chirping offstage.)*

GANDER: The goslings are hungry. I have to go find some worms, worms, worms to feed them. *(He exits.)*

GOOSE: He's such a good provider. *(She exits.)*

WILBUR: *(Looking at the web.)* "Some Pig." That may just save my life.

CHARLOTTE: For a while, I hope. But I need more words. Maybe Templeton can help. Where is he?

WILBUR: Probably sleeping next door. *(Calling out.)* Templeton, are you asleep in there?

TEMPLETON: *(Entering.)* How can anybody sleep with all this racket?

WILBUR: Did you see the message in the web?

TEMPLETON: It was there when I went out this morning. It's no big deal.

CHARLOTTE: It was a big deal to Zuckerman. Now I need new ideas. When you go to the dump, bring back a clipping from a magazine. It will help save Wilbur's life.

TEMPLETON: Let him die. I should worry.

SHEEP: You'll worry next winter when Wilbur is dead and nobody comes down here with a nice pail of slops.

TEMPLETON: *(After a pause.)* I'll bring back a magazine clipping.

CHARLOTTE: Thank you. *(A pause.)* Tonight, I will tear my web apart and write "Terrific." Now go out into the yard and lie in the sun, Wilbur. I need a little rest. I was up all night.

WILBUR: *(Leaving.)* Thank you, Charlotte. You're the best friend a pig ever had. *(He exits.)*

Think About It

1 How can Charlotte's idea solve Wilbur's problem?

2 Which character's part would you most like to play? Tell how you would play the role.

3 The playwright included many stage directions. How do they help readers as well as actors?

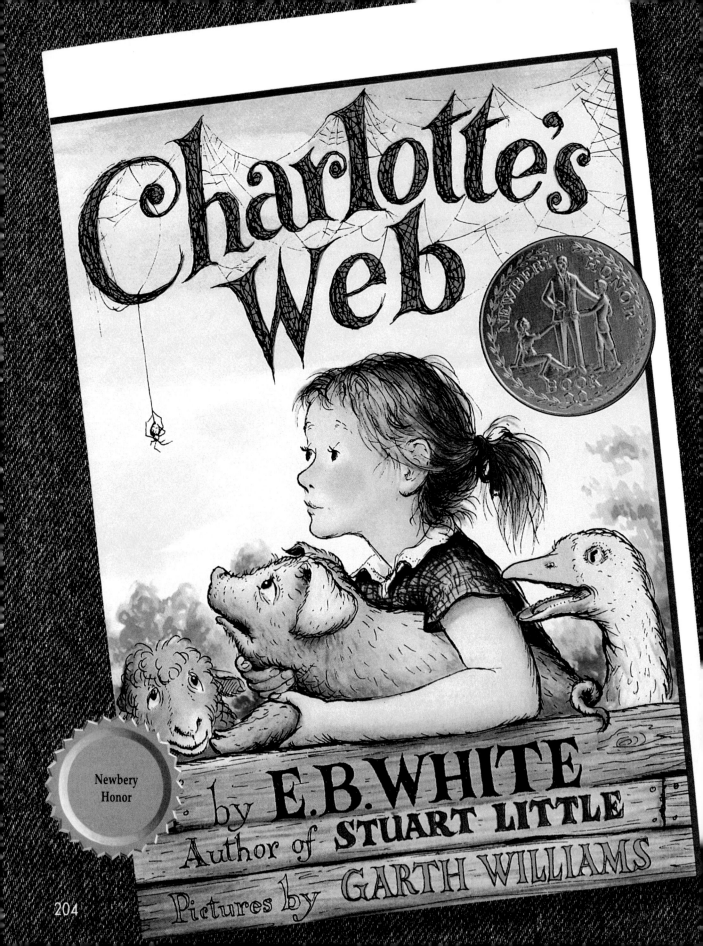

Charlotte's Web

Newbery
Honor

by **E.B. WHITE**
Author of **STUART LITTLE**

Pictures by **GARTH WILLIAMS**

The next day was foggy. Everything on the farm was dripping wet. The grass looked like a magic carpet. The asparagus patch looked like a silver forest.

On foggy mornings, Charlotte's web was truly a thing of beauty. This morning each thin strand was decorated with dozens of tiny beads of water. The web glistened in the light and made a pattern of loveliness and mystery, like a delicate veil. Even Lurvy, who wasn't particularly interested in beauty, noticed the web when he came with the pig's breakfast. He noted how clearly it showed up and he noted how big and carefully built it was. And then he took another look and he saw something that made him set his pail down. There, in the center of the web, neatly woven in block letters, was a message. It said:

SOME PIG!

Lurvy felt weak. He brushed his hand across his eyes and stared harder at Charlotte's web.

"I'm seeing things," he whispered. He dropped to his knees and uttered a short prayer. Then, forgetting all about Wilbur's breakfast, he walked back to the house and called Mr. Zuckerman.

"I think you'd better come down to the pigpen," he said.

"What's the trouble?" asked Mr. Zuckerman. "Anything wrong with the pig?"

"N-not exactly," said Lurvy. "Come and see for yourself."

The two men walked silently down to Wilbur's yard. Lurvy pointed to the spider's web. "Do you see what I see?" he asked.

Zuckerman stared at the writing on the web. Then he murmured the words "Some Pig." Then he looked at Lurvy. Then they both began to tremble. Charlotte, sleepy after her night's exertions, smiled as she watched. Wilbur came and stood directly under the web.

"Some pig!" muttered Lurvy in a low voice.

"Some pig!" whispered Mr. Zuckerman. They stared and stared for a long time at Wilbur. Then they stared at Charlotte.

"You don't suppose that that spider . . ." began Mr. Zuckerman—but he shook his head and didn't finish the sentence. Instead, he walked solemnly back up to the house and spoke to his wife. "Edith, something has happened," he said, in a weak voice. He went into the living room and sat down, and Mrs. Zuckerman followed.

"I've got something to tell you, Edith," he said. "You better sit down."

Mrs. Zuckerman sank into a chair. She looked pale and frightened.

"Edith," he said, trying to keep his voice steady, "I think you had best be told that we have a very unusual pig."

A look of complete bewilderment came over Mrs. Zuckerman's face. "Homer Zuckerman, what in the world are you talking about?" she said.

"This is a very serious thing, Edith," he replied. "Our pig is completely out of the ordinary."

"What's unusual about the pig?" asked Mrs. Zuckerman, who was beginning to recover from her scare.

"Well, I don't really know yet," said Mr. Zuckerman. "But we have received a sign, Edith—a mysterious sign. A miracle has happened on this farm. There is a large spider's web in the doorway of the barn cellar, right over the pigpen, and when Lurvy went to feed the pig this morning, he noticed the web because it was foggy, and you know how a spider's web looks very distinct in a fog. And right spang in the middle of the web there were the words 'Some Pig.' The words were woven right into the web. They were actually part of the web, Edith. I know, because I have been down there and seen them. It says, 'Some Pig,' just as clear as clear can be. There can be no mistake about it. A miracle has happened and a sign has occurred here on earth, right on our farm, and we have no ordinary pig."

"Well," said Mrs. Zuckerman, "it seems to me you're a little off. It seems to me we have no ordinary *spider*."

"Oh, no," said Zuckerman. "It's the pig that's unusual. It says so, right there in the middle of the web."

"Maybe so," said Mrs. Zuckerman. "Just the same, I intend to have a look at that spider."

"It's just a common grey spider," said Zuckerman.

They got up, and together they walked down to Wilbur's yard. "You see, Edith? It's just a common grey spider."

Wilbur was pleased to receive so much attention. Lurvy was still standing there, and Mr. and Mrs. Zuckerman, all three, stood for about an hour, reading the words on the web over and over, and watching Wilbur.

Charlotte was delighted with the way her trick was working. She sat without moving a muscle, and listened to the conversation of the people. When a small fly blundered into the web, just beyond the word "pig," Charlotte dropped quickly down, rolled the fly up, and carried it out of the way.

After a while the fog lifted. The web dried off and the words didn't show up so plainly. The Zuckermans and Lurvy walked back to the house. Just before they left the pigpen, Mr. Zuckerman took one last look at Wilbur.

"You know," he said, in an important voice, "I've thought all along that that pig of ours was an extra good one. He's a solid pig. That pig is as solid as they come. You notice how solid he is around the shoulders, Lurvy?"

"Sure. Sure I do," said Lurvy. "I've always noticed that pig. He's quite a pig."

"He's long, and he's smooth," said Zuckerman.

"That's right," agreed Lurvy. "He's as smooth as they come. He's some pig."

Think About It

Do you think Mrs. Zuckerman is right when she says "It seems to me we have no ordinary *spider*"? Tell why or why not.

ABOUT THE AUTHOR
E.B. WHITE

E. B. White wrote for *The New Yorker* magazine for many years. He started to write children's books only after he moved to a farm. One day when he was feeding his animals, he began to feel sorry about the pig's fate. He started to think of ways to save a pig. He had been watching a spider at work, and the idea for *Charlotte's Web* was born.

White's books *Stuart Little* and *Charlotte's Web* are considered children's literature classics. His works show his feelings about life. He thought simple things were important and didn't want people to forget that.

Response Activities

A Web Sight

INVENT A MESSAGE
Think of a message you could write to amaze someone or help make something good happen. (Use a thesaurus if you need help finding just the right words.) Draw your message as if it were in a web or another special place. Write a few sentences telling its purpose.

Web Weavers

CREATE SCIENTIFIC DRAWINGS

Charlotte spins an *orb web*. Learn more about different types of webs. You might find out about tangled-web weavers, sheet-web weavers, orb weavers, and funnel-web weavers. Draw some different web shapes. Label each one with the name of a spider that spins it.

Drama Club

PERFORM A READING

Work with a partner to prepare a dramatic reading of the first scene between Wilbur and Charlotte. Practice with voices that fit the characters. You will not use actions, so read with expression. Perform in front of an audience if possible.

Making Connections

COMPARE LITERARY FORMS

E. B. White wrote *Charlotte's Web*, and Joseph Robinette rewrote it as a play. Compare the story and the play. Reread the scenes in which Lurvy first sees *SOME PIG* in the web. Make a chart showing how Joseph Robinette changed the story. List what was added, what was left out, and how the order of events was changed. Then write a paragraph telling why you think the changes were made.

How to Babysit an Orangutan

**Story and Photographs by
Tara Darling
and Kathy Darling**

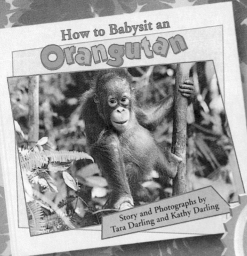

How to Babysit an

Orangutan

Story and Photographs by
Tara Darling and Kathy Darling

Award-Winning
Author

How do you babysit an orangutan? Well, first you have to find an orangutan that needs babysitting.

That's easy here at Camp Leakey. Located in the middle of a rain forest on the island of Borneo, Camp Leakey is not your average camp. It's really an orangutan orphanage.

Ordinarily, orangutan babies don't need human babysitters, but the mothers of these little red apes have been killed and the orphans are too young to survive alone in the jungle. Without babysitters, all the babies would die from disease, starvation, or injuries.

My friend Birute Galdikas is teaching me how to be an orangutan sitter. For more than twenty years she has been taking care of orangutan babies and training babysitters at Camp Leakey.

The first thing she told me was that babysitting an orangutan is not a "forever" job. A good babysitter's job is done when the baby grows up and can go off into the rain forest and live as a wild ape.

Our job is to teach the orphans the skills they need to get along on their own. That usually takes until they are seven or eight years old, the age when they would leave their natural mother. Then we must say good-bye.

Orangutans at Camp Leakey like to hug.

Study time in the rain forest

This is not easy. Orangutan babies are cute and cuddly and especially loving. These are the qualities that landed them in the orphanage in the first place. A lot of people think the adorable apes would be good pets, so greedy animal dealers can get a lot of money for one of the endangered babies. But mother orangutans will not give up their babies without a fight and they are usually killed by the baby snatchers. Then the little orphans are smuggled out of Borneo and Sumatra, the only place the remaining 5,000 wild orangs live. For every baby that reaches a circus, private zoo, or movie trainer, eight orangutans don't survive the trip.

Only a few of the babies are lucky enough to be rescued and brought back to the rain forest. They need tropical forests to find food, and the forests are disappearing as fast as the orangutans, which once numbered in the millions.

Five-year-old Nanang is my special favorite, but I am also helping with other orphans. Those under two years old take a lot of time, so all the babysitters help with them. The infants are pretty helpless for the first couple of years, much like human children.

Wild orangutan mothers nurse their babies for five or six years. So, if babies under this age come to camp, we must give them milk. Twice a day we mix up a big bucket of powdered cow's milk. Infants get the milk in a bottle. Three- and four-year-olds prefer to drink from a cup, and the wise-guy five- and six-year-olds think it is cool to slurp right from the bucket.

Milk is good for orangutan babies.

The babies depend on us for all their food. Like most children, baby orangutans are messy eaters. Babysitters must be prepared to have some food spit at them. Although we feed the babies a lot of bananas, we try to get our charges to eat foods that wild orangutans eat. Fruit is the main part of an orangutan's diet, but they also dine on nuts, flowers, leaves, and many plants that grow in the jungle. The only animals they eat regularly are termites and ants.

I want little Nanang to grow up strong. I'm willing to take a sip of milk to show him that milk tastes good. I enjoy eating bananas with him. I'll even nibble on some leaves once in a while to encourage him to try them. But I absolutely, positively refuse to eat either termites or ants. Surely, insect eating goes beyond a baby-sitter's duty!

Tom loves to slurp soap lather.

Bananas are the babies' favorite food.

This baby is jealous that Nanang has my hat and has made himself a hat out of a leaf.

In the rain forest it rains a lot. (I am sure this does not come as much of a surprise to you.) To make sure a downpour doesn't take me by surprise, I wear a rain hat. Nanang is very jealous. He snatches my hat and plops it onto his own head whenever he can. He loves wearing it even though it is so big he can't see anything with it on.

In a heavy rain, wild orangutans often hold leaf umbrellas over their heads. Orangutans don't like to get wet. That's why bath time is not fun for a babysitter. The littlest orangs get skin diseases and lose their hair in the hot months. It is the babysitter's unlucky chore to give medicine baths. There is a lot of screaming and biting during the bath.

Orangutans don't like baths, but they do love soap. When I do my wash, Tom always begs for a bar. He has rather un-usual ideas about what to do with soap. He thinks of it as food, soaping his arm and sucking the lather off with great slurps of delight. I guess he never heard that washing your mouth out with soap was supposed to be a punishment.

Princess cuddles with her son, Peter.

It isn't necessary to comb an orangutan's hair after a bath. No matter what you do, it will stick up in spiky red clumps. All the babies have this wild hairdo. As they get older, it will become more manageable. When the head hair lies flat, it is a sign that your baby is growing up. Another sign that an orangutan is almost ready to go off on its own is when the skin around the mouth and eyes turns from the pink baby color to the adult black.

When Nanang and I walk in the forest, we often meet Princess and her baby, Peter. Peter is the same age as Nanang and loves to play with him.

Peter taught me an ape-sitting lesson I never forgot: Save all snacks till you are off duty. One morning Peter snuggled up close, stuck his dirty finger into my mouth, and scooped out my bubble gum. Chuckling happily, he popped it into his own mouth.

Orangutans, big and little, are food thieves! Most humans, including me, think this is disgusting. However, it's normal, healthy behavior for a young orangutan to share food with an adult. There are hundreds of different fruits and leaves in the rain forest. Some of them are delicious, but a few are deadly poison. A baby orangutan must learn to tell them apart. So mothers allow food snatching. That way young ones can recognize the smell and taste of safe foods.

If you babysit children, you will probably see temper tantrums. Well, orangutan babies have tantrums that are much the same. There is a lot of kicking and screaming. There is also biting! Lots of biting.

Nanang is making angry kissing noises to show he doesn't want to come to bed.

221

Orangutan games almost always include biting. Not only do the apes nip each other as they play, but they will bite the babysitter if they can.

A playful orangutan shows its bottom teeth. It looks like an angry face, but it isn't. Angry orangutans stick out their lips and make kissing noises to show their displeasure. They burp a lot too. A babysitter has to be able to read the facial expressions of the orangutans. If you mistake the really angry face, with both sets of teeth showing, for a grin, you will surely feel those teeth.

Most of the time, little orangutans have a happy face. They are very playful. "Best friends" form play groups with three or four members. Sometimes we are assigned to watch one baby and other times we get a whole play group.

Best friends do everything together. The little orphans are lonesome, and it seems almost like they adopt each other and form a family. They hang around together every day. Hanging around means something

Tara is teaching Nanang to feel at home in the trees.

different to an orangutan. Any game that is fun on the ground is more fun when hanging in the trees.

One of the most important lessons we teach to the orphan orangutans is that they belong in the trees. Every day we go to the forest so they can build muscles, practice balancing, and get the judgment and coordination necessary for life in the rain forest canopy. Thank goodness the babysitter is not required to climb into the trees with her charges. I couldn't begin to go where Nanang goes with ease. He can hang on with his feet as well as his hands. His wrists allow him to swivel around without changing grip. Even so, he falls once in a while. It takes a few years to get the hang of hanging around.

Nanang knows I can't climb very well. When it is bedtime, he climbs right to the very top of a tree. He hangs up there sucking his thumb till I lure him down with a banana snack.

Princess is building a nest so she can take a nap. Peter is in it with her.

Nanang has his own way to play hide-and-seek.

Nanang isn't old enough to sleep alone in the forest. A wild orangutan would sleep in its mother's nest for five or six years. Peter, for instance, still sleeps with Princess. There are some big snakes that could kill a sleeping baby.

Orangutans like a nice, soft place to sleep. Every night they make a new nest from leaves and branches. It takes about five or ten minutes to build one. The other great apes—gorillas and chimpanzees—also build tree nests, but only the orangutans put a roof on the top to keep out the rain. We can't show our charges how to build a nest in the trees. The best we can do

is let them practice on the ground. The babies try to build a nest out of any materials they can find.

Nest building is much easier to learn if the babies have an older ape to watch. When Camp Leakey was first built, there were only human babysitters. The little orangutans they raised grew up and went out into the forest. But not for good. Many live nearby and come often to visit. Some come with babies of their own. They are wonderful role models. Adult orangutans can teach the orphans things that human babysitters can't.

Every evening when I see Princess and Peter go walking off into the forest, it makes me happy. They are free. Free to climb in the canopy and free to come and visit when they want to.

The babysitters at Camp Leakey have happily said good-bye to more than 100 orphans. These ex-captives have become wild again.

Although I love him very much, I hope someday I will be able to say good-bye to Nanang too.

Think About It

1. Why do orangutan orphans need babysitters?

2. Would you like being an orangutan babysitter? Why or why not?

3. What do you think was the authors' purpose in writing this book? Why do you think so?

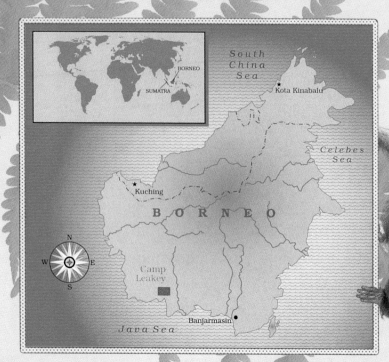

Orangutan Facts

Asian Ape

The orangutan is one of the three "great apes." The others are the gorilla and the chimpanzee of Africa.

Rain Forest Animal

Great apes are found only in tropical rain forests. Orangutans live on the islands of Borneo and Sumatra.

No Tail

A quick way to tell apes from monkeys is to look for a tail. Most monkeys have tails but none of the apes do.

Males and Females Very Different in Size

Male orangutans are two or three times bigger than the 100-pound females.

Babies Stay with Mother for Six or Seven Years

Father never babysits. All adult male orangutans live alone in the treetops.

Treetop Singers

Orangutans rarely come to the ground. Males call out in search of mates in a loud voice that can be heard for miles.

Meet the Authors
Tara and Kathy Darling

Kathy Darling edited children's books for several years before she started writing them herself. For more than twenty-five years she has been writing books that are fun and interesting. Much of her writing deals with science subjects. For example, she has written many books about animals. She raises dogs as a hobby and also writes articles for magazines about dogs.

Tara Darling, Kathy's daughter, is a photographer. This family team is a perfect combination, and the two have traveled all over the world studying different animals. In addition to orangutans, they have made books about the young of other animals.

 Visit _The Learning Site!_
www.harcourtschool.com

Response Activities

A Day in the Life

WRITE A SCHEDULE

Nanang's babysitter has a day off. Make a schedule to help the substitute sitter know what to do for the day. Use details from the selection to describe feeding, bath time, bedtime, and other activities. Give as many helpful tips as you can.

Wanted: Orangutan Sitter

WRITE A "HELP WANTED" AD

You are starting an orangutan baby-sitting service, and you need help fast! Write an ad for the local newspaper. Briefly describe the job and list the skills a person would need to babysit these animals. Before you begin, read some "Help Wanted" ads in a newspaper.

Who Helps?

REPORT ON A WILDLIFE ORGANIZATION

Find out about a group of people who help animals. Many organizations have Web pages. You might do a telephone interview with someone in your community who works for this kind of organization. Take notes, and report on your findings.

Orangutan Art

DRAW THE GREAT APES

Orangutans, like gorillas and chimpanzees, are not monkeys but Great Apes. Look for pictures and information on these animals. Then make a poster on which you draw and name each Great Ape. At the bottom, write a list of differences between the Great Apes and monkeys.

THEME WRAP-UP

Photographs at Work

WRITE A PARAGRAPH Two selections in this theme are illustrated with photographs. How are these selections different from the others in the theme? Would paintings or drawings have worked as well as photos? Write a paragraph explaining your opinion.

ADOPT A PET

Good News
PRESENT A NEWS SHOW
In a group, prepare a television news show on the topic of making the world a better place. Which people or characters from this theme would you invite to appear on the show? Choose one group member who will ask questions. Others can pretend to be people or characters in the theme and answer the questions.

What This Theme Means

Picture the Caring
USE PICTURES TO SHOW MEANING
This theme shows people and characters caring for each other and the world around them. Think of a way to show what this theme means to you. Use a web to brainstorm your ideas. You may draw or paint a picture, or you may find a special photograph. Write a caption to go with your picture or photograph.

231

CONTENTS

THEME MAKE YOURSELF AT HOME

READER'S CHOICE

Stealing Home
by Mary Stolz

REALISTIC FICTION

How can Thomas get Aunt Linzy to stop interfering with him and Grandfather? And will Aunt Linzy ever understand how important baseball really is?

Award-Winning Author

READER'S CHOICE LIBRARY

Skylark
by Patricia MacLachlan

HISTORICAL FICTION

Sarah is put to the test now that she has married Papa and has moved to the prairie. So why do she and the children move back to Maine, by the sea?

Award-Winning Author

READER'S CHOICE LIBRARY

Carlos and the Skunk

by Jan Romero Stevens

REALISTIC FICTION

Carlos is confident that he can impress his long–time friend Gloria by catching a skunk! Join in on another one of Carlos's adventures.

Chester Cricket's Pigeon Ride

by George Selden

FANTASY

Chester Cricket makes a new friend, Lulu Pigeon. Lulu gives Chester a tour of the city in an unbelievable ride across the skies of New York City.

Award-Winning Author

Pulling the Lion's Tail

by Jane Kurtz

ETHIOPIAN FOLKTALE

Almaz is impatient to win the love of her father's wife. Her grandfather tells her it is like getting hairs from a lion's tail. First, they must learn trust.

Notable Social StudiesTrade Book

SARAH, PLAIN and TALL

by Patricia MacLachlan
illustrated by Craig Spearing

Anna Witting lives on a prairie farm with her father and her younger brother, Caleb. Caleb likes to have Anna tell about Mama, who died soon after he was born and who loved to sing. One night Papa tells the children he has put an advertisement in the newspaper for a wife. Their neighbor's new wife, Maggie, had come in answer to an advertisement. Papa reads the letter he has received from Sarah, who lives with her brother near the sea in Maine.

   Papa, Anna, and Caleb write letters to Sarah. They find out that she has a cat named Seal and that she sings. Now Sarah is coming for a month's visit, "to see how it is."

Newbery Medal
ALA Notable Book
Children's
Choice

Sarah, Plain and Tall

Patricia MacLachlan

Sarah came in the spring. She came through green grass fields that bloomed with Indian paintbrush, red and orange, and blue-eyed grass.

Papa got up early for the long day's trip to the train and back. He brushed his hair so slick and shiny that Caleb laughed. He wore a clean blue shirt, and a belt instead of suspenders.

He fed and watered the horses, talking to them as he hitched them up to the wagon. Old Bess, calm and kind; Jack, wild-eyed, reaching over to nip Bess on the neck.

"Clear day, Bess," said Papa, rubbing her nose.

"Settle down, Jack." He leaned his head on Jack.

And then Papa drove off along the dirt road to fetch Sarah. Papa's new wife. Maybe. Maybe our new mother.

Gophers ran back and forth across the road, stopping to stand up and watch the wagon. Far off in the field a woodchuck ate and listened. Ate and listened.

Caleb and I did our chores without talking. We shoveled out the stalls and laid down new hay. We fed the sheep. We swept and straightened and carried wood and water. And then our chores were done.

Caleb pulled on my shirt.

"Is my face clean?" he asked. "Can my face be *too* clean?" He looked alarmed.

"No, your face is clean but not too clean," I said.

Caleb slipped his hand into mine as we stood on the porch, watching the road. He was afraid.

"Will she be nice?" he asked. "Like Maggie?"

"Sarah will be nice," I told him.

"How far away is Maine?" he asked.

"You know how far. Far away, by the sea."

"Will Sarah bring some sea?" he asked.

"No, you cannot bring the sea."

The sheep ran in the field, and far off the cows moved slowly to the pond, like turtles.

"Will she like us?" asked Caleb very softly.

I watched a marsh hawk wheel down behind the barn.

He looked up at me.

"Of course she will like us." He answered his own question. "We are nice," he added, making me smile.

We waited and watched. I rocked on the porch and Caleb rolled a marble on the wood floor. Back and forth. Back and forth. The marble was blue.

We saw the dust from the wagon first, rising above the road, above the heads of Jack and Old Bess. Caleb climbed up onto the porch roof and shaded his eyes.

"A bonnet!" he cried. "I see a yellow bonnet!"

The dogs came out from under the porch, ears up, their eyes on the cloud of dust bringing Sarah. The wagon passed the fenced field, and the cows and sheep looked up, too. It rounded the windmill and the barn and the windbreak of Russian olive that Mama had planted long ago. Nick began to bark, then Lottie, and the wagon clattered into the yard and stopped by the steps.

"Hush," said Papa to the dogs.

And it was quiet.

Sarah stepped down from the wagon, a cloth bag in her hand. She reached up and took off her yellow bonnet, smoothing back her brown hair into a bun. She was plain and tall.

"Did you bring some sea?" cried Caleb beside me.

"Something from the sea," said Sarah, smiling. "And me." She turned and lifted a black case from the wagon. "And Seal, too."

Carefully she opened the case, and Seal, gray with white feet, stepped out. Lottie lay down, her head on her paws, staring. Nick leaned down to sniff. Then he lay down, too.

"The cat will be good in the barn," said Papa. "For mice."

Sarah smiled. "She will be good in the house, too."

Sarah took Caleb's hand, then mine. Her hands were large and rough. She gave Caleb a shell—a moon snail, she called it— that was curled and smelled of salt.

"The gulls fly high and drop the shells on the rocks below," she told Caleb. "When the shell is broken, they eat what is inside."

"That is very smart," said Caleb.

"For you, Anna," said Sarah, "a sea stone."

And she gave me the smoothest and whitest stone I had ever seen.

"The sea washes over and over and around the stone, rolling it until it is round and perfect."

"That is very smart, too," said Caleb. He looked up at Sarah. "We do not have the sea here."

Sarah turned and looked out over the plains.

"No," she said. "There is no sea here. But the land rolls a little like the sea."

My father did not see her look, but I did. And I knew that Caleb had seen it, too. Sarah was not smiling. Sarah was already lonely. In a month's time the preacher might come to marry Sarah and Papa. And a month was a long time. Time enough for her to change her mind and leave us.

Papa took Sarah's bags inside, where her room was ready with a quilt on the bed and blue flax dried in a vase on the night table.

Seal stretched and made a small cat sound. I watched her circle the dogs and sniff the air. Caleb came out and stood beside me.

"When will we sing?" he whispered.

I shook my head, turning the white stone over and over in my hand. I wished everything was as perfect as the stone. I wished that Papa and Caleb and I were perfect for Sarah. I wished we had a sea of our own.

The dogs loved Sarah first. Lottie slept beside her bed, curled in a soft circle, and Nick leaned his face on the covers in the morning, watching for the first sign that Sarah was awake. No one knew where Seal slept. Seal was a roamer.

Sarah's collection of shells sat on the windowsill.

"A scallop," she told us, picking up the shells one by one, "a sea clam, an oyster, a razor clam. And a conch shell. If you put it to your ear you can hear the sea." She put it to Caleb's ear, then mine. Papa listened, too. Then Sarah listened once more, with a look so sad and far away that Caleb leaned against me.

"At least Sarah can hear the sea," he whispered.

Papa was quiet and shy with Sarah, and so was I. But Caleb talked to Sarah from morning until the light left the sky.

"Where are you going?" he asked. "To do what?"

"To pick flowers," said Sarah. "I'll hang some of them upside down and dry them so they'll keep some color. And we can have flowers all winter long."

"I'll come, too!" cried Caleb. "Sarah said winter," he said to me. "That means Sarah will stay."

Together we picked flowers, paintbrush and clover and prairie violets. There were buds on the wild roses that climbed up the paddock fence.

"The roses will bloom in early summer," I told Sarah. I looked to see if she knew what I was thinking. Summer was when the wedding would be. *Might* be. Sarah and Papa's wedding.

We hung the flowers from the ceiling in little bunches. "I've never seen this before," said Sarah. "What is it called?"

"Bride's bonnet," I told her.

Caleb smiled at the name.

"We don't have this by the sea," she said. "We have seaside goldenrod and wild asters and woolly ragwort."

"Woolly ragwort!" Caleb whooped. He made up a song.

"Woolly ragwort all around.
Woolly ragwort on the ground.
Woolly ragwort grows and grows,
Woolly ragwort in your nose."

Sarah and Papa laughed, and the dogs lifted their heads and thumped their tails against the wood floor. Seal sat on a kitchen chair and watched us with yellow eyes.

We ate Sarah's stew, the late light coming through the windows. Papa had baked bread that was still warm from the fire.

"The stew is fine," said Papa.

"Ayuh." Sarah nodded. "The bread, too."

"What does 'ayuh' mean?" asked Caleb.

"In Maine it means yes," said Sarah. "Do you want more stew?"

"Ayuh," said Caleb.

"Ayuh," echoed my father.

After dinner Sarah told us about William. "He has a gray-and-white boat named *Kittiwake*." She looked out the window. "That is a small gull found way off the shore where William fishes. There are three aunts who live near us. They wear silk dresses and no shoes. You would love them."

"Ayuh," said Caleb.

"Does your brother look like you?" I asked.

"Yes," said Sarah. "He is plain and tall."

At dusk Sarah cut Caleb's hair on the front steps, gathering his curls and scattering them on the fence and ground. Seal batted some hair around the porch as the dogs watched.

"Why?" asked Caleb.

"For the birds," said Sarah. "They will use it for their nests. Later we can look for nests of curls."

"Sarah said 'later,'" Caleb whispered to me as we spread his hair about. "Sarah will stay."

Sarah cut Papa's hair, too. No one else saw, but I found him behind the barn, tossing the pieces of hair into the wind for the birds.

Sarah brushed my hair and tied it up in back with a rose velvet ribbon she had brought from Maine. She brushed hers long and free and tied it back, too, and we stood side by side looking into the mirror. I looked taller, like Sarah, and fair and thin. And with my hair pulled back I looked a little like her daughter. Sarah's daughter.

And then it was time for singing.

Sarah sang us a song we had never heard before as we sat on the porch, insects buzzing in the dark, the rustle of cows in the grasses. It was called "Sumer Is Icumen in," and she taught it to us all, even Papa, who sang as if he had never stopped singing.

> *"Sumer is icumen in,*
> *Lhude sing cuccu!"*

"What is sumer?" asked Caleb. He said it "soomer," the way Sarah had said it.

"Summer," said Papa and Sarah at the same time. Caleb and I looked at each other. Summer was coming.

Think About It

1 How does the author show that Papa and the children feel a little nervous about getting to know someone new?

2 What makes Anna and Caleb worry that Sarah will go back to Maine? What makes them think she will stay?

3 What do you like most about Sarah?

Meet the Author Patricia MacLachlan

Dear Reader,

I wrote Sarah, Plain and Tall *as a gift to my mother. When she was a little girl growing up on the prairie, my mother knew the real Sarah, who came from the coast of Maine to become a wife and mother to a close family member. My mother remembered her fondly and told me her story.*

I began the story as a picture book. I thought that would be the perfect way to present this piece of my mother's past—as perfect as Anna's sea stone. But the book grew and changed. In the end, it included parts of the lives of all my family members—my mother, my father, my husband, my children, and me.

I always loved to read, but I didn't plan to be a writer. I thought writers had all the answers. My teachers didn't encourage writing, as teachers do today.

One of the questions children ask me most-often is why I write. I tell them I write for the same reasons they read—to see what will happen and to find out who they are. The characters I write about become real to me; they become my good friends. It is a gift for me if you believe in the truth of my stories.

Sincerely,

Patricia MacLachlan

Dear Sarah

WRITE A LETTER

Caleb and Anna worry that Sarah will feel too homesick to stay with them. Write a letter to Sarah. Do your best to persuade her to stay with Papa, Caleb, and Anna. Explain why they need her and how much their prairie home has to offer. Think about what to say to encourage someone who is making a big change.

Response

Prairie Life Guide

MAKE A GUIDEBOOK

The prairie's plants and animals are different from those where Sarah comes from. With a group, make a prairie guidebook to answer a newcomer's questions. List the plants and animals mentioned in the selection. Put them into logical groups. Then use an encyclopedia or a book about prairies to help you write a short description of each.

A Gift from Home

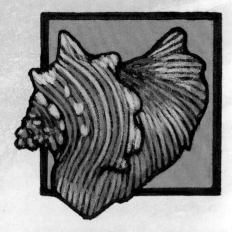

WRITE A DESCRIPTION

Sarah brings gifts from the sea. Suppose you were going to visit a friend who lives far away. What gift could you take that would tell something about your home? Draw a picture of your gift, and write a paragraph that describes it. Explain why you chose this gift.

Activities

I Have a Feeling

WRITE A POEM

Caleb, Anna, Papa, and Sarah feel many different things as they get to know each other. Think about how it feels to be nervous, excited, homesick, worried, or hopeful. Then write a poem about one of these feelings. Your poem might suggest ways for people to feel better when they are feeling bad.

Draw Conclusions

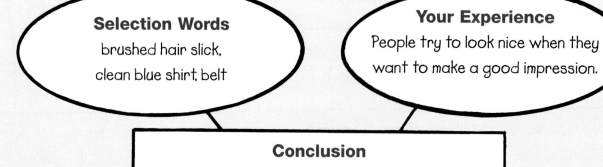

In "Sarah, Plain and Tall," these phrases tell what Papa's horses are like: "Old Bess, calm and kind; Jack, wild-eyed."

Sometimes an author tells something in a direct way. Other times, an author *shows* things without directly explaining them.

You probably figured out at the beginning of the selection that Papa wants Sarah to like him. Yet the author doesn't directly say so. She writes:

Papa got up early for the long day's trip to the train and back. He brushed his hair so slick and shiny that Caleb laughed. He wore a clean blue shirt, and a belt instead of suspenders.

From the details the author gives and what you know about the way people act, you could **draw the conclusion** that Papa wants to make a good impression on Sarah.

Selection Words
brushed hair slick,
clean blue shirt, belt

Your Experience
People try to look nice when they
want to make a good impression.

Conclusion
Papa wants to make a good impression on Sarah.

We draw conclusions all the time as we read. We need to pay close attention to the information the author gives so that our conclusions make sense.

Read the following paragraph from "Sarah, Plain and Tall." What conclusion can you draw about Anna's feelings toward Sarah?

Would the story be as interesting if the author had simply written, "I hope Sarah will like my family and want to stay"?

I shook my head, turning the white stone over and over in my hand. I wished everything was as perfect as the stone. I wished that Papa and Caleb and I were perfect for Sarah. I wished we had a sea of our own.

WHAT HAVE YOU LEARNED?

1. Find at least two places where Anna and Caleb draw conclusions about whether Sarah is happy staying with them. What information and knowledge can they use?

2. Tell whether you think Sarah will stay with the family. Make a diagram to show how you reached your conclusion.

TRY THIS • TRY THIS • TRY THIS

Think about a person you have met or a new place you have visited. How did you draw conclusions about the person or place? As you learned more, did you change your mind or draw a different conclusion? Explain your responses in a paragraph.

 Visit *The Learning Site!*
www.harcourtschool.com

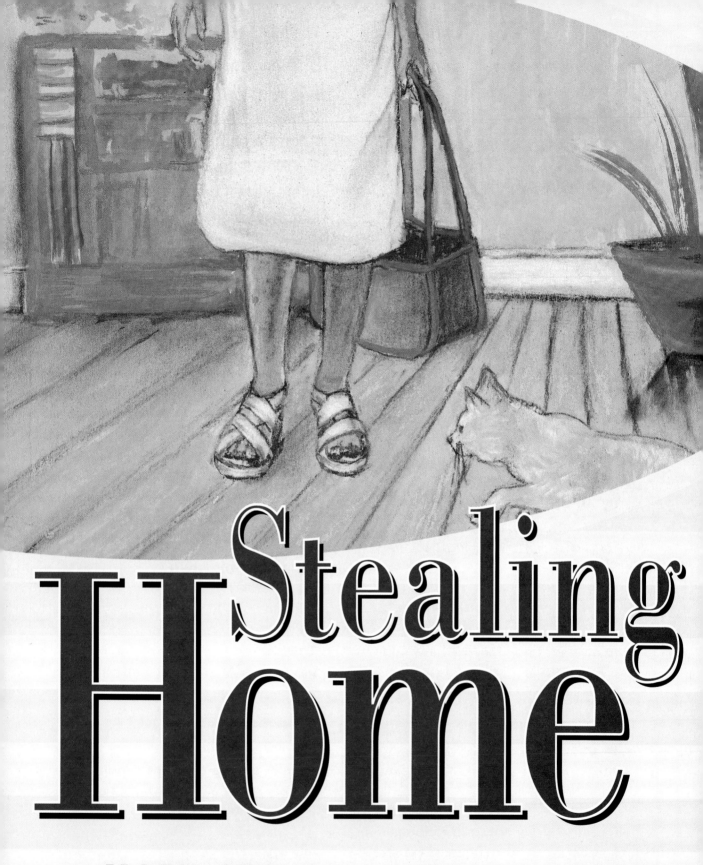

Stealing Home

BY **MARY STOLZ** • **ILLUSTRATED BY CEDRIC**

MARY STOLZ

STEALING
HOME

LUCAS

T homas likes his life with Grandfather in their small house near the beach in Florida. They enjoy gardening, playing games, collecting "treasures," and listening to baseball on the radio. Ringo, Thomas's cat, and Ivan the Terrible, a bad-tempered duck, live with them.

One day Thomas's great-aunt Linzy, with whom Grandfather does not get along, writes that she plans to come and stay for a while. When Aunt Linzy arrives, she takes Thomas's room. Thomas turns to his friend Donny for comfort.

Next morning, Aunt Linzy came into the kitchen smiling. "I slept like a baby. In spite of this awful heat, and your ceiling fans are of little help, Joseph. They just move the hot air in a circle. Nevertheless—like a *baby*. I wouldn't have believed it possible. Of course, I was desperately tired, which probably accounts for it. Thomas! Your cat is delightful! He spent the entire night at the foot of my bed. I am flattered!"

Grandfather, with a quick glance at Thomas, said, "It's the room he's used to, of course."

Thomas, with an ache in his throat, turned away. "I'm going over to Donny's."

"You haven't had breakfast—"

"I don't want any. I'll—I'll be back—sometime."

A week later, Thomas and Donny were eating cones in a yogurt shop.

"It's not going so good, huh?" said Donny.

Thomas shrugged.

"Did you get all her boxes unpacked?"

"Some of them. Grandfather told her we'd have to put the rest in a storage place. There isn't enough *room* for it all."

"Did Grandfather get a cot for you in his room, like he said?"

"Yes."

"Don't you want to talk?"

"Yes."

"So?"

Thomas burst out, "She's cleaning the whole place. I mean, the cards and checkers and dominoes and we had a Scrabble game halfway done and she just swept all the tiles into the bag, and *everything's* in drawers now, she says we can get them out when we play but isn't it tidier to tidy them away when we aren't. And Grandfather caught her just in time before she cleared all our shells and bottle glass and even the fossil into a box. . . ."

"She's cleaning the whole place."

A day or two after her arrival, Grandfather and Thomas had come in from a morning on the beach to find Aunt Linzy sitting near the bookshelves with one of her boxes on the floor beside her. She was wrapping in tissue paper, then putting in the box, all their shells, bottle glass, beachstone figures, the smaller pieces of sculpture. She was clearing from their shelves years and years of treasures.

"Linzy!" Grandfather shouted. "What the deuce are you doing?"

"As you see, Joseph. I am carefully packing your collection of—" She picked up the fossil. "Goodness, I remember this. You've had it for ages, haven't you. I think I remember Marta showing it to—"

"Why are you packing our things?"

"For safekeeping, of course. And to make room."

"They've been safe enough where they are all these years. I do not think they'll be safer in a—Room for what?"

"There is, Joseph, the matter of *my* possessions. I've only been able to empty this one box, and there are all the others on the porch. I don't think I'll be able to get much more in my room—"

Thomas swallowed hard to keep himself from saying, "*Whose* room?" He didn't dare look at Grandfather.

"So? What happened?" Donny asked.

"Grandfather made her—I mean, asked her—to put our stuff back, and they had a—a talk—about her boxes on the porch. She got a lot of the stuff out, and the rest we've put in a U-Store U-Lock over on Cortez. She says she's going to buy another dresser to put in my room. Except she calls it her room. She says she's going to tutor me in arithmetic, when school starts. So she's going to be here then. When it starts. I think she'll still be here when I get to high school. I think she's moved *in*. Period."

"Gee. It sounds—" Donny finished his cone, wiped his mouth, and asked gently, like a doctor touching a sore spot, "What about Ringo—I mean, is he—"

"She's taken him over, too. Her room, her cat. It'll be her house, probably, pretty soon."

"Oh, that's not so, Thomas. I mean, Ringo. He's *always* been your cat."

"Not anymore. Grandfather says I must make allowances for feline vagaries."

"What're they?"

"Dumb stupid ideas."

"Really?"

"No, not really."

"Grandfather knows lots of fancy words."

"He reads lots of books. You know what else he says? He says I should be *glad* that Ringo has made another friend. That's supposed to make me feel better. If you ask *me*," Thomas continued bitterly, "he's a traitor. That's what he is."

"*Grandfather?*"

"Don't be dumb. Ringo. He's turned against me."

"Gosh, Thomas—that's awful. How are you going to stand it, having her there, I mean—living with you?"

Thomas lifted his shoulders. "She's gotta live somewhere, I suppose."

"You know something?"

"Probably not."

"That's what you said about Ivan one time. You said he's gotta live somewhere."

"So—they both gotta, and we're stuck with them. And that fool Ivan is as bad as Ringo. Follows her around like she was the rainbow the pot of gold is at the end of."

"Funny."

"What's *funny?*"

"How animals like her. Maybe it makes up to her for you and Grandfather not liking her."

"What's that supposed to mean?"

"I don't know," Donny said in confusion. "I guess it doesn't mean anything."

"Nothing means anything. Let's get our bikes and go for a long ride."

"Okay."

"Goodness," said Aunt Linzy, coming into the living room on an afternoon in late August. "Is that game still going on?" Grandfather held up a shushing hand. The score was tied in the bottom of the tenth, game at Wrigley Field, Cubs batter up, count no balls, two strikes, a man on first with two out. . . .

two strikes, a man on first with two out. . . .

"Well, really! I was only going to say—"

Andre Dawson, with a line single to left, drove in the winning run and Grandfather turned the radio off.

"If their pitching doesn't fall apart," he said, "Chicago might actually win the division. Who'd have thought it, in spring training?"

"In spring training," Thomas said glumly, "I was *sure* the Pirates would."

Aunt Linzy said brightly, "I looked in the paper this morning, to see the boxing scores—"

"Box scores," Grandfather muttered.

"Oh really, Joseph. I am trying to take an interest."

"It is not necessary, Linzy. Really. Thomas and I understand that baseball isn't your sport."

Jigsaw puzzles, thought Thomas. That's her sport. She finished puzzles he and Grandfather had started, without asking if they minded. Thomas minded. By herself, she did the three hard ones a lot faster than he and Grandfather, together, could do the kind that had scenery.

"I believe," she was saying, "that family members should have interests in common. That's why I'm trying to understand the fascination of baseball even if it seems to me shocking that men get such ridiculous salaries for playing what is a—"

"Child's game. Yes, Linzy. That's been said many times. But believe me, we don't in the *least* wish to impose our pastimes on you."

We don't, Thomas thought, want to share baseball with you. Or fishing—which anyway Aunt Linzy wouldn't dream of sharing. Or our house. Or Ringo.

Ringo came in from the kitchen, briefly brushed along Thomas's leg, sprang to Aunt Linzy's lap. For Thomas, after all these weeks it still felt like a punch in the heart when Ringo, his own cat that had been his from a kitten he'd rescued from the rain, showed that he preferred somebody else. Ringo didn't absolutely ignore him, but if Aunt Linzy was in the room, to her he went. Every time.

"According to the boxing—I mean, *box* scores—your team, the Philadelphia Pirates, is sixteen games out of first place."

"Pittsburgh."

"What?"

"Pittsburgh Pirates."

"Of course. I mix them up."

Grandfather muttered, close to Thomas's ear, "She only does it to annoy, because she knows it teases."

Thomas was sure of that. Aunt Linzy was a lot of things, only dumb wasn't one of them. She knew baseball terms by now, but mixed them up on purpose. To show she was too good for it? To make him and Grandfather look silly, being crazy about a kid's game? Who knew why she did it, or why she did any of the other things that she'd been doing since she got here.

Like ironing sheets and underwear.

One day, shortly after she'd moved in, Aunt Linzy said, "I can't find your ironing board, Joseph."

"We don't have one."

"How do you iron things?"

"When we do—which is practically never—we put a blanket and a sheet on the kitchen table. Works fine."

"For my part, I think beautifully pressed clothes and bed linen are very important."

"I see. All right, I'll get an ironing board."

"Good. From now on, you can leave the laundering to me. It's the least I can do."

"That is not necess—"

"Nonsense. It will be my pleasure."

Thomas and Grandfather found their shirts, trousers, underwear, and sheets pressed and neatly stacked on their beds each week.

"Do you suppose she'd iron my sneakers if I asked?" Thomas said.

"Please. Spare me." Later Grandfather said to Aunt Linzy, "The sheets are supposed to be no-iron."

"There's no such thing. You must admit that unwrinkled bed linen is much pleasanter to sleep on."

Grandfather admitted nothing of the kind, but didn't protest. Nor did he say much when Aunt Linzy, using the sewing machine she'd brought with her, made curtains, and then slipcovers to match.

"There!" she exclaimed, when the job was finished. "Doesn't that look much nicer than blank windows and that tattered old upholstery?"

"It's pretty," Grandfather said, and added, "Thank you, Linzy."

"My pleasure."

Aunt Linzy always said, "My pleasure," when she made improvements that Thomas didn't always think improved things. Like the vacuum cleaner she bought. He and Grandfather had never had one, because they had no rugs. But Aunt Linzy found ways to use it every few days. She was bothered at how sand got tracked into the house, so she put sisal mats just inside the kitchen and front doors. They already had them on the outside. She asked, once, if it wouldn't be a good idea for them to remove their shoes before coming in the house, but Grandfather said they weren't living in Japan, and that was that.

Aunt Linzy was a good cook, and made dinner two or three times a week, using lots of vegetables and pasta. She made soup with things from the stir-fry garden, or even fruit, that Grandfather said was as good as any he made with soup bones.

"Do you suppose she'd iron my sneakers if I asked?"

265

She had made, in the time she'd been with them, lots of changes in their house, in their lives. Grandfather, trying to look on the sunny side, said it wasn't all bad, now was it, Thomas?

They were sitting on the front-porch swing, Ringo on his railing perch, listening to the evening choir of birds. Aunt Linzy had gone to visit Mrs. Price. They'd become vegetarian friends and exchanged recipes about how to make turnips exciting and amaze people with tofu. Or make soup from plums.

"Plum soup," Thomas said irritably. "That's crazy."

"Tasted pretty good, didn't it?"

Thomas wriggled. "I suppose."

"Do you want to talk about it, Thomas?"

"About what?"

"Now, now. You know about what."

"What's to say?"

"I know how difficult this is being for you. But don't you think it *could* be worse?"

"How?"

"Well—Ivan doesn't bite us anymore. There's that."

"Hah-hah."

After a short silence, Grandfather said, "Your aunt Linzy has a good disposition, which is nothing to hah-hah about. Too many people are constantly whining and

"**T**asted pretty good, didn't it?"

complaining about their lot in life. You must admit your aunt is usually pretty cheerful."

"And I think it's funny."

"What do you mean?"

"Grandfather. If you lived someplace where people were wondering how much longer you were going to stay, would you be cheerful? I wouldn't be. I'd be—" He hesitated.

"What would you be?"

Grumpy, Thomas started to say, but changed his mind. "Sad, I guess."

"Thomas, tell me. Have you once tried to look at this situation from your aunt's point of view instead of your own?"

"No. Have you?"

"Yes. Could you try?"

"No."

Grandfather continued to have the waiting look he got when he expected something more from Thomas.

"She took my room away from me."

"We're making out all right in mine, aren't we?"

"It isn't that, Grandfather—"

"I know." He held up one hand. "You needn't say what you're thinking. But *I* am thinking of what people all over the world have to endure that you and I do not. Millions of human beings hungry, hopeless, frightened. *Homeless*, Thomas. Nowhere to *live*. You and I just have to put up for a while with one lonely old lady."

"What does 'for a while' mean? I don't think it's for a while. I think she's *living* with us."

"Thomas, Thomas. You don't often disappoint me. But sometimes you do, really you do. If that should be the case — what do you suggest? Tell her to pack up and get out?"

"She stole my cat."

Thomas looked at Ringo, beautiful and composed on the railing. It made his throat, and his heart, really ache—the way Ringo had left him for Aunt Linzy.

Grandfather put an arm over Thomas's shoulders and pulled him close.

"Things never can remain the same, Thomas. It's the way life is. . . . Everything changes, and we can't stop that."

Thomas sighed. Grandfather always knew what he was thinking. "You don't bicker with her anymore, do you?"

"No. It would make things worse."

"I'm not being a good sport, am I?"

"Not especially."

"I don't want to disappoint you, Grandfather."

"I know that."

"I'll try to be better."

"Good. How about a game of Scrabble before we go to bed?"

"Okay. I mean, I'd like that."

They went into the living room, to the games table, got the Scrabble set from the drawer where Aunt Linzy had stored it, and set up.

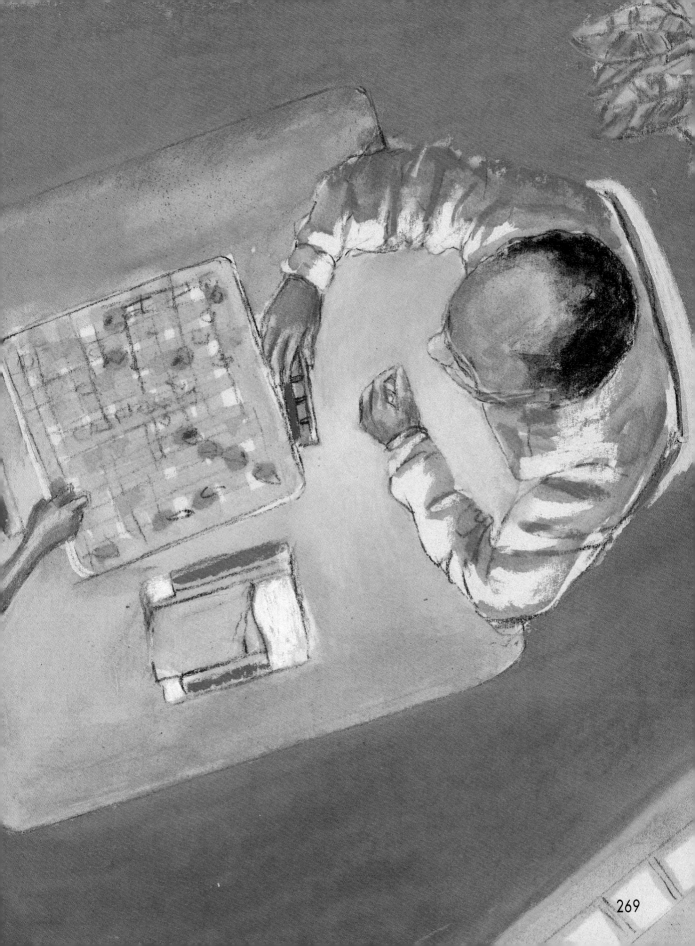

Ringo followed, leaping to Thomas's lap. He settled down and began to run his motor. Thomas, one hand on the large silky head, thought how impossible it was to hold a grudge against a cat. The same as they didn't hold grudges against people.

Think About It

1 How does Thomas's life at home change when Aunt Linzy arrives? What does Grandfather want Thomas to learn from this experience?

2 How does the author use Ringo the cat to help show the problem in the story?

3 Do you think any of the changes Aunt Linzy makes are good ones? Explain.

MEET THE AUTHOR

Mary Stolz

Besides liking cats and cooking, Mary Stolz loves reading. When she was a child, she wanted to be like characters in books she read. Mary Stolz finds that the things she learns in books, about people and life in general, help her to write interesting stories. For her, the most important goal is to capture the reader's imagination. She must be doing a good job because her books have been published in thirty languages.

"In writing, I want to entertain. Failing that, you might as well forget it."

Visit *The Learning Site!*
www.harcourtschool.com

from
Grandfather Is a Chinese Pine

Grandfather is a Chinese pine

Standing firm on the sloping hillside.

From his bright, piercing eyes

All can see the evergreen spirit

That pushed its way up from poor, stony soil.

I love, honor and revere him,

Our sturdy tree of shade and support.

From the tall height of his example

I can see my way straight and far.

—Zheng Zu, age 18
New York, New York

Response Activities

Family Meeting

ACT OUT A SCENE

Imagine that Thomas, Grandfather, and Linzy have a family meeting. Its purpose is to plan ways to get along better. Act out this scene with two classmates. Perhaps Grandfather should lead the meeting and suggest topics to discuss, such as storage problems, laundry, and meals. Before you begin, look over the story and make a list of each character's problems and feelings.

Don't Be "Board"!

WRITE A REVIEW

Thomas and Grandfather enjoy playing board games. Think of a board game you like. Write a "board game review," describing the game and telling why it is a good one. Your goal is to get your readers interested in playing the game.

Now Hear This

LIST LISTENING TIPS

Reread Thomas's conversation with his friend Donny. Figure out what makes Donny such a good listener. Think about Donny's tone of voice, the kinds of questions he asks, and the amount of time he keeps quiet while Thomas is talking. Write a list of tips that could help a person become a better listener.

Making Connections

WRITE A LETTER

Thomas is having a hard time doing what Grandfather has asked. Write a letter to Thomas from the poet Zheng Xu, telling how helpful her grandfather has been. Share thoughts about the ability of older family members to help a young person grow.

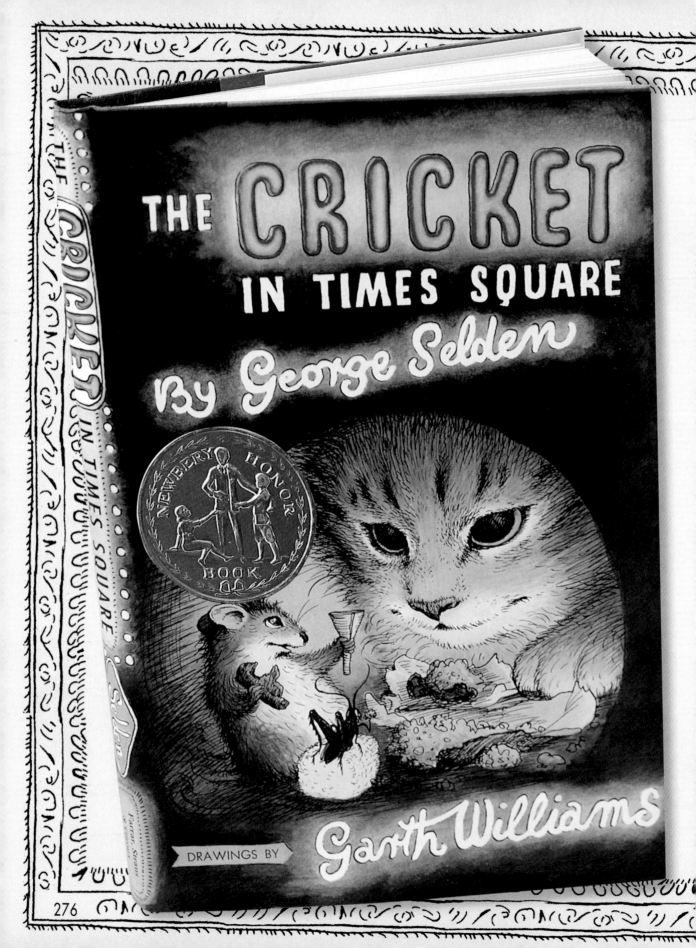

THE

CRICKET

IN TIMES SQUARE

THE CRICKET
IN TIMES SQUARE

By George Selden

DRAWINGS BY *Garth Williams*

*T*ucker Mouse lives in a drain

pipe in the Times Square subway station

in New York City, where he scrounges for

food and watches the world go by. From a

nearby newsstand, he has just overheard

a boy named Mario Bellini begging his

parents to let him keep a cricket

he found and put in a matchbox. Tucker

had heard the chirping sound also, and

now that he knows its source,

he hurries to find out more.

Newbery
Honor

*T*ucker Mouse had been watching the Bellinis and listening to what they said. Next to scrounging, eavesdropping on human beings was what he enjoyed most. That was one of the reasons he lived in the Times Square subway station. As soon as the family disappeared, he darted out across the floor and scooted up to the newsstand. At one side the boards had separated and there was a wide space he could jump through. He'd been in a few times before—just exploring. For a moment he stood under the three-legged stool, letting his eyes get used to the darkness. Then he jumped up on it.

"Psst!" he whispered. "Hey you up there—are you awake?"

There was no answer.

"Psst! Psst! Hey!" Tucker whispered again, louder this time.

From the shelf above came a scuffling, like little feet feeling their way to the edge. "Who is that going 'psst'?" said a voice.

"It's me," said Tucker. "Down here on the stool."

A black head, with two shiny black eyes, peered down at him. "Who are you?"

"A mouse," said Tucker. "Who are *you*?"

"I'm Chester Cricket," said the cricket. He had a high, musical voice. Everything he said seemed to be spoken to an unheard melody.

"My name's Tucker," said Tucker Mouse. "Can I come up?"

"I guess so," said Chester Cricket. "This isn't my house anyway."

A black head, with two shiny eyes, peered down at him.

Tucker jumped up beside the cricket and looked him all over. "A cricket," he said admiringly. "So you're a cricket. I never saw one before."

"I've seen mice before," the cricket said. "I knew quite a few back in Connecticut."

"Is that where you're from?" asked Tucker.

"Yes," said Chester. "I guess I'll never see it again," he added wistfully.

"How did you get to New York?" asked Tucker Mouse.

"It's a long story," sighed the cricket.

"Tell me," said Tucker, settling back on his haunches. He loved to hear stories. It was almost as much fun as eavesdropping—if the story was true.

"Well it must have been two—no, three days ago," Chester Cricket began. "I was sitting on top of my stump, just enjoying the weather and thinking how nice it was that summer had started. I live inside an old tree stump, next to a willow tree, and I often go up to the roof to look around. And I'd been practicing jumping that day too. On the other side of the stump from the willow tree there's a brook that runs past, and I'd been jumping back and forth across it to get my legs in condition for the summer. I do a lot of jumping, you know."

"Me too," said Tucker Mouse. "Especially around the rush hour."

"And I had just finished jumping when I smelled something," Chester went on, "liverwurst, which I love."

"You like liverwurst?" Tucker broke in. "Wait! Wait! Just wait!"

In one leap, he sprang down all the way from the shelf to the floor and dashed over to his drain pipe. Chester shook his head as he watched him go. He thought Tucker was a very excitable person—even for a mouse.

Inside the drain pipe, Tucker's nest was a jumble of papers, scraps of cloth, buttons, lost jewelry, small change, and everything else that can be picked up in a subway station. Tucker tossed things left and right in a wild search. Neatness was not one of the things he aimed at in life. At last he discovered what he was looking for: a big piece of liverwurst he had found earlier that evening. It was meant to be for breakfast tomorrow, but he decided that meeting his first cricket was a special occasion. Holding the liverwurst between his teeth, he whisked back to the newsstand.

"Look!" he said proudly, dropping the meat in front of Chester Cricket. "Liverwurst! You continue the story— we'll enjoy a snack too."

"That's very nice of you," said Chester. He was touched that a mouse he had known only a few minutes would share his food with him. "I had a little chocolate before, but besides that, nothing for three days."

"Eat! Eat!" said Tucker. He bit the liverwurst into two pieces and gave Chester the bigger one. "So you smelled the liverwurst—then what happened?"

"I hopped down from the stump and went off toward the smell," said Chester.

"Very logical," said Tucker Mouse, munching with his cheeks full. "Exactly what I would have done."

"It was coming from a picnic basket," said Chester.

"A couple of tuffets away from my stump the meadow begins, and there was a whole bunch of people having a picnic. They had hard-boiled eggs, and cold roast chicken, and roast beef, and a whole lot of other things besides the liverwurst sandwiches which I smelled."

Tucker Mouse moaned with pleasure at the thought of all that food.

"They were having such a good time laughing and singing songs that they didn't notice me when I jumped into the picnic basket," continued Chester. "I was sure they wouldn't mind if I had just a taste."

"Naturally not," said Tucker Mouse sympathetically. "Why mind? Plenty for all. Who could blame you?"

"Now, I have to admit," Chester went on, "I had more than a taste. As a matter of fact, I ate so much that I couldn't keep my eyes open—what with being tired from the jumping and everything. And I fell asleep right there in the picnic basket. The first thing I knew, somebody had put a bag on top of me that had the last of the roast beef sandwiches in it. I couldn't move!"

"Imagine!" Tucker exclaimed. "Trapped under roast beef sandwiches! Well, there are worse fates."

"At first I wasn't too frightened," said Chester. "After all, I thought, they probably come from New Canaan or some other nearby town. They'll have to unpack the basket sooner or later. Little did I know!" He shook his head and sighed. "I could feel the basket being carried into a car and riding somewhere and then being lifted down. That must have been the railroad station. Then I went up again and there was a rattling and roaring sound, the way a train makes. By this time I was pretty scared. I knew every minute was taking me farther away from my stump, but

there wasn't anything I could do. I was getting awfully cramped too, under those roast beef sandwiches."

"Didn't you try to eat your way out?" asked Tucker.

"I didn't have any room," said Chester. "But every now and then the train would give a lurch and I managed to free myself a little. We traveled on and on, and then the train stopped. I didn't have any idea where we were, but as soon as the basket was carried off, I could tell from the noise it must be New York."

"You never were here before?" Tucker asked.

"Goodness no!" said Chester. "But I've heard about it. There was a swallow I used to know who told about flying over New York every spring and fall on her way to the North and back. But what would I be doing here?" He shifted uneasily from one set of legs to another. "I'm a country cricket."

"Don't worry," said Tucker Mouse. "I'll feed you liverwurst. You'll be all right. Go on with the story."

"It's almost over," said Chester. "The people got off one train and walked a ways and got on another—even noisier than the first."

"Must have been the subway," said Tucker.

"I guess so," Chester Cricket said. "You can imagine how scared I was. I didn't know *where* I was going! For all I knew they could have been heading for Texas, although I don't guess many people from Texas come all the way to Connecticut for a picnic."

"It could happen," said Tucker, nodding his head.

Usually I don't chirp until later on in the summer—

284

"Anyway I worked furiously to get loose. And finally I made it. When they got off the second train, I took a flying leap and landed in a pile of dirt over in the corner of this place where we are."

"Such an introduction to New York," said Tucker, "to land in a pile of dirt in the Times Square subway station. Tsk, tsk, tsk."

"And here I am," Chester concluded forlornly. "I've been lying over there for three days not knowing what to do. At last I got so nervous I began to chirp."

"That was the sound!" interrupted Tucker Mouse. "I heard it, but I didn't know what it was."

"Yes, that was me," said Chester. "Usually I don't chirp until later on in the summer—but my goodness, I had to do *something*!"

*T*he cricket had been sitting next to the edge of the shelf. For some reason—perhaps it was a faint noise, like padded feet tiptoeing across the floor—he happened to look down. A shadowy form that had been crouching silently below in the darkness made a spring and landed right next to Tucker and Chester.

"Watch out!" Chester shouted. "A cat!" He dove head-first into the matchbox.

Chester buried his head in the Kleenex. He didn't want to see his new friend, Tucker Mouse, get killed. Back in Connecticut he had sometimes watched the one-sided

but my goodness, I had to do something!

Chester crept out, looking first at one, then the other.

fights of cats and mice in the meadow, and unless the mice were near their holes, the fights always ended in the same way. But this cat had been upon them too quickly: Tucker couldn't have escaped.

There wasn't a sound. Chester lifted his head and very cautiously looked behind him. The cat—a huge tiger cat with gray-green eyes and black stripes along his body—was sitting on his hind legs, switching his tail around his forepaws. And directly between those forepaws, in the very jaws of his enemy, sat Tucker Mouse. He was watching Chester curiously. The cricket began to make frantic signs that the mouse should look up and see what was looming over him.

Very casually Tucker raised his head. The cat looked straight down on him. "Oh him," said Tucker, chucking the cat under the chin with his right front paw, "he's my best friend. Come out from the matchbox."

Chester crept out, looking first at one, then the other.

"Chester, meet Harry Cat," said Tucker. "Harry, this is Chester. He's a cricket."

"I'm very pleased to make your acquaintance," said Harry Cat in a silky voice.

"Hello," said Chester. He was sort of ashamed because of all the fuss he'd made. "I wasn't scared for myself. But I thought cats and mice were enemies."

"In the country, maybe," said Tucker. "But in New York we gave up those old habits long ago. Harry is my oldest friend. He lives with me over in the drain pipe. So how was scrounging tonight, Harry?"

"Not so good," said Harry Cat. "I was over in the ash cans on the East Side, but those rich people don't throw out as much garbage as they should."

"Chester, make that noise again for Harry," said Tucker Mouse.

Chester lifted the black wings that were carefully folded across his back and with a quick, expert stroke drew the top one over the bottom. A *thrumm* echoed through the station.

"Lovely—very lovely," said the cat. "This cricket has talent."

"I thought it was singing," said Tucker. "But you do it like playing a violin, with one wing on the other?"

"Yes," said Chester. "These wings aren't much good for flying, but I prefer music anyhow." He made three rapid chirps.

Tucker Mouse and Harry Cat smiled at each other. "It makes me want to purr to hear it," said Harry.

"Some people say a cricket goes 'chee chee chee,'" explained Chester. "And others say, 'treet treet treet,' but we crickets don't think it sounds like either one of those."

"It sounds to me as if you are going 'crik crik crik,'" said Harry.

"Maybe that's why they call him a 'cricket,'" said Tucker.

They all laughed. Tucker had a squeaky laugh that sounded as if he were hiccupping. Chester was feeling much happier now. The future did not seem nearly as gloomy as it had over in the pile of dirt in the corner.

"Are you going to stay a while in New York?" asked Tucker.

"I guess I'll have to," said Chester. "I don't know how to get home."

"Well, we could always take you to Grand Central Station and put you on a train going back to Connecticut," said Tucker. "But why don't you give the city a try. Meet new people—see new things. Mario likes you very much."

"Yes, but his mother doesn't," said Chester. "She thinks I carry germs."

"Germs!" said Tucker scornfully. "She wouldn't know a germ if one gave her a black eye. Pay no attention."

"Too bad you couldn't have found more successful friends," said Harry Cat. "I fear for the future of this news-stand."

"It's true," echoed Tucker sadly. "They're going broke fast." He jumped up on a pile of magazines and read off the names in the half-light that slanted through the cracks in the wooden cover: *Art News—Musical America.* Who would read them but a few long-hairs?"

"I don't understand the way you talk," said Chester. Back in the meadow he had listened to bullfrogs, and woodchucks, and rabbits, even a few snakes, but he had never heard anyone speak like Tucker Mouse. "What is a long-hair?"

Tucker scratched his head and thought a moment. "A long-hair is an extra-refined person," he said. "You take an Afghan hound—that's a long-hair."

"Do Afghan hounds read *Musical America*?" asked the cricket.

"They would if they could," said Tucker.

Chester shook his head. "I'm afraid I won't get along in New York," he said.

"Oh, sure you will!" squeaked Tucker Mouse. "Harry, suppose we take Chester up and show him Times Square. Would you like that, Chester?"

"I guess so," said Chester, although he was really a little leery of venturing out into New York City.

The three of them jumped down to the floor. The crack in the side of the newsstand was just wide enough for Harry to get through. As they crossed the station floor, Tucker pointed out the local sights of interest, such as the Nedick's lunch counter—Tucker spent a lot of time around there—and the Loft's candy store. Then they came to the drain pipe. Chester had to make short little hops to keep from hitting his head as they went up. There seemed to be hundreds of twistings and turnings, and many other pipes that opened off the main route, but Tucker Mouse knew his way perfectly—even in the dark. At last Chester saw light above them. One more hop brought him out onto the sidewalk. And there he gasped, holding his breath and crouching against the cement.

They were standing at one corner of the Times building, which is at the south end of Times Square. Above the cricket, towers that seemed like mountains of light rose up into the night sky. Even this late the neon signs were still blazing. Reds, blues, greens, and yellows flashed down on

him. And the air was full of the roar of traffic and the hum of human beings. It was as if Times Square were a kind of shell, with colors and noises breaking in great waves inside it. Chester's heart hurt him and he closed his eyes. The sight was too terrible and beautiful for a cricket who up to now had measured high things by the height of his willow tree and sounds by the burble of a running brook.

"How do you like it?" asked Tucker Mouse.

"Well—it's—it's quite something," Chester stuttered.

"You should see it New Year's Eve," said Harry Cat.

Gradually Chester's eyes got used to the lights. He looked up. And way far above them, above New York, and above the whole world, he made out a star that he knew was a star he used to look at back in Connecticut. When they had gone down to the station and Chester was in the matchbox again, he thought about that star. It made him feel better to think that there was one familiar thing, twinkling above him, amid so much that was new and strange.

Think About It

1 For Chester, what is hard about being in a new place? What things make him feel better?

2 Which character do you like best, Chester, Tucker, or Harry? Why?

3 This story takes place in a big city. How does this setting affect the lives of the animals in the story?

About the Author

George Selden

George Selden started out as a playwright. A friend suggested that he try writing children's books. Selden became famous for writing stories about animals who act like humans. His characters show the importance of friends.

The Cricket in Times Square was an unusual story because of its city setting. Like Chester Cricket, George Selden was from Connecticut. He really heard a cricket chirp in the subway, and it made him homesick for the country. When he was asked to write a sequel, he waited ten years for an idea he thought was good enough. In the end, he wrote six more books about Chester and his friends.

 Visit *The Learning Site!* www.harcourtschool.com

293

Response Activities

Welcome to Times Square

DESIGN A SIGN

Times Square seems "terrible and beautiful" to Chester. Design a neon sign that would welcome a homesick cricket. Look at real signs for eye-catching ideas. Using black paper, create your sign with fluorescent paints or crayons. Or, you could use a computer if you have an artwork program.

Greetings from the Big City

CREATE A POSTCARD

Write a postcard from Chester to a cricket back home in Connecticut. On one side of a card, draw a city scene. On the other side, write Chester's message. Have him tell how he feels in the big city. He might also compare city life and country life and talk about getting used to a new place.

What Makes a Cricket Tick?

RESEARCH CRICKETS

Chester tells Tucker that he does not chirp until later in the summer. Is this detail based on fact? Find some interesting facts about crickets. Find out where they live and what they eat. Find out how, when, and why they chirp. Make a poster that shows what you learned. Include a drawing of a cricket.

Road Trip

MAP A ROUTE

On a map of the United States, find Chester's home, Connecticut, and Tucker's home, New York City. Also find Maine, where Sarah comes from, and Florida, where Thomas lives. Imagine you are going on a road trip to visit all these places. Find a good route for your trip. Also figure out about how far it is from place to place. Show your route to a classmate.

Sequence

In "The Cricket in Times Square," Chester tells how he got to New York City. In his words, this is the order, or sequence of events, that got him there.

> I was sitting on top of my stump.

⬇

> I smelled something, and I went off toward the smell.

⬇

> I jumped into the picnic basket, and I fell asleep.

⬇

> I could feel the basket being carried into a car and riding somewhere.

⬇

> I could tell from the noise that it must be New York.

In a **sequence,** events are described in the order in which they happen. Words that signal time order help you follow the sequence of events in a story. Signal words include *first, next, last, then, finally, before, after, earlier,* and *later.*

Copy the sequence chart on page 296. Make your boxes big enough to write in. Then write the events below in the boxes in the correct sequence.

By paying attention to sequence in a story, you can understand the ideas and events that lead to the ending.

- **Tucker Mouse bites the liverwurst into two pieces and gives Chester the bigger piece.**
- **Tucker tosses things left and right in a wild search.**
- **Chester Cricket says he loves liverwurst.**
- **Tucker carries liverwurst to Chester.**
- **Tucker dashes to his nest.**
- **Tucker Mouse asks Chester what happened next.**

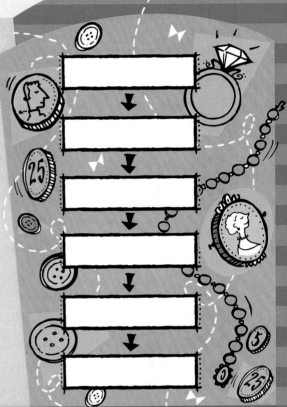

WHAT HAVE YOU LEARNED?

1 How does the author make it clear when Chester Cricket's story about his past begins and ends?

2 What sequence of events begins when Harry Cat lands beside Tucker Mouse? List four or five events that happen.

TRY THIS • TRY THIS • TRY THIS

Write a paragraph or two in which you recall something that happened in the past. First, tell the setting of the event — for example, at camp, in the classroom, in your room. Then tell about the past events in the order in which they happened. Use signal words.

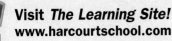

**Visit *The Learning Site!*
www.harcourtschool.com**

LOOK
to the
NORTH

A Wolf Pup Diary

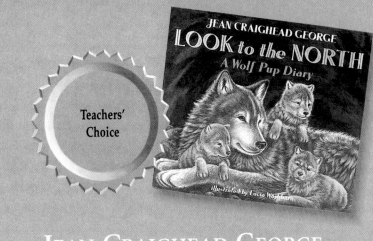

Teachers' Choice

BY JEAN CRAIGHEAD GEORGE
ILLUSTRATED BY LUCIA WASHBURN

1 *Day Old*

When you see dande-lions turning silver, look to the north. Wolf pups are being born.

Boulder, Scree, and Talus arrive. They are blind and deaf. They can't even smell. Each weighs only one pound. They are curled against their warm mother in a nursery dug deep into a hillside.

Their father is standing in the snow by the den entrance.

The wind blows ice crystals across the cold mountaintop.

10 Days Old

When the yellow warblers return from the south, look to the north. The eyes of the wolf pups are opening.

Boulder sees his sister, Scree, and jumps on her. She knocks him off. He jumps on her again. She bites him with her sharp new baby teeth. He bites her back. They growl their first growls.

Talus nurses. He is the smallest pup.

2 Weeks Old

When the redwings are flashing their bright shoulder badges, look to the north. The mother wolf will take brief vacations.

The mother wolf has not left the pups since they were born. The father fed her while she kept the pups warm. Now the pups are well furred. The mother gets to her feet. The pups are sleeping. She goes down the long tunnel into the sunlight.

She runs joyfully across the alpine tundra, then back to her pack. They run with her.

The pack is small—there are the mother and father, the alphas or leaders; an assistant, the beta; and a yearling male. They run close together like a flock of wheeling birds, never touching. Their ruffs ripple.

301

3 Weeks Old

*When the spring azure blue butterflies are flitting,
look to the north. The wolf pups can hear.*

Boulder hears his pack howl. He stands up and listens.
Scree hears the lambs of the mountain sheep bleating. Talus
not only can hear all this, but can also smell it. Talus has a
talent. He wobbles out of the den following the sweet scent
of morning. Boulder and Scree follow him into the daylight.

The outdoors is bright and big. Boulder jumps on Scree
and growls. She turns and bites his neck. He yelps. Talus follows the scent of a lemming and runs smack into his mother.
With a low growl she turns him back and stops Scree from
shaking Boulder by the neck. The pups scurry into the den.

4 Weeks Old

When you see baby robins, look to the north.
Wolf pups are almost weaned.

The mother leaves the pups. The yearling is baby-sitter.

Boulder grabs Scree by the back of her neck and shakes hard. She yelps piteously, then grabs Boulder's neck. He breaks loose. Suddenly Scree rolls to her back, flashing her pale belly fur. This is the wolves' white flag of surrender. Boulder has won. He is alpha pup.

Scree, who is now his assistant, jumps on Talus and growls. Talus smells defeat and flashes his white flag. Scree stops biting.

Each pup has found his or her place in the pup society. They know who they are. All fighting ceases

 Weeks Old

On the longest day of the year, look to the north. Wolf pups are outdoors playing.

Boulder, Scree, and Talus are jumping on the baby-sitter. They chew his tail. They knock his feet out from under him. They play rough.

The wolf pack is returning, and Talus smells the scent of good food on their breaths.

He sticks his nose in the corner of his father's mouth, which says in wolf talk, "I'm a puppy—feed me." The father coughs up food for Talus. The wolves have brought food home for the pups in their belly baskets. The mother stops all milk snacks.

⑨ *Weeks Old*

*When firecrackers shoot skyward,
look to the north. Wolf pups are
learning wolf talk.*

Boulder, Scree, and Talus can lower their ears to say to their father and mother, "You are the beloved leaders of our pack." They can spank the ground with their front paws to say, "Come play with me," and they can scent mark bones and pretty stones to say, "This is mine."

The wolf den is swathed in blue harebell flowers. The wolves stop and look at them.

10 Weeks Old

When you are eating July's abundant corn on the cob, look to the north. A change is coming to wolfdom.

Talus smells excitement in his mother's sweet scent as she prances before the den. Boulder and Scree cock their heads. The mother suddenly dashes up the den mound and away. The adults trot after her. The pups follow. Not one adult wolf steps on a harebell.

The wolf family arrives at their summer den on a hill above a river. The den is a mere tunnel in which the pups can hide from the eagle, the grizzly bear, and the intense alpine-tundra sun.

The pups play king of the hill, tug-of-war, and football. When they are bored with these games, they play "jump on the baby-sitter."

They dig holes and chew bones, rocks, and puppy tails. Sometimes they chase mice and butterflies.

12 Weeks Old

When the crickets are chirping, look to the north. Wolf pups are learning adult wolf talk.

Boulder can raise his ears straight up to say, "I am the boss pup." He can take Talus's nose gently in his mouth to say, "I'm a good leader." Talus can scent mark to say, "I am irritable." Scree can howl to say, "I am lonely." All three can show their teeth to say, "Hey, watch it." And all three can smile both with their mouths and with their tails.

3 Months Old

When you see the early goldenrod blooming, look to the north. Wolf pups are bonding.

Scree and Talus follow Boulder around berries and over wildflower seeds. They run in a knot, never bumping. They leap as one. They chase birds in a posse. They move across the ridge—until Talus smells a distant grizzly and yips. Then they break ranks and speed home.

16 *Weeks Old*

When you are eating fresh blueberries,
look to the north. Wolf pups are practicing
their hunting skills.

Boulder nips Scree the way his father nips caribou. Scree trips Talus the way her mother trips moose. Talus shakes a piece of caribou fur so hard, he gets dizzy. All three can peel hide from the bone toys their parents bring them.

This day the beta does not come home.

The wolves are having trouble getting food without their assistant. It takes the cooperation of many to fell the big game needed to feed a wolf pack. The adults hunt night

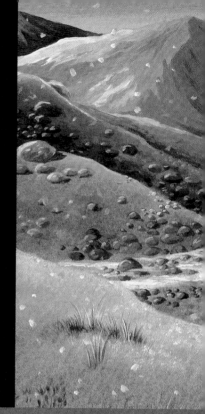

4 1/2 Months Old

When you are back in school, look to the north. Wolf pups are leaving their summer dens.

Boulder, Scree, and Talus follow their father and mother and the baby-sitter into the valley. They are gypsies. They sleep on open ridges by day and wander the river bottomlands to hunt at night.

Snow is falling in the mountains.

6 Months Old

When you are out trick-or-treating, look to the north. Wolf pups are enrolled in the wolf kindergarten of hunting.

Boulder, Scree, and Talus watch the adults stalk game. They stalk a bird, moving forward in a crouch. They pounce and miss.

Talus hunts by sniffing the air. He picks up the scent of an injured animal and jogs a mile before he finds it. He howls for his pack. They join him and feast.

Talus is no longer the wolf on the bottom. His incredible nose moves him up into a place of high rank. The baby-sitter is now on the bottom.

311

7 Months Old

When you are eating turkey and watching football, look to the north. The wolf pups are full grown.

Talus smells another wounded animal. The pack follows him through snow and wind drift. They come to a twisted spruce tree. Beneath it lies the beta. He is injured and weak from eating only voles and birds.

The adults fell a caribou. The father brings food to his friend, then scratches a shallow saucer in the snow beside him. He curls up and goes to sleep. The rest of the pack make wolf beds, too. They will take care of the beta until he is well.

10 ½ Months Old

When the day and night are of equal length, look to the north. New pups are on their way.

High up in the mountains, the young adult wolves are ready to help the pack raise their new brothers and sisters.

Think About It

1. What are three of the most important things wolf pups learn as they grow?

2. Did this selection change the way you feel about wolves? Explain why or why not.

3. Explain how the author organized the information in this

Meet the Author JEAN

Jean Craighead George loves animals. Her childhood home was full of pets—dogs, falcons, raccoons, owls, opossums, and insects. Her father, who worked for the U.S. Forest Service, took Jean and her brothers into wilderness areas to learn about plants and animals. At twenty-four, she wrote a book about a fox and discovered she was a children's book writer.

Jean Craighead George has studied wolves since 1971, when she learned to communicate with them at a research lab in Alaska. Her novel *Julie of the Wolves* won the Newbery Medal in 1973.

CRAIGHEAD GEORGE

Here, the author explains why she wrote *Look to the North*.

I love wolf pups. They have called me to Alaska's alpine tundras to lie on my stomach and watch them play. They have lured me west to my friend the wolf trainer's house, to hold them and feed them from bottles. They have included me in their pup games in Alaska and Montana. I have howled with them in Minnesota.

And I have kept notes on them.

Why do I love them so? In these nursing, tumbling, fighting, and growing children of the wild I see all children. And they are wonderful.

Jean Craighead George

Visit *The Learning Site!*
www.harcourtschool.com

MOON
of
Falling Leaves

Long ago, the trees were told
they must stay awake
seven days and nights,
but only the cedar,
the pine and the spruce
stayed awake until
that seventh night.
The reward they were given
was to always be green,
while all the other trees
must shed their leaves.

So, each autumn, the leaves
of the sleeping trees fall.
They cover the floor
of our woodlands with colors
as bright as the flowers
that come with the spring.
The leaves return the strength
of one more year's growth
to the earth.

This journey
the leaves are taking
is part of that great circle
which holds us all close to the earth.

by Joseph Bruchac
and Jonathan London

illustrated by Steve Johnson
and Lou Fancher

Thirteen Moons on Turtle's Back
A NATIVE AMERICAN YEAR OF MOONS

JOSEPH BRUCHAC and
JONATHAN LONDON

illustrated by
THOMAS LOCKER

Teachers' Choice

Outstanding
Science Trade Book

Notable
Social Studies
Trade Book

WRITE A STORY

Folk tales have given wolves a bad name. List at least two folk tales in which a wolf is the "bad guy." Then think about the real wolves described in this selection. What traits do wolves have that you admire? Write a talking-animal story in which a wolf is the hero.

RESPONSE

Growing Up

CREATE A TIME LINE

In a group, make a ten-and-a-half-month time line that begins in winter with the pups' birth and ends when Boulder, Talus, and Scree are young adults. Label your time line to show when important changes happen in their lives. Illustrate your time line with pictures showing each stage.

Follow the Leader

WRITE AN ESSAY

In a wolf pack, there are leaders and there are followers who help them. Human communities also have leaders and followers. Make a list of different kinds of leaders. Then write a few paragraphs telling what qualities someone needs to be a good leader. You may also mention a leader you admire and tell why you admire him or her.

ACTIVITIES

Making Connections

WRITE A LEGEND

The authors of both "Look to the North" and the legend about falling leaves look closely at the natural world. Write and illustrate your own legend about a plant, an animal, or a natural object. You might want to use what you learned in "Look to the North" to write a legend about a wolf.

SAGUARO
CACTUS

The Sonoran Desert is a small bit of land in the southwestern United States. The weather is hot and dry there for most of the year. It is a very difficult place for plants to grow.

Yet, rising out of the desert sand and scrub brush is an amazing sight—the giant saguaro (pronounced suh WAH row) cactus.

Habitats

SAGUARO CACTUS

PAUL AND SHIRLEY BERQUIST

by Paul and Shirley Berquist

A saguaro can live as long as 200 years. It can grow to 50 feet tall (15 meters) and weigh as much as 10 tons (9 metric tons). That's the weight of three or four automobiles.

From all over the desert, animals and birds walk, crawl, and fly to the saguaro. That's because a saguaro is much more than just a giant plant. It is the center of life for hundreds of creatures, including the tiny elf owl.

Life for a new saguaro begins in the summer, when warm rains come to the desert. This is also when the bright red fruit of a full-grown cactus falls to the ground. For desert creatures, it is time to feast!

The elf owl is only 5 inches long (13 centimeters). It is the smallest owl in the world. The elf owl is only one of the many birds that find a safe, dry home inside the cool saguaro.

Insects and birds feed on the sweet, juicy pulp of the saguaro's fruit. Mice and rabbits gobble up the soft, black seeds. By chance, a seed may stick to a mouse's paw or to a rabbit's ear. Perhaps the seed will travel with the animal to another place in the desert. And maybe it will fall to the ground and take root.

The desert is a harsh place for young saguaros. Most cactus seedlings die in the blazing heat. But a few lucky plants take root in shady spots, safe from the burning sun. In the shadow of a mesquite (mess KEET) tree, this ten-year-old saguaro is off to a good start.

The saguaro grows very slowly. After 50 years it stands only 10 feet tall (3 meters). Every spring lovely flowers appear. Each flower blooms for only one full day.

On this day, birds, bats, and insects may come to drink the nectar. This is the sweet liquid inside a flower. As the creatures drink, bits of flower dust, called pollen, stick to their bodies. At the next flower, a bit of pollen might fall off and start a new cactus.

The saguaro has long folds on its skin called pleats. These pleats allow the cactus to stretch. As it takes in water, the saguaro grows fatter and fatter. A fully grown saguaro can stretch until it holds several thousand pounds of water!

The saguaro's roots do not grow deep. They stay shallow to catch any bit of rainwater that drips through the ground. The roots spread out as much as 90 feet (27.5 meters), forming the shape of a giant bowl.

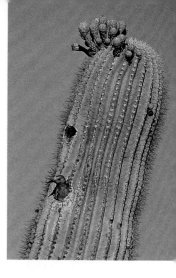

When there is no more nectar to drink, most of the creatures leave. But not the gila woodpecker. With its long, sharp beak the bird tap . . . tap . . . taps through the saguaro's tough skin to build a nest.

Soon, the woodpecker has drilled a hole that reaches deep inside the cactus. The dark hole makes a cool nesting place for the woodpecker's family. Safely inside, the birds hunt and feast on insects that would otherwise harm the saguaro.

A woodpecker family does not stay in the same nest for long. When the babies are ready to fly, the family moves on. Soon the family is tapping a new hole either in that cactus or in another.

As the woodpecker drills, a hard wall grows around the hole in the cactus's skin. This wall, called a boot, keeps the hole dry. It also keeps air from drying out the rest of the saguaro.

Even after the cactus dies, the boot stays hard and strong. No wonder the people of the desert look for cactus boots to use as dishes and bowls!

Old woodpecker nests do not stay empty. As soon as one kind of bird moves out, another moves in. Elf owls are among the first to take over. Unlike woodpeckers, however, these little owls may stay in the same hole for years.

Other birds, such as this starling, follow close behind. High up in the spiny saguaro, the birds find a safe, cool place to raise their families.

At 60 years of age, the cactus is almost 18 feet tall (5.5 meters). Now branches reach out from its sides like arms. There, white-winged doves build cozy nests. Red-tailed hawks and horned owls also find homes on the growing saguaro. Somehow, the sharp spines of the cactus do not get in their way.

By the time it is 75 years old, the saguaro is nearly 50 feet tall (15 meters) . . . and teeming with life! It is more like a crowded village than a plant.

Birds aren't the only creatures in search of a cool cactus home. Lizards, insects, and spiders also fill empty nest holes. The insects feed on the cactus. The lizards and spiders feed on the insects.

Mule deer and other animals come to eat the tender plants that grow in the shade of the saguaro. Still other creatures, such as the ringtail cat, perch at the top. Up here, they stay safe from coyotes and are free to spy on small prey.

Coyotes are members of the dog family. Although they are excellent hunters, coyotes eat just about anything. Rabbits, gophers, rats, squirrels, reptiles, and insects are all food for coyotes. So are antelope, goats, and sheep. But when necessary, coyotes will even eat berries, melons, and beans!

Keen-eyed coyotes and bobcats hunt in the brush around the saguaro. Perhaps one of them will dine on a jackrabbit tonight.

331

For 150 years or more, the saguaro provides an important habitat for many desert creatures. But, in the end, old age and disease weaken the trunk of the great plant.

When this happens, desert winds topple the dead plant to the ground. Creatures living in the saguaro must move to a new cactus home.

After the saguaro dies, it is still necessary to desert life. Now the plant becomes a cool, shady home for creatures that live close to the desert floor.

Among others, scorpions, rattlesnakes, and horned lizards come to the dead saguaro looking for food and shelter.

Very, very slowly, the dead cactus decomposes, or rots away. Over time, it will return to the earth. For now,

Beneath the cactus's tough, spiny skin are long wooden ribs. These ribs hold up the giant plant. For hundreds of years they have been used by desert people for fences, roofs, and firewood.

Javelinas are distant cousins of wild hogs. They have rough, grayish-black coats with silvery collars. Although javelinas feed mostly on roots, they sometimes prey on small animals.

though, animals such as this javelina drop by. Using all its strength, the javelina tears at the fallen cactus. Could a meal of tender young plants lie beneath it?

But look! Just behind the javelina, a young, healthy saguaro is growing. Perhaps the javelina won't harm it.

With a good deal of luck, the young saguaro will continue to grow upward and outward into a grand cactus. And if it succeeds, it too will one day become home to the many creatures of the Sonoran Desert.

Think About It

1. Why is the saguaro cactus such an important part of life in the Sonoran Desert?

2. How are this selection and "Look to the North" alike in the way they are organized?

3. List two of the most interesting facts you learned from this selection.

More About This Habitat

Desert Tortoise

With its strong legs and sharp claws, the desert tortoise is a great digger. At the end of fall, it digs a deep burrow in the sand where it will spend the winter.

Gila Woodpecker

Both gila woodpecker parents share the task of feeding and caring for their young. But at night, the father may sleep in a separate hole near the nest.

Wolf Spider

Wolf spiders are active hunters. Many stalk insects. They pounce on their prey the same way tigers do.

Mesquite Tree

The hardy mesquite tree grows where very few other plants can survive. It has many uses. Gum from its sap is even used to make candy!

Starling

The starling originally came from Europe. In 1890, about 60 starlings were set free in Central Park in New York City. Millions of starlings now live in the United States.

Bobcat

Bobcats sneak around dead saguaros, hunting for mice, pack rats, rabbits, and other small animals. Their fine senses of sight and hearing help them to catch their prey.

Paul and Shirley Berquist

When Paul and Shirley Berquist went to Arizona in 1968 on a job for the military, they decided to stay. In their years living in the desert southwest, they have made a second career out of photography. Their work has appeared on postcards and in books, magazines, and calendars. They have done educational programs for the Arizona–Sonora Desert Museum. Their photos have been used in several projects for Saguaro National Park. Although the Berquists have been as far away as Africa and South America with a camera, they especially like taking photographs of the wildlife near their home area.

Paul Berquist

Shirley Berquist

Visit *The Learning Site!*
www.harcourtschool.com

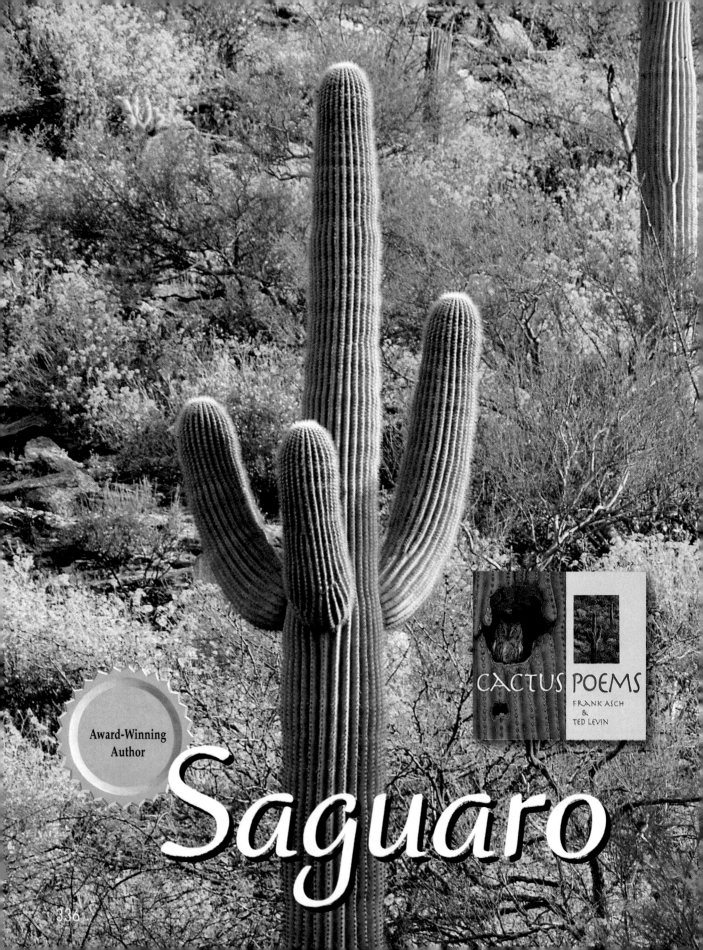

Award-Winning
Author

CACTUS POEMS
FRANK ASCH
&
TED LEVIN

Saguaro

Stand
still.
Grow
slow.
Lift
high
your arms to the sun.
Stand
still.
Grow
slow.
Lift
high
your
flowers to the sky.
Stand
still.
Grow
slow.
Hold
tight
your
water
inside.
Stand
still.
Grow
slow
and let your roots spread wide and let your roots spread wide.

by Frank Asch
photographs by Ted Levin

RESPONSE ACTIVITIES

Race Across the Desert

CREATE A GAME

With a group, make up a board game based on facts about the saguaro cactus. First, make twenty cards. On each card, write a question about the saguaro cactus. Next, create a game board. Use real board games for ideas. The starting point might show a saguaro seed, and the finish could show a large saguaro full of desert creatures. Make up rules for having players draw cards and answer questions.

Cactus Motel

CREATE A SCIENTIFIC DRAWING

Make a large drawing of a saguaro cactus. On, in, and around it, draw some of the creatures that depend on it. Using information from the selection, write a caption about each creature.

Height Chart

MAKE A BAR GRAPH

A saguaro may grow as tall as 50 feet. That is taller than some trees! Find out how tall three types of trees can grow. Look for information in an encyclopedia (in print or on-line) or in a book about trees. Create a bar graph to compare the heights of these four plants.

Making Connections

WRITE A POEM

The poem "Saguaro" presents some of the facts found in "Saguaro Cactus", but in a different way. Look at this poem again. Then find information about a plant you like. You might try gardening books or a garden shop. Write a poem about that plant. Tell how the plant changes as it grows.

THEME WRAP-UP

Growing and Changing

WRITE AN ARTICLE
Several selections in this theme show characters dealing with changes in their lives. Why is change sometimes hard? What things help people deal with change? Write a short article to answer these questions. Include examples from at least two selections in the theme.

Homes Old and New

WRITE A PARAGRAPH
Why do you think this theme is called "Make Yourself at Home"? Write a paragraph explaining your answer.

Prairie, City, Tundra, Desert

PLAN A TRIP The selections in this theme describe several very different settings or environments. Work with a group to find out more about one of the places in this theme. Imagine that you are going to visit the place. What do you need to know about the place? Make a chart to help answer these questions: What time of year should you go? How should you dress? What should you take? What would you like to learn from your trip? Choose one of the places below for your chart.

	Prairie	City	Tundra	Desert
Best Time to Visit				
Type of Clothing				
What to Pack				
What Will I Learn?				

CONTENTS

READER'S CHOICE

The Greatest Treasure
by Demi

CHINESE FOLKTALE

A wealthy man gives a poor farmer money, but the poor man is not happy with it. Find out why he returns the money and gives the rich man a flute.

Award-Winning Author

READER'S CHOICE LIBRARY

Nothing Ever Happens on 90th Street
by Roni Schotter

REALISTIC FICTION

Join Eva as she uses her creativity to write about some extraordinary people in her neighborhood and their unusual escapades.

Notable Children's Books in the Language Arts

READER'S CHOICE LIBRARY

Boss of the Plains: The Hat That Won the West

by Laurie Carlson

BIOGRAPHY

Have you ever wondered who invented the cowboy hat? Find out how John Stetson became an important part of the American frontier, the West, when every cowboy wanted a Boss of the Plains.

ALA Notable Book

Encyclopedia Brown and the Case of the Disgusting Sneakers

by Donald J. Sobol

MYSTERY

Try your hand at detective work. Can you solve these ten supersleuth mysteries?

Award-Winning Author

Fire on the Mountain

by Jane Kurtz

ETHIOPIAN FOLKTALE

A young boy accepts a challenge from his sister's rich employer. When the rich man does not honor the bet, the brother and sister decide to trick him in the same manner and win.

The Kids' Invention Book

by Arlene Erlbach

Kids Are Inventors, Too

Do you know what's unusual about earmuffs? They were invented by a kid!

Chester Greenwood wanted to keep his ears warm, so he invented earmuffs. They solved a problem for him. That's what inventions are supposed to do. Chester's invention made life easier for millions of other people.

You may already be an inventor, too, without even knowing it. You're an inventor every time you find a new way of doing something.

Have you ever made up new rules for a game? Or maybe you've wiped your mouth on your sleeve when you couldn't find a napkin. Your parents may not have been thrilled when they saw you do that, but you solved a problem for yourself.

Inventions are discoveries. An invention might be a new item, as the Koosh® Ball or Slinky® were when they first appeared in stores, years ago. Or an invention may improve something that already exists.

Think about TV. You probably see color pictures on the screen. But the first TV sets showed only black-and-white pictures. The person who invented color television improved something that people were already using.

Let's go back to earmuffs. They were invented in 1873, when Chester Greenwood was only 15 years old.

Chester lived in Farmington, Maine, and he loved to ice-skate. Anyone familiar with northeastern winters knows how hard they can be on your ears — even when you wear a hat. So Chester took a piece of wire and asked his grandmother to sew cloth pads on the ends.

At first Chester's friends thought his earmuffs looked weird, but they soon changed their minds. Chester could stay outside and skate longer than they did. His ears didn't get cold!

Soon Chester's friends wanted earmuffs, too. So he started making earmuffs and selling them. He also applied for a patent. A patent is a document issued by the U.S. government. It protects an inventor's idea so nobody else can make money from it.

Chester began manufacturing earmuffs and eventually became rich. He became famous, too. Farmington, Maine, celebrates Chester Greenwood Day each December.

Lots of kids—about 500,000 each year—invent things. Most kids don't sell their inventions or become rich. But they do have fun creating things and seeing them work.

Chester Greenwood, as an adult, still wearing his "Champion Ear Protectors"

The Prosthetic Catch & Throw Device

Inventor: Josh Parsons
Hometown: Houston, Texas

J osh Parsons wanted to help David Potter play baseball. Both of David's arms had been amputated below the elbows because of an accident he had had when he was two years old. Still, David wanted to be on a Little League team. Josh thought he could help David.

Josh's dad is the one who told Josh about David. Mr. Parsons is a Little League director. He judges kids' tryouts for teams. One evening, Mr. Parsons came home and told Josh about a kid without hands who had tried out for a baseball team.

Even without hands, David could catch and bat a ball! He caught the ball in a glove he wore at the end of his left arm. To bat, David held the bat between his left upper arm and chest. He used his right arm to push the bat. The only thing David couldn't do was throw a ball. Josh hoped he could change that.

First Josh thought about all the things David could already do. David was able to use a glove to catch. So maybe a special kind of glove could help him throw.

Josh decided to design a special glove that would replace David's lower right arm and hand. A device that replaces a missing body part is called a prosthesis (pross-THEE-sis).

Josh drew pictures of baseball gloves. Finally, he came up with a glove shaped like a scoop. Josh felt that this shape would allow David to both hold and then throw the ball.

Josh first made a model of the glove out of paper. Next, he sewed a glove from leather. The glove fit onto the end of David's right arm.

Josh hit a ball to David. David caught it in his left glove. Then he dumped the ball into the prosthetic glove and threw the ball into the air!

David started playing right field for the Spring Branch Mustangs. They won first place that season.

Josh's invention drew a lot of attention. He and David were interviewed on *Good Morning America* and the Cable News Network. Stories about the glove appeared in newspapers across the United States. Josh received an award from the Easter Seal Society, an organization that helps people with disabilities. He and Dave even threw out the first pitch at a Houston Astros game.

Josh also received a prize from the Houston Inventors' Association—a 291-piece tool kit. He can make plenty of things with that. But, Josh says, "The most important part was that the glove helped David. That's why I invented it."

★★★ DAVID ★★★

The All-in-One Washer/Dryer

Inventor: Reeba Daniel
Hometown: Palos Park, Illinois

"I wanted to design an automatic rabbit feeder for my school invention project," Reeba Daniel said. "But my teacher told me that automatic pet feeders had already been invented."

Then Reeba's mom gave her a suggestion. "Invent something everyone could use—something that saves time."

A few days later, Reeba was folding laundry. She thought about how doing laundry is a two-step job. First the clothes go into the washer. Then, when they're damp and heavy, somebody needs to lift them into the dryer. Reeba thought about inventing a machine that would wash and dry clothes in one step.

Reeba began drawing pictures. Her first idea involved placing the washer and dryer side by side. A conveyor belt would move the clothes from the washer to the dryer. The idea certainly seemed useful—but too complicated! It would also be very expensive to manufacture.

Reeba thought of a simpler way to make her idea work. The washer could be on top of the dryer. Her washer would have a trapdoor that would open following the drain cycle. The clothes would drop into the dryer, making it start. A computerized device could time each of the cycles.

Reeba didn't make a working model of her invention. It would have cost thousands of dollars to build. Instead, she did what many inventors do: Reeba drew a diagram of her invention. Then she made a model of it, from cardboard. From her diagram and model, people could see how her invention would look.

Reeba's invention won a prize at her school's invention fair. She also won a prize from a national organization that included a trip to Washington, D.C.

These aren't the first prizes Reeba has won. She has also won awards for acting and has received an American Legion award for courage, honor, patriotism, scholarship, and service. Reeba is also a straight "A" student.

Reeba hopes to become a doctor, engineer, or senator. She believes that the ability to keep trying is the key to anyone's success.

The Conserve Sprinkler

Inventor: Larry Villella
Hometown: Fargo, North Dakota

One of Larry Villella's chores was watering the lawn, which included watering eight trees and eight shrubs. He had to hose each tree and shrub separately or keep moving the sprinkler around.

Larry thought he was wasting a lot of water every time he would change the sprinkler or move the hose. He thought a sprinkler that actually fit around a tree or shrub would save water — and time. And the plant would get more water if the sprinkler had holes on the top *and* bottom.

Larry believed a circular sprinkler could do the trick. He'd just need to cut an opening in the sprinkler so it would fit around a tree or shrub. Then he'd need to seal the ends.

Larry and his dad cut a section from a sprinkler with a power saw. They sealed the ends by gluing on pieces of thin plastic. Then they drilled holes in the bottom of the sprinkler that were wider than the tiny holes on top. The bigger holes would allow water to seep into the ground and soak the plant's roots.

Larry's sprinkler won his school's invention contest. Then he and his dad showed it to Dr. Ron Smith, a professor of agriculture at North Dakota State University. Dr. Smith suggested a change. He thought the holes on the bottom should be even bigger, so more water would go into the ground and aerate (supply air to) the soil.

Larry began making Conserve Sprinklers by hand and selling them. They sold so well that Larry didn't have time to make them all. At first, he turned the manufacturing over to a training center for people who are handicapped. But sales grew even more, and Larry needed a place that could mass-produce the sprinklers. A company called Terhorst in Minot, North Dakota, began manufacturing them, and thousands of people have bought Larry's sprinklers.

You Can Do It

When you invent, you think up ideas. Then you make them work, step by step.

Steps to Creating an Invention

1. Think of ways to make life easier or better for you or people you know. Think of problems that need to be solved. Think about what goes on in your home or at school. Observe your friends, families, and pets. They may have problems you've never thought about before.

2. Make a list of these problems in a notebook. This note-book will be your invention journal. Whenever you think of another problem that needs solving, write about it in your journal. Some inventors take their journals with them wherever they go.

Problems
① Outgrow clothes wear out.

Arms too short t trombone.

3. From your list of problems, choose one that you think you can solve. Make sure it's one you find important and interesting enough to keep working on.

4. Think about how to solve the problem. Lie down on your bed or sit in a comfortable chair. Think of lots of solutions to the problem. Some of them won't make any sense. Some will sound good. Some will seem absolutely terrific. This process is called *brainstorming*. It allows you to come up with many ideas, answers, and plans.

5. List the best solutions in your journal. Next, describe how the solutions might look if you turned them into something tangible—something you can see and touch.

Solutions

① a) Expandable clothes made from super-stretchy fabric.
   b) Sectional clothes—attach additional pieces as you grow.

② a) Hand-held slide mover extends arm length.
   b)

③ a) Scrolling map attaches to handlebars.
   b) Transparent map stickers to stick on back of sunglass

④ a) Sunhat based on baseball cap design with multiple movable brims.

357

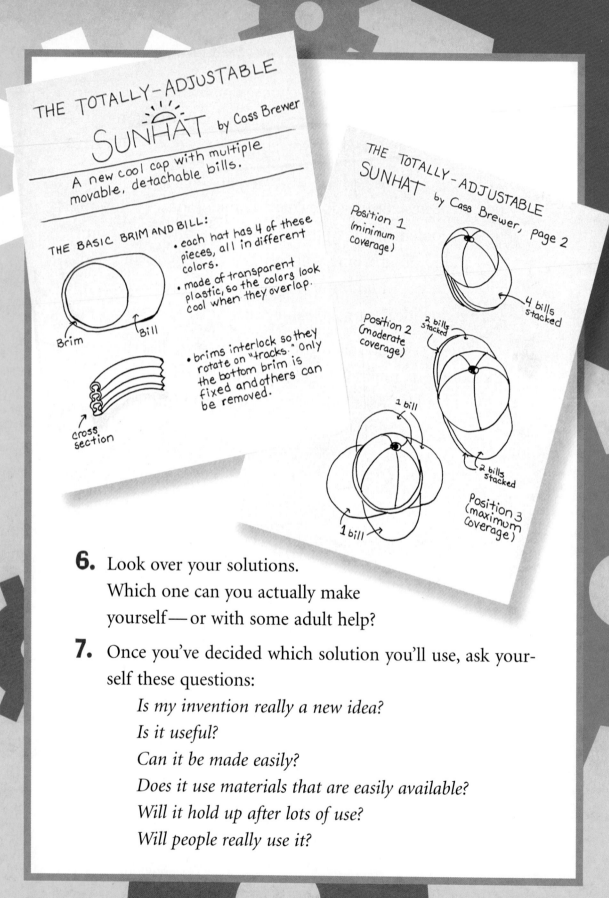

THE TOTALLY-ADJUSTABLE SUNHAT by Cass Brewer

A new cool cap with multiple movable, detachable bills.

THE BASIC BRIM AND BILL:

• each hat has 4 of these pieces, all in different colors.

• made of transparent plastic, so the colors look cool when they overlap.

Brim

Bill

• brims interlock so they rotate on "tracks." Only the bottom brim is fixed and others can be removed.

cross section

THE TOTALLY-ADJUSTABLE SUNHAT by Cass Brewer, Page 2

Position 1 (minimum coverage)

4 bills stacked

Position 2 (moderate coverage)

2 bills stacked

1 bill

2 bills stacked

1 bill

Position 3 (maximum coverage)

6. Look over your solutions. Which one can you actually make yourself—or with some adult help?

7. Once you've decided which solution you'll use, ask yourself these questions:

Is my invention really a new idea?

Is it useful?

Can it be made easily?

Does it use materials that are easily available?

Will it hold up after lots of use?

Will people really use it?

If any of the answers to your questions are "no," think of how you might modify, or change, your idea. Inventors change ideas all the time.

8. Once all the answers to your questions are "yes," draw pictures of how your invention should look. You don't need to be a great artist to do this. Simple line drawings will do. Your first drawing is a rough draft. It shows the basic idea of what the invention will look like. A rough draft is meant to be changed.

9. Next, you need to refine the drawing of your invention. This means redrawing until it looks exactly right. Sometimes this process takes lots of tries. On your final drawing, label all the parts. On the back of your paper, list the materials you'll need to make your invention.

10. Now comes a very important step—building the model. You might need an adult to help you. That's okay. Lots of adult inventors pay people to make models for them. You may need to build your model more than once. Sometimes inventions don't work as you had hoped.

11. Once your model is exactly the way you want it, have some of your friends and relatives use it. Use it a few times yourself. Does it hold up and work? Congratulations! You've just created a new invention!

Think About It

① Give some examples of how the young inventors used the steps the author gives for creating an invention.

② Which invention in the selection interested you the most? Explain why.

③ Why do you think the author chose to write about young inventors rather than adult inventors?

MEET THE AUTHOR

Arlene Erlbach

To: students@anyschool.edu
From: editors@harcourt.com
Date: 09/12 01:04:36 PM
Subject: Arlene Erlbach

We are writing in response to your interest in the author of *The Kids' Invention Book*. Arlene Erlbach liked to make up stories when she was in elementary school, but she wasn't sure at first that she could be a writer. When teachers liked her writing, she decided to try.

Arlene Erlbach has written both fiction and nonfiction books. She gets ideas from her childhood, from her son Matthew, and from the news. Since she is a school-teacher, she also gets ideas from experiences at school. She is in charge of the Young Authors' Program at her school in Illinois.

Visit *The Learning Site!*
www.harcourtschool.com

Response Activities

Bright Ideas

WRITE A REPORT
Learn about an inventor such as Louis Braille or Grace Hopper, or research an invention such as the microwave oven or the ice-cream cone. You might choose an invention that, like the one Josh Parsons made, helps people with special physical needs. Write a short report about the inventor or invention you choose.

Million-Dollar Ideas

WRITE A PERSONAL NARRATIVE

The author says, "You're an inventor every time you find a new way of doing something." Write about an "invention" you or someone you know created without meaning to. You may have invented a game, a great recipe, or a creative way to solve a problem.

Ad Campaign

CREATE ADS

Work with a group to create a magazine ad for the All-in-One Washer/Dryer or for the Conserve Sprinkler. Draw a picture of the invention. Write a snappy slogan to convince people that they should have one. Before you begin, look at some ads to get ideas. You might also create a radio ad, using a tape recorder. Think carefully about the wording, since a radio ad has no picture with it.

Be an Inventor

DRAW A DIAGRAM

Think of an invention that would make your life easier. Then follow the steps on pages 356–360 to develop your idea. Make a diagram, and write captions to describe how the invention works. Think of a name for your invention.

Main Idea and Details

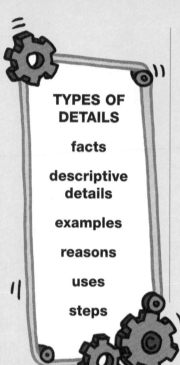

TYPES OF DETAILS

facts

descriptive details

examples

reasons

uses

steps

What is "The Kids' Invention Book" about? What are some examples of things you learned? If you can answer these questions, you can identify the main idea and details.

The **main idea** of a selection is what it is mostly about. The details give information to explain and support that main idea. Details usually answer questions starting with *Who, What, Where, When, Why,* and *How*. This chart shows the main idea and some of the details in "The Kids' Invention Book."

Main Idea

Kids can come up with inventions that will solve problems or make life easier.

Supporting Details

Kids have created successful inventions that

- keep people's ears warm.
- help a person without hands throw a ball.
- wash and dry clothes.
- water plants more efficiently.

364

Many writers state the main idea and then give supporting details. It's a good way to organize a paragraph. It's as if the writer says, "Here's what I'm writing about, and here's how I support my ideas."

The main idea of a passage may instead be stated at the end, or it may not be stated at all. If it is not stated, the reader must get it from the details.

Read the following paragraph. Then make a chart like the one on page 364. State the main idea and fill in the details that support it.

The bicycle is an invention that has been improved many times. The first bicycles had wooden wheels and no pedals. Riders moved by pushing their feet against the ground. An inventor added pedals in the 1830s. Early bikes had a huge front wheel and a tiny rear wheel. About 120 years ago, bikes with wheels the same size were built. Thanks to many different inventors, the modern bicycle was born.

WHAT HAVE YOU LEARNED?

1. How does the author use details to make her writing interesting? Give examples from the selection.

2. What is the main idea given about the invention of earmuffs? What facts support that idea?

TRY THIS • TRY THIS • TRY THIS

Write a paragraph about something you use often that you think is a great invention. Begin with your main idea. Then write four or five detail sentences that explain why the object is important.

Visit *The Learning Site!*
www.harcourtschool.com

Encyclopedia Brown helps his father, the Idaville Chief of Police, solve cases. In the summer he runs a detective agency from the family's garage with the help of his friend Sally Kimball. True to his nickname, Encyclopedia has the answers, even to problems that stump everyone else.

THE CASE OF PABLO'S NOSE

by **Donald J. Sobol**

illustrated by **Matthew Archambault**

Award-Winning Author

Pablo Pizzaro, Idaville's greatest boy artist, burst into the Brown Detective Agency.

"My nose," he wailed. "It's been stolen!"

"Whoever stole it returned it in very good shape," Sally observed.

"I don't mean *my* nose," Pablo said. "I mean Abraham Lincoln's."

He explained. Last month the nose on the statue of Abraham Lincoln in South Park had been smashed to pieces by a baseball. So the mayor had announced a New Nose Now contest. The winning nose would be put on the statue. The winning sculptor would get a cash prize.

"I thought I had a good chance of nosing out everyone else," Pablo said proudly, and told why.

First he had made a mold of the statue's face. Then, using photographs of Abraham Lincoln, he had built a nose in soft wax. Next he had ground down a piece of the same stone from which the statue had been carved to make sure he had the right texture and color. Then he had mixed that with his special glue. Finally he had shaped the mixture into a copy of the wax model.

"Golly, Pablo!" Sally exclaimed. "You're a regular plastic surgeon!"

Pablo smiled a weak smile. "The nose was my masterpiece," he said. "There isn't time to make another. The contest ends Thursday."

"Are you sure it was stolen?" Encyclopedia asked.

"Sure I'm sure," Pablo said. "I've been leaving the nose on the front lawn to weather so it would make an even better match with Lincoln's face."

Half an hour ago, he went on, he had discovered that the nose was gone. At the same time he'd noticed a girl biking away from his house like mad. She'd been holding something the size of the nose in her right hand.

"Did you see who she was?" Sally asked.

"I only saw her back," Pablo said sadly. "She wore a blue shirt and rode a purple bicycle."

He paused for a strengthening breath of air.

"I should have kept my nose a secret," he muttered. "Like a blockhead, I bragged all over the neighborhood."

He laid a quarter on the gas can beside Encyclopedia.

"Find my nose!" he pleaded.

"There are three purple bicycles in the neighborhood," Sally said. "Desmoana Lowry has one. So do Martha Katz and Joan Brand."

The detectives and Pablo started at Martha Katz's house. From Mrs. Katz they learned that Martha was spending the summer with her grandparents in Maine.

The news was no better at Joan Brand's house. Joan had gone off to Camp Winiwantoc in North Carolina a week ago.

"That leaves Desmoana Lowry," Sally said.

"She has to be the thief," Pablo said. "She's been jealous of me since I beat her in the tulip drawing contest last year."

"Being jealous isn't being a thief," Encyclopedia said quietly. "Let's pay her a visit."

Desmoana came to the front door herself. "What do you want?" she demanded, giving Pablo an unfriendly look.

Pablo accused her straightaway. "About an hour ago, you stole my nose, didn't you?"

"No, but I should have," Desmoana retorted. "I'd have improved your looks."

"He means Abraham Lincoln's nose," Sally said. "The thief wore a blue shirt and rode a purple bicycle."

"Does this look like a blue shirt?" Desmoana asked.

The shirt she had on looked very red to Encyclopedia.

"You could have changed your shirt," Sally said. "But you can't have repainted your purple bicycle in an hour."

"I didn't need to," Desmoana retorted. "I didn't steal anything."

She led the detectives and Pablo to the garage. A purple bicycle stood half hidden behind the water heater.

"When was the last time anyone saw me ride my bike?" she said. "Not for a long time, right? Fact is, it hasn't been ridden for nearly a year."

"That's the most unheard-of thing I ever heard of!" Pablo yelped.

Sally seemed uncertain. She glanced nervously at Encyclopedia.

Encyclopedia was uncertain, too. He tried to recall when he'd seen Desmoana on her bike last.

It was a bad moment.

Then a happy thought struck him.

"Why did you try to hide your bicycle?" he asked.

"I wasn't hiding it," Desmoana replied. "I put it out of the way. I'm into roller skating now. It's more fun."

"That's not the reason," Encyclopedia said. "Come on, tell the truth. You were never much good at riding a two-wheeler."

"Who says?" Desmoana snapped.

She rolled the purple bicycle out to the street.

"Slam your eyes on this," she invited, and forthwith did some trick riding.

She rode in a circle no-handed.

She sat on the handlebars and pedaled backward.

She lifted the front wheel off the ground and whipped through a figure eight.

"There!" she sneered. "I showed you how I can ride a two-wheeler."

"You showed me, all right," Encyclopedia agreed. "You showed me you're guilty!"

How did Encyclopedia know?

Solution to THE CASE OF PABLO'S NOSE

Desmoana denied being the girl who Pablo had seen riding away on a purple bicycle.

To give herself an alibi, she claimed that her purple bicycle hadn't been ridden for nearly a year.

Encyclopedia had his doubts. So he got her to show off how well she rode a two-wheeler.

That was her mistake!

She couldn't have done tricks if the bicycle had really been unused for nearly a year. The tires would have lost air and been flat! Pablo got his nose back. Since it was the only nose entered in the New Nose Now contest, it won.

Think About It

1 How does Encyclopedia Brown show that he is a creative problem solver?

2 Before you read the solution to the case, did you think Desmoana was the thief? Explain why or why not.

3 What kind of person is Desmoana? What details does the author use to show you what she is like?

Donald J. Sobol

When Donald Sobol was a boy, he read Sherlock Holmes mysteries and dreamed of becoming a detective. Now, for more than thirty years, he has been writing stories about boy detective Encyclopedia Brown. His books have been published in thirteen languages and in Braille.

When asked if Encyclopedia is a real boy, Donald Sobol says, "The answer is no. He is, perhaps, the boy I wanted to be—doing the things I wanted to read about but could not find in any book when I was ten."

Visit *The Learning Site!*
www.harcourtschool.com

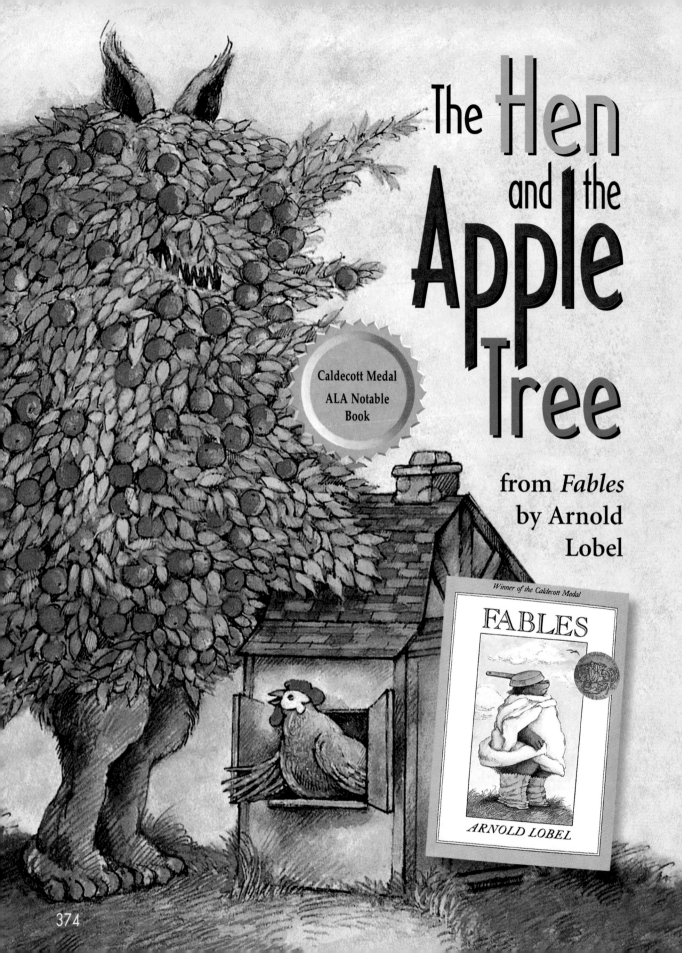

The Hen and the Apple Tree

Caldecott Medal
ALA Notable
Book

from *Fables*
by Arnold
Lobel

Winner of the Caldecott Medal

FABLES

ARNOLD LOBEL

One October day, a Hen looked out her window. She saw an apple tree growing in her backyard.

"Now that is odd," said the Hen. "I am certain that there was no tree standing in that spot yesterday."

"There are some of us that grow fast," said the tree.

The Hen looked at the bottom of the tree.

"I have never seen a tree," she said, "that has ten furry toes."

"There are some of us that do," said the tree. "Hen, come outside and enjoy the cool shade of my leafy branches."

The Hen looked at the top of the tree.

"I have never seen a tree," she said, "that has two long, pointed ears."

"There are some of us that have," said the tree. "Hen, come outside and eat one of my delicious apples."

"Come to think of it," said the Hen, "I have never heard a tree speak from a mouth that is full of sharp teeth."

"There are some of us that can," said the tree. "Hen, come outside and rest your back against the bark of my trunk."

"I have heard," said the Hen, "that some of you trees lose all of your leaves at this time of the year."

"Oh, yes," said the tree, "there are some of us that will." The tree began to quiver and shake. All of its leaves quickly dropped off.

The Hen was not surprised to see a large Wolf in the place where an apple tree had been standing just a moment before. She locked her shutters and slammed her window closed.

The Wolf knew that he had been outsmarted. He stormed away in a hungry rage.

It is always difficult to pose as something that one is not.

Think About It

What is the hen's problem, and how does she solve it?

Response Activities

Case Closed

ROLE-PLAY A SCENE

In a group, act out the scene in which Encyclopedia, Pablo, and Sally go to Desmoana Lowry's house and solve the case. Be sure to rehearse your parts. The person who plays Desmoana can pantomime the bicycle tricks.

Sincerely Yours

WRITE A LETTER

Write a letter of apology from Desmoana to Pablo. In the letter Desmoana should tell why she stole Pablo's nose and why she lied about it. You might also have her offer to do something nice to make up for what she did.

Creativity at Work

RESEARCH JOBS

Artists and detectives both use creativity to solve problems. Learn about another type of job that requires creative thinking and problem-solving skills. Examples might be the work of an architect or a computer-game designer. If possible, talk to someone who does this kind of work, or search the Internet for career Web sites. Take notes so that you can share what you learned.

Making Connections

WRITE COMPARISONS

How is Encyclopedia Brown like the hen in "The Hen and the Apple Tree"? How is Desmoana Lowry like the wolf? Write one paragraph about the problem solvers and another paragraph about the suspects.

In the Days of King Adobe

retold by Joe Hayes
illustrated by Gerardo Suzán

THERE WAS ONCE AN OLD WOMAN who lived all alone in a tiny house at the edge of a village. She was very poor, and all she had to eat was beans and tortillas and thin cornmeal mush. Of course, she ate a few vegetables from her garden, but most of them she took into the village on market day to sell or trade for what little she needed for her simple life.

But the old woman was very thrifty, and by saving carefully—a penny a day, a penny a day—she was able to buy herself a big ham. She kept it hanging from a hook in a cool, dark closet behind the kitchen, and she only cut a thin slice from the ham on very special days— or if she was lucky enough to have company join her for a meal.

One evening a couple of young men who were traveling through the country stopped at the old woman's house and asked if they could have lodging for the night. The old woman had no extra beds, but she offered to spread a blanket on the floor for the young men to sleep on. They said that would be fine, and thanked the old woman for her kindness.

"It's nothing," the old woman told them. "I'm happy to have the company. I'll get busy and make us all a good supper."

She got out her pots and pans and then went to the closet and cut three slices from the ham— two thick, generous slices for the travelers and a thin one for herself.

The young men were delighted to see the old woman preparing ham for their supper. Seldom were they offered such good food in their travels. But those two young men were a couple of rascals, and right away a roguish idea came into their minds. They decided to steal the ham that night while the old woman was asleep.

After they had all eaten their fill, the old woman spread out a bed for the young men on the floor. She said good night and wished them good dreams and then went into her own room to sleep.

Of course, the young men didn't go to sleep. They lay on the floor joking and talking about how nice it was going to be to have a whole ham to eat. When they felt sure the

old woman was asleep, the young men got up and crept to the closet. They took the ham down from the hook and wrapped it in a shirt. One of the young men put the ham in his traveling bag. Then the two young men lay down to sleep with smiles on their faces. They had very good dreams indeed!

But the old woman hadn't gone to sleep either. In the many years of her life she had become a good judge of character, and she had noticed the rascally look in the young men's eyes. She knew she had better be on her guard. When she heard the young men getting up from their pad on the floor, she went to the door and peeked out. She saw everything the young men did.

Later that night, when the young men were sound asleep, the old woman crept from her room. She took the ham from the traveling bag and hid it under her bed. Then she wrapped an adobe brick in the shirt and put it in the traveling bag.

When the young men awoke in the morning, they were anxious to be on their way. But the old woman insisted they stay for a bite of breakfast. "It will give you strength," she told them. "You have a long day of walking ahead of you. And you may not have anything else to eat all day."

One of the young men winked at the other as he sat down at the table and said, "You're probably right, *abuelita*, but who knows? Last night I dreamed that today my friend and I would be eating good food all day long."

"Is that right?" the old woman replied. "Tell me more about your dream. I'm fascinated by dreams. I believe they are sometimes true."

The young man thought he'd really make fun of the old woman. He smiled at his friend and then said, "I dreamed we were sitting under a tree eating. It was in a beautiful land. And the king of that country was named Hambone the First."

"Aha!" spoke up the second young man. "Now I remember that I had the same dream. And I remember that the land in which Hambone the First was king was named Travelibag."

The young men had to cover their mouths to keep from bursting out laughing. But the old woman didn't seem to notice. In fact, she seemed to be taking them very seriously.

"I had a similar dream last night myself!" she exclaimed. "I was in a land named Travelibag, and Hambone the First was king of that country. But then he was thrown out by the good people and replaced by a new king named Adobe the Great. And for some people, that meant a time of great hunger had begun."

"Isn't that interesting," the young men said, biting their lips to keep from laughing. "Oh, well, it was just a dream." They hurried to finish their breakfast and then went on their way, laughing at the old woman's foolishness.

All morning long the two rascals joked about the old woman as they traveled down the road. As midday approached, they began to grow tired. They sat down under a shady tree to rest.

"Well, now," said the first young man as he leaned back and closed his eyes. "Don't you think it's time for dreams to come true? Here we are sitting under a tree, just as I dreamed. Open up the land of Travelibag. My stomach tells me I need to visit the king of that land."

"By all means," said the other. "Let's see how things are going with our old friend Hambone the First."

The young man opened his bag and pulled out the bundle wrapped in his shirt. Chuckling to himself he slowly unwrapped the shirt. Suddenly the smile disappeared from the young man's face. "Oh, no," he gasped. "The old woman knew more about dreams than we thought."

"What do you mean?" asked the other.

"Well," he said, "she told us Hambone the First had been thrown out, didn't she?"

"Yes."

"And do you remember who was put in his place?"

The young man laughed. "Adobe the Great! Where do you suppose she came up with a name like that?"

"Probably right here," said his friend. "Look."

The first young man opened his eyes. "I see what you mean," he groaned. "And I see what the old woman meant about the time of great hunger beginning. I'm starved!"

After several hungry days the two young men met another kind old woman who fed them a good meal. This time they didn't even think about trying to play any tricks.

Think About It

1 How does the old woman stop the thieves from stealing her ham? Why do you think she chooses this way of stopping them?

2 Were you surprised at any point in the story? Explain when and why.

3 What traits make the old woman a likable character? How does she show these traits?

Meet the Author
Joe Hayes

"*Kids will ask me, 'How long did it take you to write that book?' And I have to tell them, 'Well, I had been telling those stories for about four years before I wrote them down. So you could say it took four years. On the other hand, since I already had the stories in my head, it only took me about four hours to type them into my computer. So you could say it took four hours.'*"

Joe Hayes has received several awards in the southwestern United States. He has written other stories based on Hispanic and Native American folktales told there.

Joe Hayes

Visit *The Learning Site!* www.harcourtschool.com

Response Activities

Old Stories, New Forms

CREATE A COMIC STRIP

Magazines for children sometimes include famous stories rewritten in comic-strip form. With a partner, retell part of "In the Days of King Adobe" as a comic strip. Invent your own dialogue as needed. Discuss the differences between the comic strip and the story.

Wise Woman

WRITE A CHARACTER SKETCH

The old woman outsmarted the thieves, yet she did not hurt them or even become angry with them. Write a character sketch describing the kind of person the woman is. Use details and quotations from the story to support your conclusions.

Shame on Them!

WRITE A LETTER

Suppose the old woman had not discovered that her ham was gone until after the young men were on their way. Write a letter to the young men telling them what you think of the way they have behaved. Think of a creative way to convince them that they must return the ham at once.

What Is Adobe?

TAKE NOTES

Many houses in the southwestern United States and Mexico are made of adobe. With a partner, find out how long adobe has been used, where it is used, and how it is made. Take notes from two sources on what you find. Then have classmates ask you about adobe. See how many questions you can answer.

Summarize and Paraphrase

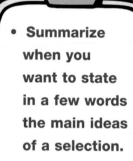

If a friend asked you what "In the Days of King Adobe" is about, you might say,

- Summarize when you want to state in a few words the main ideas of a selection.

- Paraphrase when you want to restate in your own words what someone else wrote or said.

> In this folktale an old woman fools two thieves who try to fool her. When two travelers ask her for a night's lodging, the kind woman shares a ham with them. They decide to steal the ham, but she overhears their plan. Late that night she exchanges the ham for an adobe brick. They discover her trick only after they have traveled a long way from her house.

If you described the story this way, you would be **summarizing** it. When you give a summary, you retell the story using a lot fewer words. If you rewrote a sentence or a paragraph from the story in your own words, you would be **paraphrasing** that part. Here's an example of a paraphrase:

Original Sentence
Tricksters can be found in the folktales of countries throughout the world.

Paraphrase
Folktales from many lands include tricksters as characters.

Summarizing and para-phrasing are good ways to check your understanding. In both, you are restating the writer's ideas, not giving your own opinions.

A summary is much shorter than the original story. You have to leave out a lot of details and tell only what is most important. A paraphrase uses different words, but it may not be any shorter. When you paraphrase, you should not change the meaning.

Tell which statement below belongs in a summary of "In the Days of King Adobe." Then find one statement that is not accurate, one that includes unimportant details, and one that expresses the reader's opinion.

- **I enjoyed reading "In the Days of King Adobe."**
- **Nearly all the old woman ate was beans and tortillas.**
- **The old woman did not want to share her ham.**
- **The young men learned not to play tricks.**

WHAT HAVE YOU LEARNED?

1. If you were writing a book review, would you include a summary or a paraphrase? Explain.

2. Read a short article in a newspaper or a magazine. Write one sentence that summarizes the article.

Visit *The Learning Site!*
www.harcourtschool.com

TRY THIS ● TRY THIS ● TRY THIS

Write two or three sentences telling what you thought of a story you have read recently. Exchange papers with a classmate, and write a paraphrase of your classmate's sentences. Discuss whether the paraphrases change the original words without changing the meaning.

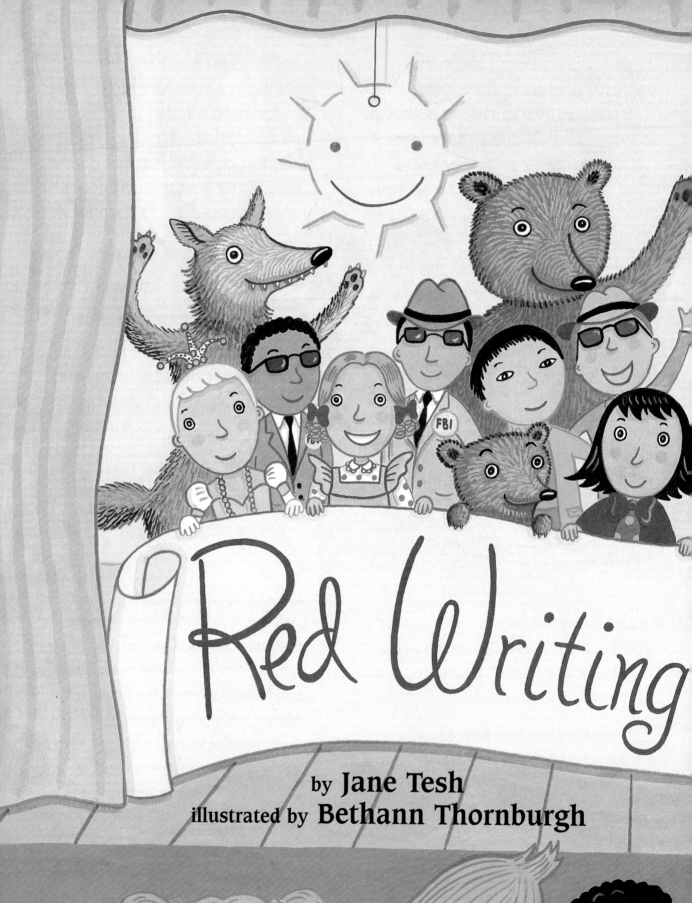

Red Writing

by **Jane Tesh**
illustrated by **Bethann Thornburgh**

CAST OF CHARACTERS

RED RIDING HOOD
WOLF
LITTLE MISS MUFFET
1ST PRINCE CHARMING
GOLDILOCKS
FATHER BEAR
MOTHER BEAR
BABY BEAR
BO PEEP
CINDERELLA
2ND PRINCE CHARMING
GOLDILOCKS' MOTHER
GOLDILOCKS' FATHER
AGENT GRIMM
AGENT ANDERSEN
AGENT RACKHAM

TIME: *Long ago.*

SETTING: *A forest. A few trees are scattered about.*

AT RISE: RED RIDING HOOD *skips on, whistling a happy tune, carrying a basket of goodies.* WOLF *comes out from behind a tree.*

WOLF: Hello there, little girl. What do you have in that basket?

RED RIDING HOOD: Oh, hello, Mr. Wolf. I have some treats for my dear grandma.

WOLF: Treats? That sounds nice. And where does your grandma live?

RED: In a little house at the edge of the forest.

WOLF (*Aside, to audience*): I'll just go along to grandma's and have a tasty treat of my own! (WOLF *starts to exit.*)

RED: Hold on! Wait a minute. (WOLF *halts. Aside*) I don't like the way this story's headed. I'm going to change a few things.

WOLF (*Puzzled*): What? (RED *takes a pencil and notepad out of her basket*). Hey, what are you doing?

RED: Changing the script.

WOLF (*Alarmed*): You can't do that! (RED *erases and scribbles.*)

RED: There! (*Reads*) "The wolf became a ballet dancer and never came near Red or her grandma again."

WOLF: What? A ballet dancer! (*Starts to dance*) Hey, this isn't the way the story goes! What about "What big ears you have"? "What big teeth you have"? (*Against his will, he pirouettes off, still protesting.*)

RED: This is great! I wonder what else I can do? (MISS MUFFET *enters, carrying tuffet and bowl.*)

MISS MUFFET: Oh, hi, Red. I was just about to have some curds and whey. Would you care to join me?

RED: No, thanks, Miss Muffet, but I may be able to help you out.

MISS MUFFET: Really? How?

RED: You do know a big ugly spider is going to sit down beside you and frighten you away.

MISS MUFFET (*Sighing*): That's usually how it goes.

RED (*Triumphantly*): Not any more! (*Takes pencil and notepad, erases, and writes*) Try this! (MISS MUFFET *sits on tuffet and starts to eat when* 1ST PRINCE CHARMING *enters, sits beside her, and smiles.*)

MISS MUFFET: My goodness! Prince Charming!

1ST PRINCE: That looks delicious! May I have some?

MISS MUFFET: Of course! But what in the world are you doing here? (RED *grins, taps pad with pencil.*)

RED: I decided a few things needed changing around here.

1ST PRINCE (*Taking MISS MUFFET's hand*): Miss Muffet, I would be honored if you'd share your curds and whey with me. Why don't we go to my palace?

MISS MUFFET: That sounds wonderful! (*To* RED) Thanks, Red! Goodbye! (MISS MUFFET *and* 1ST PRINCE *exit.*)

RED (*Smiling*): Now, who's next? (GOLDILOCKS *dashes onto stage.*)

GOLDILOCKS: Oh, Red Riding Hood! You have to help me! Those bears are after me again!

RED (*Scolding*): Did you break their furniture again?

GOLDILOCKS: I didn't mean to, but you know how it always is: too hard, too soft, too hot, too cold.

RED: Leave everything to me. (*Thinks a moment and then writes on her notepad. Growls are heard offstage.*)

GOLDILOCKS (*Looking off*): Oh, here they come! I'd better hide! (*She ducks behind tree as FATHER BEAR, MOTHER BEAR, and BABY BEAR enter.*)

RED (*Finishing writing*): That should do it. O.K., Goldie, you can come out now. (GOLDILOCKS *comes out from behind tree. She is now wearing bear ears.*)

FATHER BEAR: My goodness, what a cute little bear!

MOTHER BEAR: She's darling! Let's adopt her, Henry!

BABY BEAR: I've always wanted a sister!

GOLDILOCKS (*Patting ears and face*): Oh, wow! I'm a bear! This ought to be fun! (*To* RED) Thanks, Red! (GOLDILOCKS *and* BEARS *exit.*)

RED: This is neat! I wonder why I didn't think of it before? (BO PEEP *enters, sobbing.*)

BO PEEP: Oh, Red Riding Hood! Have you seen my sheep?

RED: Bo Peep, have you lost those sheep again?

BO PEEP: It does seem to be a habit, doesn't it?

RED (*Taking out pencil and paper*): I can find them for you. In fact, I can find as many as you want. Let's see, how about fifty to start?

BO PEEP: Fifty? That would be wonderful. (RED *writes. After moment, loud baaing noises are heard off.*)

RED: There they are! Go round 'em up! (BO PEEP *claps in delight.*)

BO PEEP: Thanks so much! (*She exits.* CINDERELLA *enters.*)

CINDERELLA: Red, have you seen Prince Charming? He's late for the ball.

RED (*Anxiously, to herself*): Gosh, it's Cinderella! The Prince went off with Miss Muffet. What can I do? (*Thinks a moment*) I know! I'll just bring in another prince! (*Writes hurriedly*) There! (2ND PRINCE CHARMING *enters.*)

2ND PRINCE: Cinderella, my dear!

CINDERELLA (*Hands on hips*): There you are! You're late for the ball. (1ST PRINCE *enters, followed by* MISS MUFFET.)

1ST PRINCE: Cinderella, my dear!

CINDERELLA (*Confused*): What's this? Are there two of you?

MISS MUFFET: I thought I was going to the ball with the prince! (*As MISS MUFFET and CINDERELLA stare from one prince to another, GOLDILOCKS' MOTHER and FATHER enter.*)

MOTHER: Red, have you seen Goldilocks?

RED (*To herself*): Oh, dear! Goldilocks' parents! I can't tell them I changed their daughter into a bear! (*To MOTHER and FATHER*) I think she went to visit the Three Bears.

FATHER: She does that every now and then, but she's usually home by now. We're getting a little worried. (*GOLDILOCKS enters, followed by THREE BEARS.*)

GOLDILOCKS: Red, I need to talk to you! (*MOTHER and FATHER, when they see GOLDILOCKS, react in horror to her appearance.*)

MOTHER and FATHER (*Ad lib*): Goldie! What's happened to you? What have they done? (*Etc.*)

GOLDILOCKS: You have to change me back! I don't like being a bear!

BABY BEAR: And she's eating us out of house and home!

RED: O.K., O.K., hang on! (*Gets out pencil and paper and starts to erase. Stops and stares at the end of pencil*) Oh, no! I've used up all my eraser!

GOLDILOCKS (*Alarmed*): What? You mean you can't change me back?

CINDERELLA: I don't need two Prince Charmings!

FATHER BEAR: We don't want to be the Four Bears!

MOTHER (*Desperately*): My baby! (BO PEEP *enters, frantic. Loud baaing is heard offstage.*)

BO PEEP: Red, you've given me too many sheep! I can't keep up with them! They're driving me crazy! (*Everyone begins to talk and complain. WOLF enters, dressed in tutu and ballet slippers, and begins to dance, getting in everyone's way. BEARS argue with GOLDILOCKS and her parents. RED stands in the middle of all the confusion, trying to scratch out words on her paper.*)

RED: If everyone could just be quiet a moment! (AGENTS GRIMM, ANDERSEN, *and* RACKHAM *come up aisle, dressed in dark suits, dark glasses, and carrying briefcases.*)

AGENTS (*Ad lib*): Wait! Stop! (*All stop talking and stare at AGENTS. Baaing stops.*) This has gone on long enough! (*Etc.* AGENTS *come up on stage.*)

RED: Who are you?

AGENTS (*Showing badges*): FBI.

RED: FBI?

AGENT GRIMM: Fairytale Believers, Incorporated. I'm Agent Grimm, this is Agent Andersen, Agent Rackham. (*Other agents nod.*)

RED: Fairytale Believers, Incorporated? I've never heard of you.

AGENT ANDERSEN: We believe fairy tales and nursery rhymes ought to be left alone.

AGENT RACKHAM (*To* RED): By changing the original stories, you're doing the world a terrible injustice.

RED (*Repentant*): I'm sorry! I only wanted to help. . . .

GRIMM (*Holding out hand*): The script, please. (RED *hands it over.* GRIMM *takes pencil from* ANDERSEN *and begins to write.*) Let's see now. Miss Muffet first. (*Writes. Large spider drops from trees.* MISS MUFFET *screams and runs off.*)

401

GRIMM: Cinderella needs only one Prince Charming. (2ND PRINCE *exits.*)

CINDERELLA: Thank you so much, sir. (*Exits with* 1ST PRINCE)

GRIMM: Goldilocks and the Four Bears would never be acceptable. (GOLDILOCKS *takes off bear ears and runs to her parents.*)

RACKHAM: I'll erase about forty sheep. That should do it. (BO PEEP *looks off and nods.*)

BO PEEP: Thank you so much!

GRIMM (*Starting to put pencil away*): There. All done.

WOLF: Hey, what about me?

GRIMM: Oh, right, sorry. (*Erases a little more.* WOLF *discards tutu and ballet slippers.*)

WOLF: Whew! My toes are killing me!

GRIMM: There! I think that takes care of everything.

ANDERSEN (*To* RED): I hope you've learned a lesson, Miss Riding Hood.

RED: I didn't mean for things to get so out of hand, but I didn't want to be eaten, and I didn't want my granny to be eaten, either.

ANDERSEN: But don't you remember?

RED: Remember what?

RACKHAM: The woodsman saves you and your grandmother.

GRIMM: He kills the wolf. (*All turn and look at* WOLF.)

WOLF: Give me that pencil! (*Snatches pencil and paper from* GRIMM)

AGENTS: Wait! (WOLF *writes something hurriedly*

and hands it back. AGENTS *read it, look at each other, and nod.*)

ANDERSEN: I think, under the circumstances, we can allow this.

WOLF (*To audience, reads*): "And they *all* lived happily ever after!"

ALL: The end! (*Curtain*)

THE END

Think About It

1. What is Red Riding Hood's goal in rewriting the script? Does she achieve this goal?

2. Do you agree with the agents that fairy tales should be left alone? Tell why you think as you do.

3. Give two examples of ways the author uses stage directions to make the play funnier. Explain why each is humorous.

Response Activities

SET THE SCENE

ILLUSTRATE A SCENE

Choose your favorite scene from the play and illustrate it. You might show a stage with actors playing the characters or draw the characters themselves in a fairy-tale setting. Looking at illustrated books of fairy tales might give you some ideas.

BE A FAIRY TALE WRITER

REWRITE A TALE

In the play, Red Riding Hood rewrites some old fairy tales. Rewrite another fairy tale, making it as funny as you can. Then give your tale to a classmate. See if he or she can identify the tale it is based on and the changes you made to it.

404

CREATIVE PROBLEM SOLVING

CREATE A SOLUTION

Red Riding Hood solves some problems, but she creates some new problems, too. Choose one of the characters she tries to help. Create a new solution to that character's problem that will not cause other problems. Describe the problem in one paragraph and the solution in another.

PLAN A PRODUCTION

MAKE A CHART

Imagine that your class is going to stage the play "Red Writing Hood." With a partner, brainstorm ideas for the costumes, props, and forest scenery. You might also think of ideas for lighting, sound effects, and music. Make a chart that shows your ideas.

One Grain of Rice

A Mathematical Folktale

Demi

Teachers'
Choice

Notable
Social Studies
Trade Book

Long ago in India, there lived a raja who believed that he was wise and fair, as a raja should be.

The people in his province were rice farmers. The raja decreed that everyone must give nearly all of the rice to him.

"I will store the rice safely," the raja promised the people, "so that in time of famine, everyone will have rice to eat, and no one will go hungry."

Each year, the raja's rice collectors gathered nearly all of the people's rice and carried it away to the royal storehouses.

For many years, the rice grew well. The people gave nearly all of their rice to the raja, and the storehouses were always full. But the people were left with only just enough rice to get by.

Then one year the rice grew badly, and there was famine and hunger. The people had no rice to give to the raja, and they had no rice to eat.

The raja's ministers implored him, "Your Highness, let us open the royal storehouses and give the rice to the people, as you promised."

"No!" cried the raja. "How do I know how long the famine may last? I must have the rice for myself. Promise or no promise, a raja must not go hungry!"

ime went on, and the people grew more and more hungry. But the raja would not give out the rice.

One day, the raja ordered a feast for himself and his court—as, it seemed to him, a raja should now and then, even when there is famine.

A servant led an elephant from a royal storehouse to the palace, carrying two full baskets of rice.

A village girl named Rani saw that a trickle
of rice was falling from one of the baskets.
Quickly she jumped up and walked along beside
the elephant, catching the falling rice in her skirt.
She was clever, and she began to make a plan.

t the palace, a guard cried, "Halt, thief! Where are you going with that rice?"

"I am not a thief," Rani replied. "This rice fell from one of the baskets, and I am returning it now to the raja."

When the raja heard about Rani's good deed, he asked his ministers to bring her before him.

"I wish to reward you for returning what belongs to me," the raja said to Rani. "Ask me for anything, and you shall have it."

"Your Highness," said Rani, "I do not deserve any reward at all. But if you wish, you may give me one grain of rice."

"Only one grain of rice?" exclaimed the raja. "Surely you will allow me to reward you more plentifully, as a raja should."

"Very well," said Rani. "If it pleases Your Highness, you may reward me in this way. Today, you will give me a single grain of rice. Then, each day for thirty days you will give me double the rice you gave me the day before. Thus, tomorrow you will give me two grains of rice, the next day four grains of rice, and so on for thirty days."

"This seems still to be a modest reward," said the raja. "But you shall have it."

And Rani was presented with a single grain of rice.

The next day, Rani was presented with two grains of rice.

And the following day, Rani was presented with four grains of rice.

On the ninth day, Rani was presented with two hundred and fifty-six grains of rice. She had received in all five hundred and eleven grains of rice, only enough for a small handful.

"This girl is honest, but not very clever," thought the raja. "She would have gained more rice by keeping what fell into her skirt!"

On the twelfth day, Rani received two thousand and forty-eight grains of rice, about four handfuls. On the thirteenth day, she received four thousand and ninety-six grains of rice, enough to fill a bowl.

On the sixteenth day, Rani was presented with a bag containing thirty-two thousand, seven hundred and sixty-eight grains of rice. All together she had enough rice for two full bags.

"This doubling adds up to more rice than I expected!" thought the raja. "But surely her reward won't amount to much more."

On the twentieth day, Rani was presented with sixteen more bags filled with rice.

On the twenty-first day, she received one million, forty-eight thousand, five hundred and seventy-six grains of rice, enough to fill a basket.

On the twenty-fourth day, Rani was presented with eight million, three hundred and eighty-eight thousand, six hundred and eight grains of rice—enough to fill eight baskets, which were carried to her by eight royal deer.

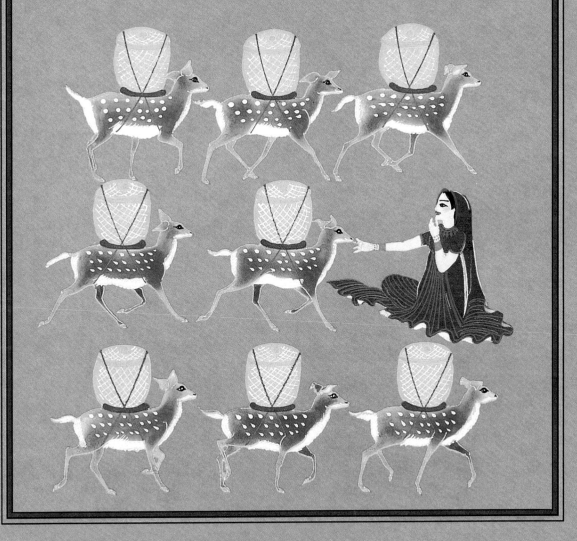

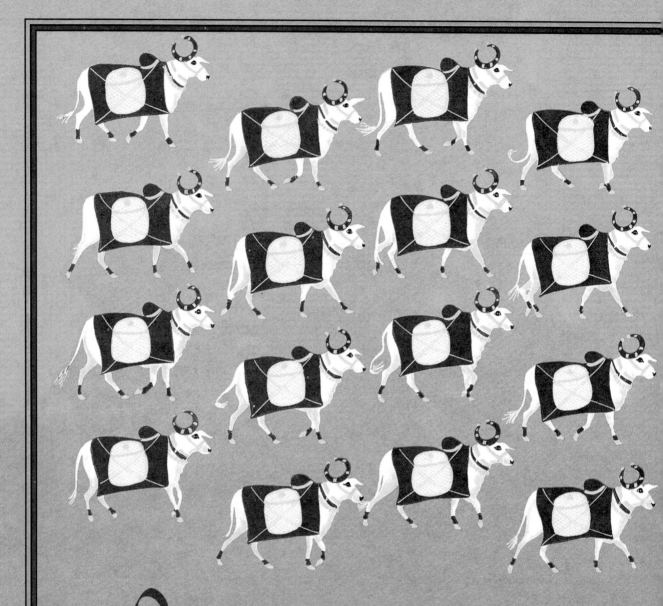

On the twenty-seventh day, thirty-two Brahma bulls were needed to deliver sixty-four baskets of rice.

The raja was deeply troubled. "One grain of rice has grown very great indeed," he thought. "But I shall fulfill the reward to the end, as a raja should."

On the twenty-ninth day, Rani
was presented with the contents
of two royal storehouses.

On the thirtieth and final day, two hundred and fifty-six elephants crossed the province, carrying the contents of the last four royal storehouses—five hundred and thirty-six million, eight hundred and seventy thousand, nine hundred and twelve grains of rice.

All together, Rani had received more than one billion grains of rice. The raja had no more rice to give. "And what will you do with this rice," said the raja with a sigh, "now that I have none?"

"I shall give it to all the hungry people," said Rani. "And I shall leave a basket of rice for you, too, if you promise from now on to take only as much rice as you need."

"I promise," said the raja.

And for the rest of his days, the raja was truly wise and fair, as a raja should be.

From One Grain of Rice to One Billion

Each day, Rani received double the amount of rice as the day before. See how quickly one grain of rice doubles into so much more.

To count how many grains of rice Rani received in all, add all of these numbers together. The answer: 1,073,741,823—more than one billion grains of rice!

DAY 1	DAY 2	DAY 3	DAY 4	DAY 5
1	2	4	8	16
DAY 6	DAY 7	DAY 8	DAY 9	DAY 10
32	64	128	256	512
DAY 11	DAY 12	DAY 13	DAY 14	DAY 15
1,024	2,048	4,096	8,192	16,384
DAY 16	DAY 17	DAY 18	DAY 19	DAY 20
32,768	65,536	131,072	262,144	524,288
DAY 21	DAY 22	DAY 23	DAY 24	DAY 25
1,048,576	2,097,152	4,194,304	8,388,608	16,777,216
DAY 26	DAY 27	DAY 28	DAY 29	DAY 30
33,554,432	67,108,864	134,217,728	268,435,456	536,870,912

Think About It

1 Describe the problem in the story, and tell why Rani's solution is such a good one.

2 Why does the raja keep giving away rice even after he sees what is happening?

3 How does the raja change at the end of the story? What do you think he learned?

Meet the Author and Illustrator

✳ DEMI ✳

As a child, Charlotte Dumaresq Hunt was nick-named Demi. She now writes and illustrates books under that name. She comes from a family of artists.

Demi has studied art in several countries. She lived in India for two years and became interested in Indian art and culture. She also loves Chinese painting, and it has had a strong influence on her work. Demi's husband is from China. He has told her the folktales and fables he heard as a child. Demi retells the tales in her books.

Demi's work has been shown in museums across the country. She has created murals, mosaics, puppet toys, scroll paintings, and Chinese paper objects.

Visit *The Learning Site!*
www.harcourtschool.com

Demi

It's Just Math

by Linda O. George

illustrated by Barbara Emmons

TRICKS WITH NUMBERS can be fun. Here's one you can try with your friends:

1. Think of a number.
2. Add 3 to this number.
3. Multiply your answer by 2.
4. Subtract 4.
5. Divide by 2.
6. Subtract the number you started with.

If you did everything right, your answer will be 1. Try the trick again using a different number. Your answer will still be 1.

Here's another example. Since we can start with any number, let's pick 5.

1. Think of a number.	5
2. Add 3.	$5 + 3 = 8$
3. Multiply by 2.	$8 \times 2 = 16$
4. Subtract 4.	$16 - 4 = 12$
5. Divide by 2.	$12 \div 2 = 6$
6. Subtract the original number.	$6 - 5 = 1$

Is this magic? No! Math is magic only for people who don't understand it. There is a reasonable explanation for every number trick.

Let's use pictures. If we pretend that our numbers represent buttons, we can see what happens in this trick.

1. **Think of a number.**
   Since we can start with any number of buttons, let's hide them in a bag.

2. **Add 3.**
   Our bag of buttons and 3 more buttons.

3. **Multiply by 2.**
   Now we have 2 bags and 6 buttons altogether.

4. **Subtract 4.**
   Take away 4 buttons.

5. **Divide by 2.**
   That leaves us with 1 bag and 1 button.

6. **Subtract the original number.**
   Take away the bag of buttons we started with, and we are left with 1 button!

This will happen every time. Remember that the bag of buttons could hold any number of buttons, and we did not do anything to change the buttons inside the bag. So we will always end up with 1 lone button at the end of this trick. This lone button stands for 1.

The next time you see a number trick, try to figure out why it works. You can be sure that if it's math, it isn't magic.

Think About It

Do you think the buttons and bags example is a good explanation of the trick? Explain your answer.

Response Activities

Tales of Justice

WRITE A COMPARISON

Compare this tale with "In the Days of King Adobe." Think about what is unfair, what trick solves the problem, and what some traits of the characters are. Write a few paragraphs comparing the stories.

Palace Pantomime

USE MOVEMENT TO TELL A STORY

Many times storytellers use movement or dance as they tell their tales. In a group, make up a pantomime of a scene from "One Grain of Rice." Use gestures, facial expressions, and body language to tell the story. A narrator may introduce the scene.

Rice Count

ESTIMATE QUANTITY

The story says that there are 511 grains in a small handful of rice. Have a contest in your classroom. Fill a small, clear bottle with dried beans or grains of uncooked rice. Then challenge classmates to guess the number of beans or grains.

Making Connections

RESEARCH EVERYDAY MATH

Both the story and the magazine article contain number tricks. You may already know some tricks of your own, like adding a zero to the end of a number if you want to multiply by 10. Find out more neat number shortcuts. You might learn about estimating or about ways to figure the tip in a restaurant. Start by looking in your math book. Take notes to help you remember the strategies you learn!

THEME

WRAP-UP

Character Encounter

WRITE A CONVERSATION
"Red Writing Hood" includes conversations between characters from different stories. Write a conversation between two characters from different selections in this theme. Have them first introduce themselves and then tell each other about the problems they solved.

From Story to Play

REWRITE A SCENE In a group, choose a story from this theme that would make a good play. Work together to write a scene from the story in play form. Act out the scene for classmates, and ask them to compare and contrast the story and the play.

Creative Minds, Good Ideas

MAKE A WEB What kinds of creative ideas are described in this theme? Show your answer in a web. Include the names of characters who use each kind of idea.

Good Ideas

431

Theme
Community

Contents

Ties

433

Lucita Comes Home to Oaxaca
by Robin B. Cano

REALISTIC FICTION

At first, Lucita feels strange, revisiting her birthplace in Mexico, but she soon discovers many wonderful things about her family and her heritage.

READER'S CHOICE LIBRARY

Celebrating the Powwow
by Bobbie Kalman

NONFICTION

Join in the festivities as the powwow celebrates the Native American heritage and traditions.

READER'S CHOICE LIBRARY

Reader's

Fair!
by Ted Lewin

NONFICTION

The county fair is coming to town, and there's a lot to see and do. Enjoy the sights, smells and tastes as excitement fills the air.

Notable Social Studies Trade Book

The Blue Hill Meadows
by Cynthia Rylant

REALISTIC FICTION

Four stories, each in a different season, are shared by Willie Meadow of Blue Hill, Virginia. He tells of everyday family life with some of its adventures and all of its pleasures.

Award-Winning Author

Going Home
by Eve Bunting

REALISTIC FICTION

When Carlos and his family go home to Mexico for the holidays, he and his brothers and sisters find a new appreciation for their roots.

Award-Winning Author

Choice

FIRE!

There are 35,000 fire departments in the United States and about 1.5 million firefighters. This selection from the book *Fire!* shows the importance of firefighters to their communities, both now and long ago. It also shows how their work is important to the firefighters themselves. It gives them the sense of belonging to a community, as well as the satisfaction of saving lives.

BY JOY MASOFF

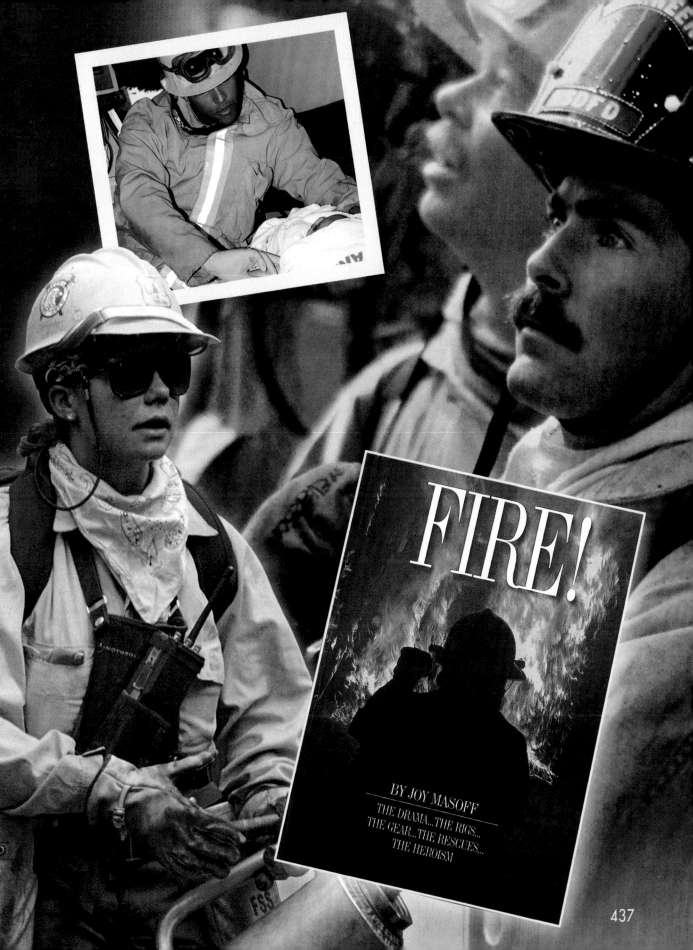

FIRE!

BY JOY MASOFF

THE DRAMA...THE RIGS...
THE GEAR...THE RESCUES...
THE HEROISM

Different...Yet the Same

When a call comes in—whether it's a report of flames at a country farm or smoke on the forty-eighth floor of a skyscraper—firefighters feel the same emotions. What will it be like? Will I be able to help? But every town is different; every department does things a different way.

They all have different names for their equipment and different systems for getting things done. In big cities, people get paid to be firefighters. In small towns, they usually don't. But one thing is the same. It's *always* challenging, always demanding...always thrilling.

In big cities, firefighters can answer a dozen calls a day. City firefighters stay at the station house.

In small towns, many firefighters are volunteers. There are almost one million volunteer firefighters in the United States.

438

Answering the Call

Y ou are a firefighter. People count on you to come the moment they call. But you never know when that call will happen, so you are always ready. You check your equipment. You check your equipment again. You might sleep at the fire station a few nights each month or you might sleep in your house with a beeper at your bedside. But you always wait for that moment when you hear the call for help.

The station house is a second home to you. The people you work with are more than just your co-workers. They are the people you trust with your life. They have become like family—brothers and sisters you love fiercely, even if sometimes you get on one another's nerves.

You wait and check and practice. And then it happens. . . .

When the bells and buzzers sound in the station house, there is a great burst of activity. Poles are slid down, gear is pulled on.

Firefighters call these runs JOBS or WORKERS. Let's pretend that for just one day, *you* are a big-city firefighter. You've got a worker!

YOUR ASSIGNMENT: ENGINE 21

Unlike small-town fire departments, which keep all their equipment in one place, big-city fire departments keep their trucks in buildings all over town, just a few trucks to each building.

Each truck has a team. There's a DRIVER (who takes care of the rig), an OFFICER (who's in charge of the crew), and FIREFIGHTERS (who tackle the flames or mount the rescues). In the old days, those firefighters were called "back-steppers" because they used to ride on the back of the truck, hanging on for dear life. This was very dangerous, so new trucks carry them inside.

You will work on a shift—usually a 24-hour period when you live at the station, eating and sometimes sleeping there. Remember, fire doesn't take vacations. Accidents never take the night off.

LIFE IN THE HOUSE

When you arrive for your shift, you pull out your gear and get it set up near your rig. If you're going to be working at night, you make your bed and help clean up the station house. There are usually training sessions to attend. You might even shop for groceries and cook dinner. There's always a lot to do.

The calls will come in to DISPATCH via the 911 network, and you never know what they will be. A child locked in a bathroom, a car that hit a stop sign, a burst pipe, a funny smell, a cat stuck inside a wall . . . people call the fire department for help with *everything*.

▶ *These bunker pants are already tucked into boots, ready to be pulled on at a second's notice.*

STRUCTURE FIRE, CORNER OF PARK AND MAIN

But a fire call is something special. And now, just before lunch, a call has come in. Smoke is billowing from a store downtown. You hear your truck number called. In many fire stations you slide down the pole and slide into your turnout gear. Then, with your heart racing, you hop on your rig.

ALL ABOARD

The sirens are on, the lights flashing. You're on your way. You try to imagine what's waiting for you, and all the time your mind is racing along with your heart. You feel excited. This is what you've trained for.

▶ *Pull on your hood, pull on your mask, check the airflow, and head on in!*

OUT OF CONTROL

When you get to the scene, the crew breaks up into teams. Some of you pull in the attack hoses to cool the flames. Some set the bigger discharge lines. Others are part of SEARCH AND RESCUE, looking for people or pets. Still others ventilate the building by breaking windows or cutting holes in the roof.

When it is all over and the fire is almost KNOCKED DOWN, you shovel up the cinders and toss outside anything that might still burn, then soak it until you can touch it with your bare hands. This is called the OVERHAUL.

The one word firefighters never want to hear is REKINDLE . . . a fire they thought was out but wasn't.

Three hours after the first alarm, it's back to the station, into a quick shower, and finally it's time for a very late lunch.

Eat Like a Firefighter

Firefighter McNulty's Four-Alarm Chicken

Ask a grown-up to help you whip up this reheat-and-eat dinner. Serves an entire firehouse (6–8 people)

4 cups cut-up boneless chicken breasts

2 cups celery, thinly sliced

$\frac{1}{4}$ cup chopped green pepper

$\frac{1}{4}$ cup chopped red pepper

2 tsps. lemon juice

$1\frac{1}{2}$ cups spaghetti sauce

1 cup bread crumbs

1 tablespoon melted butter

1 cup grated cheddar cheese

For a spicier dish add $1\frac{1}{2}$ *tbsps. Worcestershire sauce and 1 tsp. Tabasco sauce.*

Combine all the ingredients except the bread crumbs, butter, and cheese. Pour into a baking dish. Top with grated cheese. Toss the bread crumbs with melted butter and sprinkle over the top. Bake at 350° for 40 minutes. Can be reheated whenever a rescue interrupts.

Firefighting Long Ago

In 1607, Jamestown, Virginia, became the first English settlement in America, and in 1608 it burned to the ground. Life in this "new world" seemed to be one big fire after another. Year after year people built homes only to see them go up in flames. Here's why. . . .

THE FIRST LITTLE PIG BUILT HIS HOUSE OF STRAW

The first homes in our country were built quickly, using easily

▲ *It's easy to see why Jamestown, Virginia, kept burning down. The houses were made of campfire ingredients.*

found materials such as brush, tree limbs, clay, and grasses. The roofs were made of thatch (which is made from bundles of straw lashed together) and mud. If you've ever been to a campfire, you know that a lot of those things make for a mighty flame. There was no heat or hot water and no electric stoves, so people kept fires going all day long in poorly constructed hearths.

EVEN CHILDREN WERE FIREFIGHTERS

If you lived in the 1600s you would have been a part of the firefighting force. It took the whole town to stop a blaze. Every single home had a leather bucket hanging near the door just for putting out fires. Unlike today, when you just turn on a faucet to get water, townspeople had to get water from ponds, rivers, or wells. When a fire broke out, people formed a BUCKET BRIGADE.

Two lines stretched from the town's water source, everyone armed with a bucket. The men would fill the buckets and pass them toward the fire; the women and children would send the empty ones back to be filled. Most times it was too little water, too late. Town after town burned to the ground.

IT'S 9 P.M. IS YOUR FIRE OUT?

Wisely, the elders knew things had to change. Laws were passed forbidding the use of flammable building materials such as thatch. And because most fires occurred at night, while people slept, their fire-places still lit for warmth, a curfew (which comes from the French for "cover the fire") was ordered. You could not have a fire going between 9 P.M. and 4:30 A.M. If you broke the law, you paid a heavy fine, and the money went toward big buckets, ladders, hooks, and rope.

▼*Women are firefighters, too. The first American woman firefighter on record was Molly Williams, who lived in the late 1700s. By the early 1900s there were all-woman companies like this one in Silver Spring, Maryland.*

THE RATTLE WATCH

In the quickly growing cities, more and more houses were being built, all packed in close together. When one caught on fire, dozens ended up burning. In some cities, men were appointed to wander the streets at night to watch for fires. They carried big wooden rattles that made an alarming sound when twirled.

▲ When Ben Franklin wasn't flying kites in lightning storms, he was busy improving day-to-day life.

WHO INVENTED THE FIRE DEPARTMENT?

Benjamin Franklin, one of the greatest Americans ever, convinced a group of Philadelphia's leading citizens to band together to form the Union Fire Company. Willing to drop what they were doing to rush to the scene, they brought with them a great sense of dedication and loyalty—the true spirit of fire-fighting to this day. Franklin also published an important newspaper, and he frequently printed articles urging people to be more careful. He came up with the phrase "an ounce of prevention is worth a pound of cure" to keep people from carrying hot coals on shovels from room to room. George Washington, Paul Revere, and Thomas Jefferson were all volunteer firefighters, along with many other patriots. It was the right thing to do for a growing country.

447

Tools of the Trade

ou wouldn't go out to play in the snow and ice in a bathing suit, would you? Just as you depend on gloves, a hat, a warm coat, and boots to protect you, firefighters depend on their turnout gear. That gear can mean the difference between a successful rescue and disaster.

HOOD
(Underneath helmet)

HELMET

EYE SHIELD

FACE MASK
(Underneath eye shield)

AIR CYLINDER

FIRE TOOL

REGULATOR
(Controls the flow of air in and out)

FIRE-RESISTANT LINED GLOVES

WALKIE-TALKIE
(Worn on left side of coat)

PRESSURE GAUGE
(Shows how much air is left in the tank)

GEAR POCKET

BUNKER PANTS

BOOTS

Total weight of the average turnout gear: 68 pounds!

Think About It

1 List some of the many things a firefighter might do during a 24-hour shift.

2 What is the most surprising or interesting fact you learned from this selection? Explain.

3 Why do you think the author addresses the reader directly in the section "Answering the Call"?

Meet the Author

Joy Masoff is a writer and art director in advertising. As a scout leader, she took her troop to visit the fire station that sponsored it. There she developed an admiration for the job firefighters do for the community. *Fire!* is her first book. Ms. Masoff visited many fire stations and museums and talked with firefighters to get the information for this book. She tries to capture the danger and the excitement of firefighting, and possibly inspire young people to choose this important job as a career. Continuing her interest in careers that help the community, her second book is *Emergency!*

Joy Masoff

RESPONSE ACTIVITIES

Fire Safety Tips

MAKE A POSTER

The best way to fight fires is to prevent them. Read an encyclopedia article on fire prevention, or write to your county's health department or a local fire station for information about preventing fires. Use some of the most important information to create a fire safety poster. Display your poster in a hallway at your school.

Firefighters in Action

WRITE A NEWS STORY

Make up a newspaper story about a fire and a rescue. Answer the questions *who, what, when, where, why,* and *how.* Give your article an attention-getting headline.

Pros and Cons

MAKE A CHART

Imagine that you are trying to decide whether to apply for a job as a firefighter. Think of reasons for and against choosing this line of work. Write your reasons in a chart.

In Case of Fire

MAP A ROUTE

Make sure you know what your class should do in case of a fire. Work with a partner to make a map of your school that shows the best escape route. You might also show where you are to go if it is lunchtime or recess time.

451

Fact and Opinion

In "Fire!" the author tells many facts about the life of a firefighter. A **fact** is a statement that can be proven to be true. Now and then the author gives an **opinion**, something she believes to be true but cannot prove. This chart shows examples of facts and opinions from the selection:

Facts can be proven to be true.

Opinions are ideas someone believes. They cannot be proven.

Facts

City firefighters stay at the station house.

Early houses were built of materials that caught fire easily.

George Washington, Paul Revere, and Thomas Jefferson were volunteer firefighters.

Opinions

Being a firefighter is always thrilling.

A fire call is something special.

Joining a volunteer fire department was the right thing to do.

Knowing how to tell the difference between fact and opinion can help you make decisions about what you read.

Read the paragraph below. Use a chart like the one on page 452 to separate the facts from the opinions.

Many firefighters are paramedics trained to give emergency medical treatment. This is an exciting part of a firefighter's job. When a medical call comes in, paramedics jump into the ambulance and speed to the scene. They give first aid and often take the victim to the hospital. Paramedics save lives. We should all appreciate them.

WHAT HAVE YOU LEARNED?

1. What are some facts you learned about fire fighting? What is an opinion that you agree with?

2. Tell whether you would expect to find more facts or more opinions in each of the following—a news story, a letter from a friend, a TV commercial. Explain your answers.

TRY THIS • TRY THIS • TRY THIS

Can boys and girls your age do anything to help prevent fires? State an opinion. Then give some facts to support your opinion. Make another chart like the one on page 452 to record your ideas.

Visit *The Learning Site!*
www.harcourtschool.com

A Very Important Day

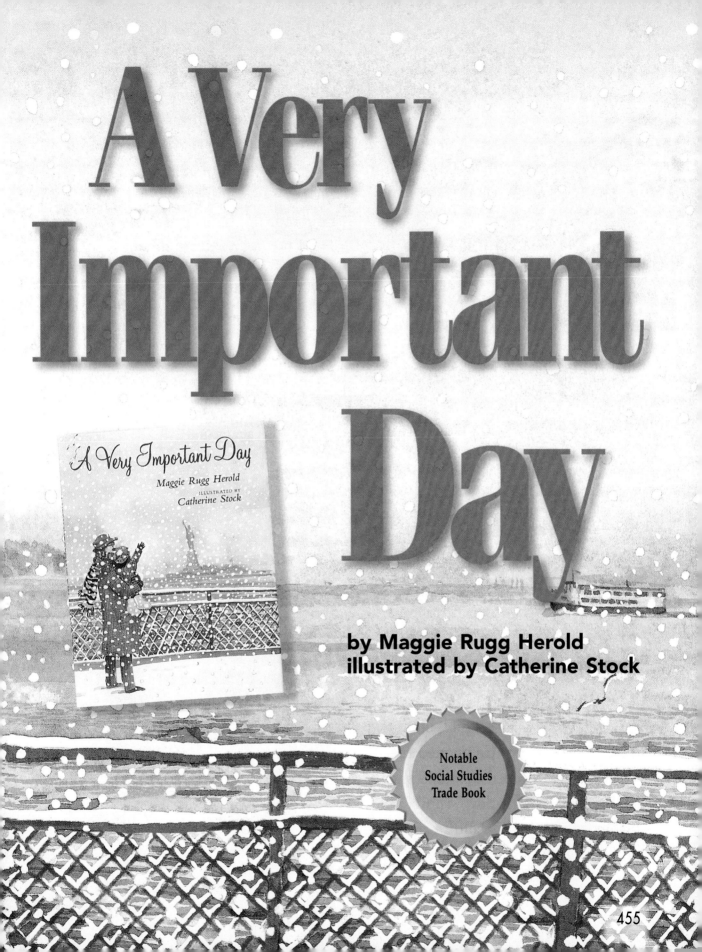

A Very Important Day

Maggie Rugg Herold

ILLUSTRATED BY
Catherine Stock

by Maggie Rugg Herold
illustrated by Catherine Stock

Notable
Social Studies
Trade Book

Nelia Batungbakal (NEL-i-ah bah-TUHNG-bah-KAHL) was too excited to sleep. She was looking out her window, listening to music on her Walkman, when she thought she saw snow!

Sure enough, before long the station DJ came on. "It's three A.M. here in New York City, and it's snowing. Four to six inches are expected by noon."

Nelia's mind raced. Imagine, snow on such a very important day. This would never happen in the Philippines. Her son and daughter-in-law and the grandchildren were fast asleep. She would need to awaken them early, to allow extra time for the trip downtown.

"Wake up, Miguel (mee-GEL). It's snowing," Rosa Huerta (ROE-sah WHERE-tah) called to her brother. "There are at least two inches on the fire escape."

"All *right!*" said Miguel, bounding from his room. He opened the window and scooped up some snow.

"Close that window," their father ordered. "It's cold in here, and—Miguel, is that snow in your hand?"

"Yes, Papa, the first this year."

"Back outside with it before it melts. And on such a very important day. This would not happen in Mexico, at least not in the south."

"Let's move quickly," urged their mother. "It's six-thirty. We can get an early start downtown."

Veena Patel (VEE-nah pah-TEL) had just set the table when the doorbell rang. "That will be the children," her husband, Mohandas (moe-HAHN-dahs), said.

But it was their neighbors, the Pitambers (pi-TAHM-buhrs). They apologized for stopping by so early. "We were afraid of missing you, and we wanted to wish you well on this very important day."

"Join us for breakfast," said Veena. "Our daughter and her family will be here any minute. They think we must allow extra time, that the snow will slow us down. That's one worry we never had in India."

The doorbell rang again, and this time it was the children. Everyone gathered quickly at the table, talking eagerly about the special morning ahead.

Out the door and down the steps came the Leonovs (lay-OH-nufs)—first Eugenia (yev-GAY-nee-ah), then her brother, Lev (LEF), followed by their grandfather, grandmother, mother, and father.

457

"Snow reminds me of Russia," said their mother.

"I love snow!" exclaimed Eugenia.

Her grandfather stooped, grabbed two handfuls, and threw them at his grandchildren.

The fight was on.

Just then Mr. Dionetti (dee-on-ET-ee) lobbed a snowball from the door of his corner grocery. "Is this the big day?" he called out. "Are you headed downtown?"

"Yes," answered their father.

"This snowball fight is headed for the subway."

"Congratulations!" cried Mr. Dionetti. And tossing a big handful of snow straight up in the air, he crossed the street to shake their hands.

Kostas and Nikos Soutsos (KOS-tahs and NEE-kose SOO-tsose) were clearing the sidewalk in front of the family restaurant when their mother came out the side door from their apartment above. She was carrying their baby sister, Kiki (ki-KEE).

458

"And read this sign, everyone. What does it say?"

They chorused together, "Closed for a very important day."

"Finally! There's the bus," said Duong Hao (ZUNG HAH-oh). He and his older sister, Trinh (CHRIN), brushed snow off each other and followed their mother on board. It was crowded at first, but a few stops later they all got seats.

"Here we are," said their mother, "in the middle of a snowstorm on the most important day since we arrived from Vietnam—"

Suddenly the driver braked hard.

They were all thrown forward.

"Car skidded at the light and couldn't stop," the driver yelled. "Everybody okay?"

Fortunately only bundles had landed on the floor.

"That was close," said their mother.

"Yes," said Trinh, "but our driver's good."

Duong nodded. "Maybe he knows that today of all days we just have to get downtown."

"Kiki, this is snow," said Kostas.

"How do you like it?" Nikos asked.

Kiki seemed puzzled by the flakes that hit her nose.

Their mother laughed. "She'll get used to it, living here. Not like Greece, where it snows maybe once in ten years. But where's your father? We should be on our way."

"He went to make a sign for the door. See, there he is."

"Set those shovels inside, and let's be off," their father called.

"I love the ferry," said Jorge Báez (HOR-hay BYE-es).

"So do I," agreed his cousin Pedro Jiménez (PAY-droe hee-MAY-nes), "especially in snow. Let's go up on deck."

"Not by yourselves, but I'll go with you," said Pedro's father.

"And I'll keep you company," Jorge's father added.

"Me too," begged Jorge's sister. "I want to go outside."

"All right," said her father. "You are old enough."

They went up on deck, leaving the little ones inside with Jorge's mother and aunt.

"I'm so glad this day takes us across the harbor," said Pedro's father. "I never tire of the ride."

"Neither do I," said Jorge's father. "Even in snow, this view is the best in the city. And now we will all remember it as part of the most important day since we came from the Dominican Republic."

Through the narrow streets on the unshoveled sidewalks the Zeng (DZENG) family made their way on foot. Suddenly, from above them, a voice called out.

Yujin's (EEOO-JING) friend Bailong (BYE-LONG) was leaning out the window. "I've been watching for you," he said. "Don't open this until later. Catch!"

Down through the snowflakes came a small brightly wrapped package, straight into Yujin's outstretched hands.

"Thanks, Bailong."

"Thanks for remembering."

"This is such an important day."

"The most important since we arrived from China."

Yujin tucked the package safely inside his coat, and with waves and good-byes the Zengs set off again, heading south.

Jihan Idris (ji-HAN i-DREES) and her parents had also left home early to make the trip downtown. Now their subway ride was over, and there was time for breakfast.

"I see a coffee shop ahead," Jihan's mother called out.

"I want to sit at the counter!" Jihan exclaimed.

They entered and sat on three stools, Jihan in the middle.

"I'd like waffles," Jihan told their waitress.

"And I'll have pancakes," said her father. "With coffee and grapefruit juice."

"Scrambled eggs and a toasted bagel, please," said her mother. "With orange juice and tea."

Quickly the waitress was back with their breakfasts. "What brings you out so early on a snowy day like today?" she asked.

"Can you guess?" said Jihan's mother.

"It's the most important day for us since we came from Egypt," said Jihan's father.

She nodded.

"On your mark, get set, go!"

And off they dashed, down the sidewalk.

"Tie," Efua declared at the bottom of the steps.

"I used to run in Ghana," Kwame said, "but never in snow."

"Wait," said Efua, taking a camera from her purse.

"Before we go in on this very important day, let's get someone to take our picture."

So they asked a stranger, who gladly obliged, and then hand in hand they climbed the courthouse steps.

"And I'm celebrating with waffles," said Jihan. "I never get them at home."

"There's the courthouse," said Kwame Akuffo (KWA-mee ah-KOO-foo) to his wife, Efua (eh-foo-WAH), as they rounded a corner, walking fast.

She stopped. "Only two blocks to go. I'll race you to the steps."

He stopped, too. "Are you crazy?"

"It's not slippery."

"You're on! Ready?"

As Robert MacTaggart came through the courthouse door, he heard familiar voices calling, "Robert. Over here."

Near the entrance stood his friends Elizabeth and Alan. Each of them gave him a big hug.

"You made it," Robert said. "Thank you so much for coming. I was afraid the snow would stop you."

"Oh, no, not on such an important day," said Elizabeth.

"We were getting worried about *you*, though," said Alan.

Robert chuckled. "A few snowflakes defeat a man from the highlands of Scotland? Come on. Let's find the chamber. It's on this floor."

Leaving relatives and friends to wait in the hall outside, Alvaro Castro (AL-vah-roe CA-stroe), his wife, Romelia (roe-MAY-lee-ah), and their children entered the crowded chamber. They were among the last to find seats.

Soon the examiner appeared, and the room became quiet. "When I call your name," he said, "please come forward to receive your certificate."

Many names were called; many people went forward. Then, "Alvaro and Romelia Castro and children Marta, José, and Oscar."

The Castros approached the examiner.

"Please sign here," he said to Alvaro. "And here," he said to Romelia. "These are your papers."

"Thank you," said Alvaro. "This is a proud moment."

The Castros returned to their seats. "The long journey from El Salvador has ended," Romelia whispered to her husband, and he squeezed her hand.

When the examiner had finished, he said, "Please open the door to relatives and friends."

People poured in. There were so many they filled the aisles and lined the walls at the back and sides of the chamber.

"Everyone please rise," said the examiner, and as everyone did, a judge entered the chamber.

"Your Honor," said the examiner, "these petitioners have qualified for citizenship in the United States of America."

"Then," said the judge, "will you repeat after me the oath of citizenship. Let us begin. 'I hereby declare, on oath . . .' "

"I hereby declare, on oath . . ."

Echoing the judge phrase by phrase, sentence by sentence, the many voices resounded as one, swearing loyalty to the United States of America.

"Congratulations," said the judge. "Those of you who can be, please be seated."

As the room became quiet again, the judge cleared his throat. "Two hundred nineteen of you from thirty-two countries

have become United States citizens here today. You are carrying on a tradition that dates back to the earliest days of our country, for almost all Americans have come here from somewhere else. May citizenship enrich your lives as your lives enrich this country. Welcome. We are glad to have you. This is a very important day."

Everyone then rose and joined the judge in the Pledge of Allegiance.

Family and friends and strangers turned to one another. "Best wishes!" "I'm so happy for you." "You must be so proud." "Isn't it wonderful?" "What a day!" "Let me shake your hand." "Let me give you a kiss." "Let me give you a hug."

Zeng Yujin tore open the package from his friend Bailong. Inside he found small American flags, a dozen or so, enough to share with everyone in his family and with other new citizens surrounding him.

In a wave of excitement, they all made their way out of the chamber, through the hallway, and back to the courthouse door.

"Look!" they exclaimed, everybody talking at once. "The snow has stopped." "The sun is shining." "It will be easy to get home and go on celebrating." "This has become our country on this very important day!"

Think About It

 How are the people in this story different from each other? How are they alike?

 What do these words mean to you: "May citizenship enrich your lives as your lives enrich this country"?

 Why do you think the author waits until the end of the story to tell readers what the special day is?

MEET THE AUTHOR
Maggie Rugg Herold

MEET THE ILLUSTRATOR
Catherine Stock

468

A book review tells about a book and gives an opinion. It might look like this.

Books on America: Top Picks

If you're looking for good books on citizenship, one to check out is *A Very Important Day*. This colorful picture book is written by Maggie Rugg Herold and illustrated by Catherine Stock.

On a snowy day in New York, people from all over the world make their way downtown. At the turn of each page, readers meet a new family with the same plans. Herold's text keeps readers guessing what is so important, and Stock's bright watercolors set the happy mood.

The author and illustrator are a good team for a book like this one. Herold has made her career in children's book publishing. Stock is both an author and an illustrator, and many of her books celebrate special days such as holidays. Stock lives in New York City, and Herold lives in nearby Montclair, New Jersey.

This is a book about the true meaning of citizenship that any reader will enjoy.

Visit *The Learning Site!* www.harcourtschool.com

469

Response

Welcome!

GIVE A SPEECH

At the courthouse the judge welcomes the new citizens with a speech. Write your own welcoming speech for people who are new to your community. You might wish them luck and tell how their coming will enrich the community. Practice your speech, and then present it with expression.

From Far and Wide

LOCATE COUNTRIES

The people at the ceremony came from thirty-two different countries. Work in a group to list the twelve countries mentioned in the selection. Then find each one on a flat map of the world. Look in an almanac to find basic facts about each country. Write some facts on self-stick labels, and use the labels to mark each country's location on the map.

Activities

Ellis Island

WRITE A REPORT

In the early 1900s many thousands of immigrants entered the United States at Ellis Island, near New York City. Look at social studies books or an encyclopedia to learn more about this historic place. Find out what immigrants experienced as they passed through Ellis Island. Write a short report about what you learn.

Liberty Songs

PRESENT SONGS

The Statue of Liberty is a symbol of freedom. Work in a group to find songs and poems about liberty. Use them to make a presentation to classmates. You may want to use props and play taped background music.

Award-Winning
Author

HOUSE, HOUSE

In the early 1900s, the Howes brothers took pictures of people in front of their houses. One of the towns they visited was Hatfield, a little farm community in Massachusetts. There, they photographed over one hundred houses. Almost a century later, Jason Stemple has done the same thing. The photos in this selection show how the houses and their surroundings have changed, and the author describes how life has changed.

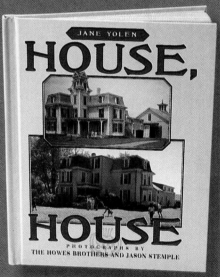

by **Jane Yolen**

photographs by **the Howes brothers and Jason Stemple**

In 1900, a boy and his dog could ride from Hatfield to nearby Northampton on an electric trolley, though heavy winter snows often closed the trolley lines down. Fifteen years later, automobiles started showing up on local streets. A new car then

N O W

In 1934, buses took the place of trolleys and the trolley tracks were removed. Many roads began to be paved. Today there is no public transportation in or out of Hatfield, but almost every household has a car, often several. A new car costs well over $10,000.

In the early 1800s, Hatfield girls went to school four months of the year, because the town would not vote more money than that for the education of females. But by 1900, Hatfield classes were finally co-ed the entire school year.

N O W

Today children of Hatfield—boys and girls—go to a school that has computers, a gymnasium, a library, a PA system, a lunchroom serving hot meals, and organized after-school sports programs. None of these things were in that earlier school.

THEN The first telephones came to western Massachusetts in 1877, one year after Alexander Graham Bell received his patent. Within the first five years, only one hundred phones were installed in valley homes, very few of them in Hatfield.

N O W **T**oday, every single house in Hatfield has at least one telephone; most have jacks for several phones. And many of the houses have computer modems and faxes running through the telephone lines, as well.

In 1890, a housewife might wait a long time till the grocery wagon came by. The horse-drawn wagon was used for delivering meat, bread, milk, butter, cheese—almost all from local farmers. She stored those things in an ice box, where they were kept cold by the use of ice. The first household refrigerator was not built until 1913. The house-wife knew the grocer and driver by name.

N O W

Today, a trip by car to a supermarket takes only a few minutes. Distances may be farther, but the choices are greater: oranges from Israel, cheese from Holland, rice from India, Australian beef. These can be kept fresh in a refrigerator or freezer, cooked on a gas or electric stove, reheated in a microwave. The customer will not know the supermarket owner's name.

T H E N

In 1898

Sugar: 4 cents a pound.

Butter: 25 cents a pound.

Hamburger on toast sandwich: 7 cents.

A ride to the next town took well over an hour.

N O W   **In 1998**

Sugar: $2.00 a five-pound bag, or 40 cents a pound.

Butter: $2.19 a pound.

Hamburger on a bun: 69 cents.

A ride to the next town takes eight minutes by car.

T H E N

In 1906, when this picture was taken, a maid lived in the attic, in a little room with bright yellow-flowered wallpaper. The room was freezing in the winter and sweltering in the summer. She did all the work in the house from sunup to sundown.

N O W

Today, the writer of this book works in the same little attic room. The flowered wallpaper is now faded and brown. There is an air conditioner to keep the room cool in summer and electric baseboard heat to keep it warm in winter. The author works at her writing from sunup to sundown.

Think About It

 How has the town of Hatfield changed over time?

 Which time would you choose for living in Hatfield—then or now? Explain why.

3 How do the photographs and the author's description help you understand what has happened in Hatfield in the last hundred years?

MEET THE AUTHOR

JANE YOLEN

Jane Yolen began her writing career as a journalist and a poet before turning to children's literature. She has written over 150 children's books, including the Piggins mystery series, and has won many literary awards. She says she comes from a family of storytellers, so writing children's tales continues the family tradition. Jane Yolen also includes family in her stories, having fashioned several characters after her husband and children. Her son, Jason Stemple, even did the photography for *House, House.*

Visit *The Learning Site!*
www.harcourtschool.com

RESPONSE ACTIVITIES

Turn of the Century

PLAN A TIME CAPSULE

The photographs taken by the Howes brothers help us understand what life was like about one hundred years ago. With a partner, plan a time capsule that would tell children one hundred years from now what your life is like today. Decide what kind of container to use, and make a list of items to include.

Dear Editor

WRITE AN OPINION

Imagine that there is an old building in your neighborhood. The owners would like to replace it with a new building instead of making repairs. Write a letter to the local newspaper, giving your opinion on the matter and reasons to support it.

Housework

MAKE A SEQUENCE CHART

There is a lot of work to be done before a house is ready for a family to move in. Make a list of all the workers who are involved in building a house. Draw a sequence chart to show what kinds of workers are needed, starting from the empty lot and ending with a family moving in.

Home, Future Home

DRAW A HOUSE PLAN

Throughout history, house builders have used materials that were practical for and available in their time and place. What kind of house might people build in the future? Design a house, and add labels to explain how it is different from today's houses.

Author's Purpose and Perspective

In "House, House," Jane Yolen tells about the town of Hatfield. She wants readers to know how the town has changed with the times. The reason an author has for writing is called the **author's purpose.** Sometimes an author may have more than one purpose. The chart below shows the three main purposes an author may have for writing. What was Jane Yolen's purpose?

to persuade

to encourage readers to act or believe a certain way

to inform

to tell readers the facts about something

to entertain

to give readers enjoyment

The writer's viewpoint is called the **author's perspective.** Knowing something about the author helps you understand his or her perspective. What do we know about Jane Yolen?

She lives in one of the houses shown in the pictures.

Perspective:

She is able to tell the story of Hatfield from a personal viewpoint.

Her son is one of the photographers.

The author's perspective affects the way he or she writes. Read the two paragraphs below. For each, identify both the author's purpose and the author's perspective.

My dad works at an auto plant. He says that the car is a great invention that has made life easier. With a car you can go places without having to wait for a bus. You can visit relatives who live far away. Before cars were invented, some people never left their own town! I think everyone should have a car.

For social studies, my class observed city traffic from the school playground. We found that traffic was heaviest just before 9 A.M. and again between 12:15 and 1 P.M. Out of 100 cars, 20 had license plates from out of state. The most common colors were green for cars and black for trucks.

WHAT HAVE YOU LEARNED?

1. Do you trust the author of "House, House"? Do you think she told the history of Hatfield accurately? Support your opinion.

2. Think of something else you have read recently in which the author shows you a new way of looking at a topic or an issue. Describe the author's perspective and purpose.

TRY THIS • TRY THIS • TRY THIS

Choose an advertisement for a product for young people, and write a few sentences about it from your own perspective. Tell what parts of the ad appeal and do not appeal to you. Tell whether you believe the ad and why or why not.

 Visit *The Learning Site!*
www.harcourtschool.com

Janey's father works in the fields, picking crops. Her family, like those of many other migrant workers in the 1940s, must always move on to wherever workers are needed. The family takes only basic necessities with them, except for a blue willow plate that belonged to Janey's great-great-grandmother. To Janey, the plate is a reminder of the time when they had a home. When she discovers a place that reminds her of the picture on the plate and finds a friend, Lupe, she begins to hope that this time they will stay.

BLUE

PUFFIN NEWBERY LIBRARY

Blue Willow

DORIS GATES

Newbery
Honor

WILLOW

by Doris Gates
illustrated by Robert Crawford

Janey and Dad were on their way to the cotton fields. Dad was going to work; Janey was going to school. It was October now. The sun, though bright and warm, was not hot as it had been a month ago, and the mountains, as if rewarding the valley for milder weather, were allowing their blue outlines to be seen. Wild sunflowers turned bright faces to the east, and occasional dust devils went spiraling off across the plain in merry abandon. But Janey, huddled in a corner of the ragged front seat, was sulkily indifferent to the world around her. The corners of her mouth sagged, her lower lip protruded in something close to a pout, and her eyes glowered darkly. She wasn't glad to be going to school, not this school at any rate. If only she were being taken to the town school, the one where Lupe and all the other children of the district went! That is, they did if they belonged to the district. Janey was well aware that actually she herself could have attended that school, too. There was no law forbidding it. But it was a fact, too, that in some communities she would have been extremely unwelcome, and Dad, knowing this, had made his own law in respect to Janey.

"We'll keep with our own kind," he had once said when she had remonstrated with him. "The camp schools are put there for us to use and so we'll use them and be thankful. Besides, a body can learn anywhere if he's a mind to."

Janey hadn't argued further with him on that occasion and she had no desire to do so today. She knew that going to the "regular" school would no longer satisfy her anyway, for just going there couldn't make her really belong. Since she had begun to want to stay in this place, merely going to the district school was no longer enough. What Janey wanted was to belong to this place and to go to the district school because as a member of the community it was her right to go there. The camp school would now be a daily and forceful reminder of the fact that she didn't belong, and so she dreaded it.

She knew what the camp school would be like. No two of the children would have learned the same things, and it would all be a jumble. In some lessons, Janey would find herself way ahead of most of the boys and girls her age, and she would be expected as a matter of course to know other things she had never had a chance to learn. Most of the time she wouldn't know whether she was going or coming and there would be endless questions and much tiresome fussing.

Besides, it was much too early in the day for school to start and she would have to wait around until it did. She would have asked Dad to let her go into the field with him if she had thought it would do any good. But she knew from past experience that it wouldn't. Never had she been allowed to do any field work. Other children did and sometimes Mom, but never Janey. Dad, so easy-going about most things, was firm on this. So Janey sat with a frown on her face as the old car jolted along its way, and came very near to feeling sorry for herself.

She would have known the school house as soon as they came in sight of it even if Dad hadn't bothered to point it out. She had seen many of them before and they all looked alike. Some were newer than others and that was about the only difference. This was one of the newer ones. It was a rather large square building, its unpainted boards gleaming in the bright light. In front of it a flagpole, also unpainted, towered against the morning sky. As yet no flag was in evidence,

so Janey knew for sure that school had not
yet started. Her father let her off at the front
steps, then drove over to park beside a row of
cars that looked as if they might all have come
from the same junk pile. Janey sat down to wait,
her package of lunch beside her.

Across from her were the cottages, row upon row,
that comprised the camp. Looking at these little one-room
sheds so close together that their eaves almost touched, she
was thankful for their own shack and the spreading country
around it. Of course there was plenty of country spread
around here. But the camp itself was squeezed into
as small a space as possible so as not to use up any
more of the cotton ground than was absolutely
necessary. The deep green of the cotton plants
reached in every direction almost as far as the eye
could see. And here and there against the green of every
bush a gleam of white showed clearly. That was where a
cotton boll had burst open to free the fluffy fibers which
would be picked by hand from each boll. There would be
thousands, perhaps millions, of these little white bunches
and it would take many fingers working many hours a day to
pick all the ripening cotton. That is why there was a village
of little houses at this place with a school house at hand.
During the picking season hundreds of people lived here
and worked here until the day should come when all the
cotton was harvested. Then they would load their cars with
what household goods they owned, and with their boys and
girls the cotton pickers would move on to some other part
of the country which needed their hands and their heads.

Of course, Janey wasn't thinking of all this while she sat on the steps of the school house. It was so much a part of her life that she didn't bother to think about it any more than she bothered to think about the processes of breathing when she drew fresh air into her lungs.

For perhaps ten minutes, Janey sat there, a blue-overalled figure of gloom, when all at once she caught a movement in the dust in front of her. It was so slight a movement that at first she thought her eyes were playing her tricks. But in the next second, the dust was again stirred, and then she was off the school house steps in one lunge. Flat on the ground she hurled herself, one arm reaching out ahead of her. Slowly she drew in her arm, her hand tightly closed, and gathered herself up. From head to foot she was coated with fine dirt, but she didn't care. She didn't even stop to brush herself off before she slowly began to open her fingers, squinting closely at what she held there. A smile widened across her face, for in the shadowy hollow of her palm was a small horned toad. Its eyes, mere pinheads of glistening black, stared fiercely at her, and its chinless mouth was set grimly. But Janey was not alarmed. She had captured many horned toads before this and knew that for all their fierce expression and spiky covering, they were quite harmless creatures. Slowly she lowered herself onto the school house steps once more to inspect her captive. To most people he would have appeared far from beautiful, but to Janey he seemed an object of delight. His four tiny feet with their minute claws were perfect, and from the fringe of miniature scales outlining what should have been his chin, to the last infinitesimal spike on the end of his brief tail, he was finished and complete. Janey loved him at once and began cautiously to draw her finger across his hard little head.

Suddenly an idea occurred to her. She would use this horned toad to test the new teacher. In every school she had ever been, someone had always solemnly assured her whenever she happened to mention a "horned toad" that she should call them "horned lizards," for they were not really toads at all. Janey had always been entirely willing to accept the fact that they were not, strictly speaking, "horned toads," but to call them anything else just wasn't possible. The minute you said "horned lizard" you turned a perfectly good horned toad into a new and unattractive animal. She would loathe having anyone refer to her new pet as a horned lizard, and if the new teacher did so, Janey's respect for her as a human being would be completely shattered. It would be, she thought, like saying "It is I" instead of "It's me." If you used the former, you would be correct, but you wouldn't be a friend. She was determined to discover whether the new teacher was a friend or merely correct.

She and the horned toad had not long to wait. Janey had hardly got some of the dirt brushed off when a dusty sedan rolled to a halt in the shade of the school house and a fat and smiling woman got out of it. Janey felt hopeful.

"Hello," called the woman. "No ten-o'clock-scholar about you, is there?"

Janey felt increasingly hopeful as she rose to meet this stranger who was undoubtedly the teacher. Surely no one who quoted Mother Goose to you before she had asked your name would call a horned toad a horned lizard. More than that, she would know what to do with you if you were good in reading and poor in arithmetic. Suddenly the whole tone of the day was changed. But the final test was yet to come.

"Look," said Janey, holding out her captive.

"Well, bless my soul," said the woman heartily, bending over Janey's hand, "a horned toad! Did you catch it?"

Janey nodded, too delighted for the moment to speak, then: "But I haven't named him yet."

"Can't let him go without a name. Let's see." The woman thought a moment. Then, "I have it. Let's call him Fafnir. He was a first-class dragon when giants ruled the earth. And this fellow looks a lot like a dragon. A fairy dragon. Does Fafnir appeal to you?"

Janey nodded.

The teacher chuckled. "I suppose the proper thing would be to let the horned toad decide such an important matter for himself. But from the look of him I should say that he wasn't quite on speaking terms with us yet."

She looked at Janey with eyes that were merry and direct. Trustworthy eyes with friendly secrets in their depths.

"I am Miss Peterson," she said.

"I'm Janey Larkin."

A stout arm encircled Janey's narrow shoulders and for a brief moment she felt herself squeezed against Miss Peterson's warm and well-cushioned side.

"Welcome to Camp Miller school, Janey. Come on inside. We'll start the day together."

No questions, no fussing. Just "Come on in," as if she had known you always. Janey slid an arm around Miss Peterson's ample waist and together they entered the building, the small girl walking on tiptoe, to her teacher's secret amusement. Miss Peterson would have been surprised to know she was the innocent cause of that strange behavior. For Janey was thrilling to the certainty that this very morning, unexpectedly and alone, she had discovered the most wonderful teacher in the world. That was enough to make anyone prance on tiptoe! A few minutes ago she had been feeling sorry for herself and all the time there had been Fafnir and Miss Peterson. Not even Lupe going to the "regular" school could possibly have enjoyed such luck as that!

During the next half hour Janey helped Miss Peterson prepare for the day's work. She cleaned the blackboards and put the tables and benches in order. Some pink petunias were blooming in a window box and Janey watered them from the standing pipe outside the door. Then she picked off the withered blossoms, which left her fingers so sticky she had to return to the water pipe to wash her hands. Soon the boys and girls began to arrive. The school day started at nine o'clock when one of the boys carried the flag out to the unpainted pole and fastened it to the rope neatly secured there. While the whole school stood grouped at attention, the flag was drawn slowly up into the morning sky until at last it came to rest at the pole's very top and the Stars and Stripes was unfolded above the school and the camp. The little ceremony ended, they all trooped to their lessons.

As the morning advanced, Janey's regard for Miss Peterson increased, if that were possible. Because they were crowded on the benches, and because their legs were not all long enough to reach the floor, she saw to it that the children were given time to move around and rest. And it seemed to be the custom for two or three of the children to tell the others each day which part of the country they had thought the most interesting in their traveling around. Janey, listening to the others this morning, decided, when her turn came, to tell about the place by the river which she had discovered the other day. The place like the willow plate.

Think About It

1 How do Janey's feelings about the camp school change during the story? Why do they change?

2 Why do you think Janey's parents will not allow her to do field work?

3 Why is the horned toad important to the story's plot?

504

About the Author
Doris Gates

Some encyclopedias give facts about one subject, like animals or music. Here is an entry from an encyclopedia of authors.

GATES, Doris (1901–1987) Born November 26, 1901, in Mountain View, CA; daughter of Charles and Bessie Gates. Died September 3, 1987, in Carmel, CA.

Education: Fresno State Teachers College, Los Angeles Library School, Case Western Reserve University

Career: library director, writer, teacher, editor

Doris Gates grew up on a ranch, where she met migrant fruit pickers who had to move from place to place to find work. Later she taught children whose families were poor because of damage to farms in the Dust Bowl. These experiences inspired *Blue Willow*, her most famous book, published in 1940. Gates often wrote about the importance of home to a child.

Visit *The Learning Site!*
www.harcourtschool.com

Horned Lizard

Still as a rock,
you watch bees, ants,
your wriggly lunch.
    I watch you,
carefully put you, bellybulge
pincushion, in my palm,
just for a minute touch
your prickly top.
    Puff. A warm balloon
puffs in my hand.
                    Plop
away you hop across hot sand,
soft, spiny desert creature,
    like me.

by **Pat Mora**
pictures by **Steve Jenkins**

Award-Winning
Author

The Right One for the Job

WRITE A WANT AD

Suppose Miss Peterson leaves the camp school someday. Write an ad that the camp school could use to find another wonderful teacher. Tell a little about the students who go to the school, and list the traits their teacher needs. Look at newspaper want ads for models.

RESPONSE

First Day

WRITE A JOURNAL ENTRY

Write a diary entry Janey might have written after her first day at the camp school. Tell about Fafnir, Miss Peterson, and the schoolroom. Also tell how Janey now feels about the camp school and why.

Making Connections

WRITE A DESCRIPTION

Reread the descriptions of horned toads in "Blue Willow" and "Horned Lizard." Think about how each author uses details to help readers "see" and "feel" the animal. Then study a close-up photograph of a small animal. Write a clear, colorful description of it. If you need help finding just the right word, use a thesaurus or a synonym finder.

Comparing Notes

ROLE-PLAY A CONVERSATION

Imagine that Janey meets one of the children from "A Very Important Day." What might the characters say about their experiences? What might they say about wanting to belong? With a partner, act out their conversation. Before you begin, make notes on your role.

In My

Every time I paint, it serves a purpose—to bring about pride
in our Mexican American culture. The paintings and stories
in this book are my memories of growing up in Kingsville,
Texas, near the border with Mexico. — Carmen Lomas Garza

Family

by Carmen Lomas Garza

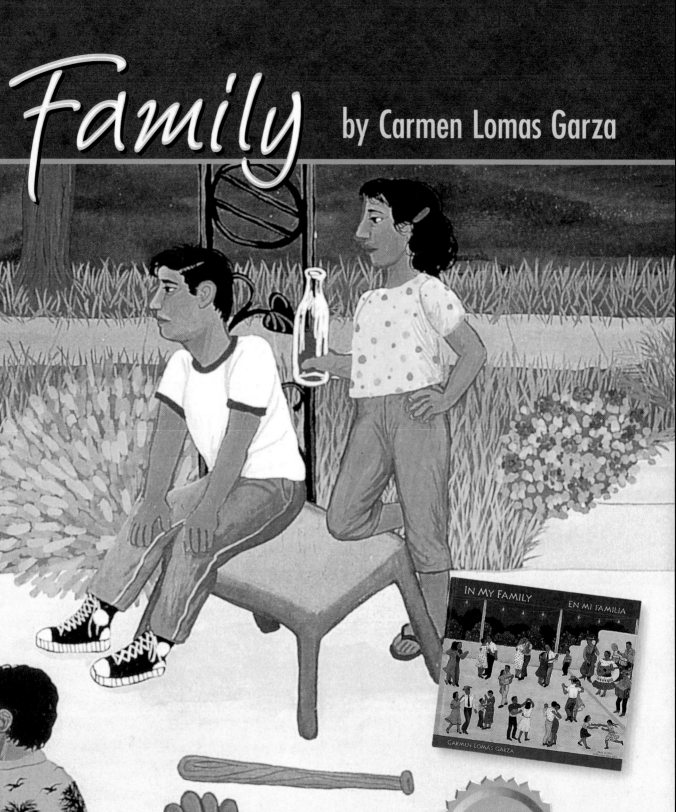

IN MY FAMILY   EN MI FAMILIA

CARMEN LOMAS GARZA

**Award-Winning
Author/Illustrator**

The Horned Toads

When we were kids, my mother and grandmother would get mad at us for playing in the hot sun in the middle of the day. They'd say we were just like the horned toads at high noon, playing outside without a care.

I was fascinated by the horned toads. They're shaped like frogs, but they're not frogs. They're lizards. They have horns all over their bodies to protect them from bigger animals that want to eat them.

Here's my brother Arturo, trying to feed an ant to a horned toad. I'm behind him, on my toes, because I don't want the ants to crawl up on me. Those are fire ants. They can really sting.

Cleaning Nopalitos

This is my grandfather, Antonio Lomas. He's shaving off the thorns from freshly-cut cactus pads, called *nopalitos*. My sister Margie is watching him work.

 Nopalitos are called "the food of last resort," because back when there were no refrigerators and your winter food supply would run out, you knew you could eat the cactus pads through the last days of winter and the early days of spring.

 My grandmother would boil the *nopalitos* in salt water, cut them up, and stir-fry them with chile and eggs for breakfast.

Empanadas

Once every year my Aunt Paz and Uncle Beto would make dozens and dozens of *empanadas*, sweet turnovers filled with sweet potato or squash from their garden. They would invite all the relatives and friends to come over, and you could eat as many as you wanted. They lived in a little one-bedroom house, and every surface in the house was covered with a plate of *empanadas*. There was no place to sit down.

There's Uncle Beto, rolling out the dough. Aunt Paz, in the yellow dress with the red flowers, is spreading in the filling. My mother and father are drinking coffee. That's me in the blue dress.

Birthday Barbecue

This is my sister Mary Jane's birthday party. She's hitting a piñata that my mother made. My mother also baked and decorated the cake. There she is, bringing the meat that's ready to cook. My father is cooking at the barbecue, which he designed and built himself. My grandfather is shoveling in the coals of mesquite wood.

Underneath the tree are some young teenagers, very much in love. My great uncle is comforting my young cousin, who was crying, and encouraging him to hit the piñata. My grand-mother is holding a baby. She was always holding the babies, and feeding them, and putting them to sleep.

Easter Eggs

This is my parents' dining room. My mother and brothers and sisters and I are gathered around the table decorating eggshells, *cascarones*, for Easter Sunday. We would fill them with confetti, which we made by cutting up newspapers and magazines.

On Easter Sunday, after church, we would go swimming. After swimming, we'd eat, and after eating, we'd bring out the *cascarones*. We would sneak up on our brothers or sisters or friends, break the *cascarones* on their heads, and rub the confetti into their hair. Sometimes my brothers would put flour into the eggshells, so that when they broke them on your wet head, the flour would turn to paste. That's how sneaky my brothers were sometimes.

Dance at El Jardín

This is a Saturday night at *El Jardín*, a neighborhood restaurant in my home town. It's the summer, so warm that you can dance outside. A *conjunto* band is playing — drums, accordion, guitar, and bass. This is the music I grew up with. Everybody's dancing in a big circle: the young couples, the older couples, and the old folks dancing with the teenagers or children. Even babies get to dance.

I learned to dance from my father and grandfather. This is where my love of dance started. To me, dance means *fiesta*, celebration. You have the music, the beautiful clothes, and all the family members dancing together. It's like heaven. It is heaven.

Think About It

1. How does the author feel about her childhood? Use the paintings to help you answer the question.

2. Which painting do you like best? Why?

3. How does the author give information about Mexican American culture through her paintings and words?

Meet the Author and Illustrator
Carmen Lomas Garza

How old were you when you started making art?

I was thirteen years old when I decided to become an artist. I taught myself how to draw by practicing every day. I drew what-ever was in front of me—books, cats, my left hand, my sisters and brothers, chairs, chilies, paper bags, flowers—anything or any-body that would stay still for a few minutes.

How long does it take you to make a painting?

It takes from two to nine months to complete a painting. I can paint for about six hours a day and then my fingers and eyes get tired. I do not paint every single day because I also have to work in my office to write letters, make telephone calls, and keep records for my art business.

Answers Questions from Children

Do you sell your artwork?

I have sold most of my paintings and lithograph prints. Sometimes it is very difficult to let go of paintings because I get very attached to them—just like parents get very attached to their children and do not want them to move out of their home.

Which painting is your favorite?

I can't really say which painting is my favorite, but I do like to paint interiors like bedrooms and kitchens. My favorite thing to paint is clothing. I can still remember some of the colors and designs of the clothing that my mother sewed for me.

CARMEN LOMAS GARZA

Visit *The Learning Site!*
www.harcourtschool.com

Did you go to college?

I have three college degrees. When I was in high school I could hardly wait to graduate so I could go to college and study art. My parents insisted that all of us go to college to study whatever we wanted.

My Village

by Isaac Olaleye
illustrated by Stéphan Daigle

Èrín is the name
Of my African village.
Laughter is what Èrín means
In the Yoruba language.

In streams,
Women and children
Still collect water in gourds and clay pots,
Which they balance on their heads.

Electric light has not shone in my village.
With ruby-red palm oil
Poured into a clay vessel
We see at night.

My village of Èrín is peaceful,
Like a hidden world.
It's ringed by radiant green
And surrounded by five streams.

Like a stream,
The love
For my village
Flows.

Response Activities

Special Events

DRAW A SCENE

Carmen Lomas Garza's paintings show special events she enjoys with her family and friends. Make a color drawing that shows a happy event you attended. Write some paragraphs to describe your picture, as the author does.

Word Pictures

WRITE A POEM

What is the best celebration you've ever been a part of? Write a poem about it. You could describe where you were, who else was there, what you ate, or what you did.

Let's Eat

WRITE A RECIPE

Carmen's family makes *empanadas* together. Find out how to make a dish your family loves to eat. Write the recipe for the dish. Look at some cookbooks to see how recipes are written. If you can, input your recipe on a word processor.

Making Connections

WRITE A PARAGRAPH

Imagine that you have visited one of the communities you read about in "In My Family" or "My Village." Write a paragraph describing the interesting things you saw or did. Use details from the story or poem and the illustrations to describe the surroundings.

Theme
Wrap-Up

Meaningful Quotes

FIND QUOTATIONS
Find two sentences or short passages in this theme that express the importance of belonging or of community ties. Write each sentence or passage on an index card. On the back, write the name of the selection the quotation is from, and tell why you chose the quotation.

Fascinating Facts

LIST AND DISCUSS Look back at the selections in this theme. What did you learn that was especially interesting or surprising? Choose two or three items and write them in a list, along with the page numbers where you found them. You may need to put the information in your own words. Share your list in a small group. Discuss why the information was interesting or surprising.

Community Roles

MAKE A CHART The selections in this theme show some of the roles people play in a community, both at home and on the job. Look back at the selections, and make a chart showing the roles you find. In the first column, write the names of the selections. In the second column, list the roles. In the third, briefly describe the importance of each role.

Selection	Role	Why Role Is Important

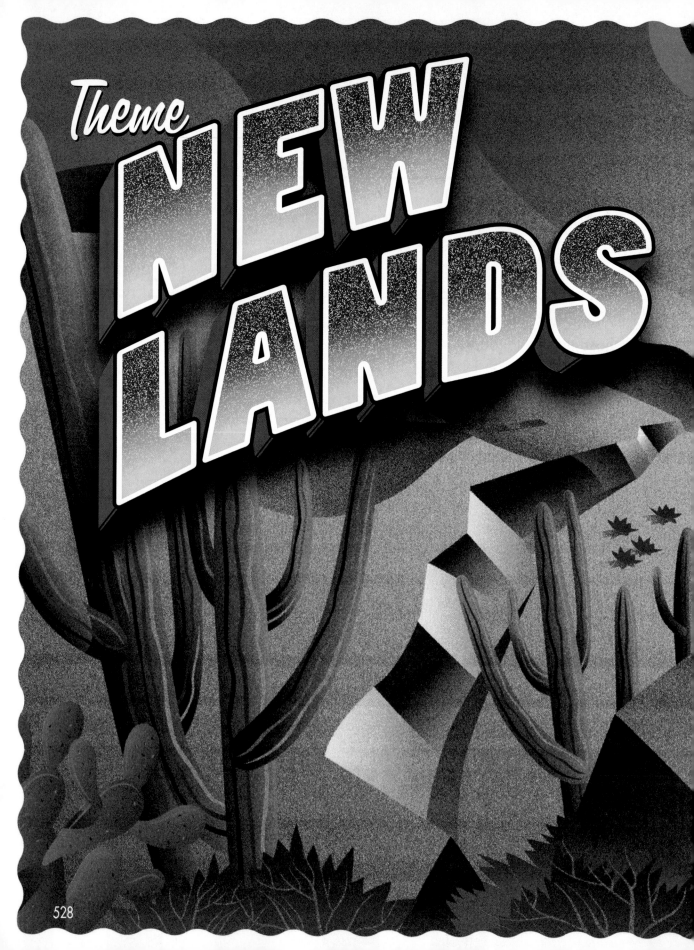

Theme

NEW LANDS

Contents

READER'S CHOICE

Flute's Journey
by Lynne Cherry
NONFICTION

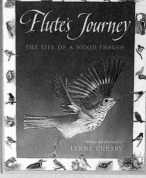

Flute, a young wood thrush, makes its way from Maryland to Costa Rica and then back again. This is the story of the migration of a wood thrush and how it survives the journey.

Notable Social Studies Trade Book
READER'S CHOICE LIBRARY

The Down and Up Fall
by Johanna Hurwitz
REALISTIC FICTION

Bolivia is going to a new school with old friends Rory and Derek. Then she meets Aldo and De De. Join Bolivia in her adventures with friends, both old and new.

Award-Winning Author
READER'S CHOICE LIBRARY

Homesteading: Settling America's Heartland

by Dorothy Hinshaw Patent

NONFICTION

People left their homes for a chance to own land in America's heartland when the Homestead Act was signed. Explore the prairie in the spirit of the pioneers who built soddies and met each challenge along the way.

Award-Winning Author

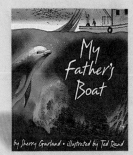

My Father's Boat

by Sherry Garland

REALISTIC FICTION

Three generations of a family of fishermen are separated by time and place. Even though the grandfather is still in Vietnam, the father tells his son they have never forgotten each other. **Award-Winning Author**

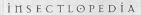

Insectlopedia

by Douglas Florian

POETRY

Twenty-one witty poems about spiders and insects, delightfully portrayed, make you want to read this book again and again.

ALA Notable Book

I Have Heard of a Land

ALA
Notable Book

Coretta Scott
King Honor

I Have Heard of a Land

BY JOYCE CAROL THOMAS

ILLUSTRATED BY FLOYD COOPER

Heard

I have heard of a land
Where the earth is red with promises
Where the redbud trees catch the light
And throw it in a game of sunbeams and shadow
Back and forth to the cottonwood trees

I have heard of a land
Where a pioneer only has to lift up her feet
To cast her eyes on the rocks
The fertile earth, the laughing creek
Lift up her feet running for the land
As though running for her life
And in the running claim it
The stake is life and the work that goes into it

I have heard of a land
Where the cottonwood trees are innocent
Where the coyote's call is a lullaby at night
And the land runs on forever
And a woman can plant her crop and
    walk all day and never come to the end of it

537

I have heard of a land
Where the imagination has no fences
Where what is dreamed one night
Is accomplished the next day

I have heard of a land where the flapjacks
Spread out big as wagon wheels
Where the butter is the color of melted sun
And the syrup is honey
Stirred thick by a thousand honeybees

I have heard of a land
Where winter brings storm warnings
And pioneers wonder whether
The scissortail in spring will ever sing

I have heard of a land where the children
Swing in homemade swings strung from
The strong limbs of trees

I have heard of a land
Where the crickets skirl in harmony
And babies wrapped to their mothers' backs in the field
   laugh more than they cry

I have heard of a land where worship
Takes place in an outdoor church
Under an arbor of bushes
And the hymns sound just as sweet

I have heard of a land
Where a woman sleeps in a sod hut
   dug deep in the heart of the earth
Her roof is decorated with brush
A hole in the ground is her stove
And a horse saddle is her pillow
She wakes thinking of a three-room log cabin

And soon that morning her neighbors
  and their sons and daughters
Help lift the logs and chock them into place
Together they hoist the beams high
After dinner, they finish the porch
  where they sit and tell stories
Finally when everyone else has gone home
She saws the planks for the steps
  by herself

That night by the glow of an oil lamp
She writes in her journal:

I raise nearly everything I eat
The land is good here
I grind corn for meal
Raise me some cane and make sorghum syrup
And if I feel real smart
I make hominy grits from scratch

I have heard of a land
Where the pioneer woman still lives
Her possibilities reach as far
As her eyes can see
And as far as our imaginations
   can carry us

Think About It

1. What are the good things that make pioneers want to travel to this land? What are some hardships they must face?

2. Which pictures and descriptions of the land do you like best? Give several examples.

3. How do you think the author wants readers to feel about the pioneers? Explain.

MEET THE AUTHOR
Joyce Carol Thomas

Question: Why did you write *I Have Heard of a Land*?

Joyce Carol Thomas: I wanted to tell my family stories. Slaves who were set free were given land if they settled in the Oklahoma Territory. In the book I imagine the feelings of my great-grandmother, who traveled to Oklahoma from Tennessee to establish a homestead.

Several of my other books are also set in Oklahoma, where I was born.

Question: How did you prepare to become a writer?

Thomas: I read many books as a child and made up songs, poetry, and plays. I studied at California State University and at Stanford University. I taught in middle schools, community colleges, and universities before I became a full-time writer.

Question: You write poetry. Do you think that influences the way you write stories?

Thomas: Yes. The words, even when I write stories, must have a singing rhythm.

**Visit *The Learning Site!*
www.harcourtschool.com**

554

MEET THE ILLUSTRATOR

Floyd Cooper

Question: Do you have any personal connections to *I Have Heard of a Land*?

Floyd Cooper: Yes. My great-grandparents ran for the land in Oklahoma. I was born and raised in Tulsa, and I studied at the University of Oklahoma.

Question: What made you want to be an artist?

Cooper: When I was in the second grade, my teacher hung my sunflower art on the wall. Everyone else's picture was on the wall, too, but I felt so proud to see mine displayed. I thought, this is what it is like to be an artist.

After college I worked for a greeting card company. I didn't feel I could be creative doing greeting cards. I tried advertising for a while. Then I discovered the world of children's book illustrating.

Question: How did you paint the pictures in *I Have Heard of a Land*?

Cooper: I worked with a kneaded rubber eraser. First I painted a background on paper glued to cardboard. Then I rubbed shapes onto the background with the kneaded eraser. Then I applied color—very thin washes of oil paint. This is the technique I use for all my paintings now.

555

Response

Westward Ho!

DRAW A DIAGRAM

The woman in "I Have Heard of a Land" traveled in a covered wagon. Learn about the Conestoga wagon, the "prairie camel" that carried many pioneers west. Create a diagram of a Conestoga wagon. Draw and label some of the foods, tools, and other supplies the wagons carried.

Is It Worth the Trouble?

WRITE A LETTER

Suppose that you have moved west in the 1880s. Write a letter to a friend or relative back home. Describe the good things and the bad things about your move and about pioneer life. Decide whether you want to persuade your friend or relative to move west, too.

Activities

Home on the Range

LEARN A SONG

Many pioneers wrote songs about their new home. Look in a children's book of folk songs for songs about the West. Learn one of the songs, and teach it to your classmates.

Then and Now

MAKE A COMPARISON CHART

Moving to a new place and building a house are both very different today from what they were like in pioneer times. Make a chart to compare these activities in the past and the present. List details in one column about what they were like in pioneer times, and in another column about what they are like today.

557

TYPES OF CONTEXT CLUES

a short definition near a word

a synonym or an antonym near a word

descriptive details

illustrations and diagrams

Did you read some new words in "I Have Heard of a Land"? Had you ever heard of a *scissortail* before? Did you know what it means to *skirl*?

As you read, you often come across new words. Sometimes you look them up in a dictionary or ask an adult for help. Often you just read on and use clues right in the story to figure out what the new word means. These are called **context clues**. The context is made up of the words, sentences, and illustrations around a word.

This chart shows how a reader might use context clues:

New Word in Context	How I Used Context Clues
pioneers wonder whether the <u>scissortail</u> in spring will ever sing	I know birds sing in spring, so I think a <u>scissortail</u> is a type of bird.
the crickets <u>skirl</u> in harmony	Harmony has to do with music, so <u>skirl</u> must mean "make music."
Her roof is decorated with <u>brush</u>	A brush can be a tool with bristles, but here <u>brush</u> is part of a roof. I see from the picture that it looks like small branches.

Some words, such as *brush*, are multiple-meaning words. The context tells the reader which meaning makes sense.

Using context clues will make you a faster reader because you won't have to look up every new word. You will also be a more active reader because you will be making connections between words.

Read the paragraph below. Explain how you can figure out what each underlined word means.

When Grandpa's family didn't have milk or eggs, they'd make <u>corn pone</u>. Corn pone was a lot like cornbread, only it wasn't as tasty. Grandpa would dip it in dark, sweet <u>molasses</u>. Grandpa says that whenever he smells molasses, it <u>catapults</u> him right back to his boyhood.

WHAT HAVE YOU LEARNED?

1. In "I Have Heard of a Land," how can you figure out what *chock* and *hoist* mean?

2. Find an unfamiliar word in a book you are reading on your own. What context clues help you figure out what the word means?

Visit *The Learning Site!*
www.harcourtschool.com

TRY THIS • TRY THIS • TRY THIS

Think of a word your classmates may not know, such as the name of an unusual food, plant, or animal. Write a short paragraph in which you use the word and give clues to its meaning. See if a classmate can figure out from the context what the new word means.

Award-Winning
Author

Paul Bunyan and

Retold by Robert D. San Souci   Illustrated by Andrew Glass

Paul Bunyan, the greatest logger of all time, the giant who pretty much invented the lumber industry, was born and raised in Maine. He had logged off the better part of that state before he turned twenty. After that he did some work in Canada, before he turned up in Michigan. He became boss of a camp on the Big Onion River, where he would cut down so much timber in a day that three hundred mule drivers would have to work day and night to haul his logs to the river. He headed a campful of mighty men, including French Canadians, Swedes, Irishmen, Scots, and any other logger who could give a good account of himself.

But his truest companion was Babe the Blue Ox.

Babe the Blue Ox

from *Larger Than Life: The Adventures of American Legendary Heroes*

There are different stories of how the two met. One story is that Paul found Babe during the Winter of the Blue Snow.

On that special morning, Paul woke just before dawn, broke up the ice on a little lake nearby and washed his face, parted his hair with a hand ax, and combed his beard with a crosscut saw. Then he went out looking for a stand of trees to cut down, walking through the blue snow that filled the woods. Suddenly he heard bellowing from the direction of the frozen river. There he discovered a young ox, already bigger than a full-grown steer, splashing in the water where the ice had given way under it.

"Hold on!" cried the soft-hearted logger. Kneeling down on the snowy bank, he fished out the soggy calf. The poor thing had been white when he had fallen in, but had turned bright blue from the cold before Paul pulled him out of the icy river.

Paul carried the creature back to camp through a blue blizzard, saying, "There, there, poor little baby." When they reached Big Onion Camp, Paul built a barn for the ox he had already begun to call "Babe." Then he searched the mountains around for moose moss to make soup for the calf.

As it turned out, when Babe was spoon-fed love and soup, he grew so fast, that the next morning, Paul found the barn he had built sitting on the ox's back. Then Paul put his hands on his hips and said with a smile, "You're sure gonna be something t' reckon with." Then he scratched at his beard thoughtfully, and added, "You have so much power, it shouldn't be wasted. When you're grown up, I'll find you some useful work."

Babe made a soft, chuckling sound, as if to say, "That's fine with me."

Paul kept on feeding Babe, and pretty soon the animal was up to full size, measuring forty-two ax handles between the eyes. An ordinary person standing at Babe's head or tail would have to use a telescope to see what was happening at the other end.

Some people say that Paul dug the Great Lakes so that Babe would always have fresh water. A lot of the smaller lakes in Wisconsin and Minnesota, they add, are simply Babe's hoofprints filled with water.

Babe's shoes were made by the blacksmith Ole Olsen, who sank to his knees in solid rock the first time he tried to carry one.

At first there was a lot of grumbling, because Paul put part of his crew to work bringing in enough hay to feed Babe. "That critter's a waste of hay and time," some men said.

The matter was settled by Johnny Inkslinger, Paul's bookkeeper. He used a special fountain pen that was eighteen feet long and connected by a three-foot hose to thirty-eight barrels of ink on the shelf over his desk. Always looking for a way to save a penny, Johnny once saved nine barrels of ink over a winter by not crossing his t's or dotting his i's. He pointed out, "Babe really *saves* us money. He can haul the lumber in one trip that we needed three hundred mule drivers for. Thanks to him, we make more money. That means your paychecks are bigger."

This fact—if not the milk of human kindness—quickly made the blue ox popular with the loggers.

Babe, who could haul anything, was a great worker who could drag 640 acres of timberland to the river at one time—all in one piece. There, Paul's crew chopped down the trees. Then the blue ox hauled the cleared land back into place.

Paul would also use the blue ox in plenty of other ways. Once, when one of Paul's men sent the wrong lumber down the Mississippi to New Orleans, Paul was faced with the problem of getting the lumber back upstream. What would have seemed impossible to anyone else just needed a little thinking on Paul's part. He simply fed Babe an extra-big salt ration, then led him to the Mississippi to drink. Babe was so thirsty, he drained the river dry, sucking the water upstream, so that the logs came back faster than they had gone down.

Babe was a fine pet. When he was happy, he would chortle and roll his big blue eyes and stick out his tongue to lick Paul behind the ear or on the back of the neck. This would always send the giant logger into roars of laughter that made folks miles away think thunder was rolling down the mountains.

But Babe loved to play jokes on Paul's crew, and this could make the men angry. He would sometimes go to the lake from which the men got water, and drink it dry in a single swallow. Then the men would have to go thirsty and dirty until the lake filled up again. Once he lay down in the river and dammed it up, not moving until Paul drew him away with a sandwich made of two giant flapjacks with a filling of clover hay.

But even with all of his joking, Babe helped Paul to keep the money rolling in. Paul added more and more men to his crew, building bunkhouses so long that it took three days to walk from one end to the other. To keep his men well fed

and happy, Paul hired the best camp cooks around, including Hot Biscuit Slim, Joe Muffinton, Sourdough Sam, Pea Soup Shorty, and Cream Puff Fatty, who made desserts.

At Round River Camp, Paul built a cooking stove so big that it took three hundred cooks standing shoulder to shoulder to keep it going, and a special crew just to supply firewood. When it was time to make flapjacks, a griddle would be lowered onto the stove, and this was greased by the kitchen workers skating along with bacon slabs tied to their feet.

Meals were served by men on roller skates, who raced up and down the long tables Paul had built.

When they were ready to move on to the next camp in North Dakota, Paul got the bright idea of tying all the camp buildings together, with the cookhouse in the lead, and having Babe haul the camp to Red River.

When he yelled, "Gee! Haw! Yay!" Babe pulled the camp over mountains and plains, while the loggers leaned out the cabin windows, waving to anyone they happened to see—though, for the most part, only the wild creatures of the woods saw them pass.

One winter Paul logged off North Dakota with the Seven Axemen, his finest lumberjacks. Stories about the height and weight of the Seven Axemen are different, but people say that they used four-foot logs as toothpicks. When they got working along with Paul, their axes often flew so fast, they sometimes came close to setting fire to the forests.

In the Dakotas, they all got carried away and logged off the whole of the state, until there wasn't much left but bushes. Looking around and feeling a little bad, Paul said, "I think maybe we shoulda stopped a while back."

Sitting on a big stump, Babe beside him, Paul looked out over the sorry wasteland he had helped make. To Babe he said, "I won't let this happen again. It isn't good for the land. And there's nothing left for an honest logger to make a living from."

True to his spirit of making the best of the worst, Paul got up, took a big hammer, and pounded down the stumps into the ground. He turned the Dakotas into smooth, rolling plains that became fine farmland.

But Paul was never able to cross the Dakotas without thinking of the great forests that had disappeared under his ax.

When Paul and his men returned to the North Woods, they found that pine trees, loggers, and a certain blue ox were not the only things that came big-sized there. They were attacked by giant mosquitoes that had to be fought off with pikes and axes. When they tried to escape into a cabin, these monsters would tear off the roof or chew through the log walls.

Paul decided to fight fire with fire, so he sent Sourdough Sam back to Maine for some of the giant bees Paul remembered from his boyhood. Sourdough had to bring the insects back on foot, with their wings tied, because they could not be controlled if they were allowed to fly. He collected their stingers, gave them boots, and marched them two by two to Paul's camp.

But when Paul let the bees go, thinking they would chase away the mosquitoes, he found he had planned wrong. The bees and mosquitoes intermarried, producing offspring with stingers in front and behind, and they got Paul's men coming and going.

Paul got rid of them by sending ships full of sugar and molasses out to the middle of Lake Superior.

The insects, who had a bee-like hunger for sweets, swarmed over the ships, eating so much sugar they could not fly, and they drowned trying to get back to shore.

The following year, Paul decided to try his luck among the tall trees of Oregon and Washington, on the Pacific Coast. Since both he and the blue ox were getting a little on in years, Paul bought several thousand oxen to help Babe with the hauling. This worked out fine for several weeks, until tragedy struck.

On the fateful day, one of Paul's crew tied all the oxen together, with Babe in the lead, to haul lumber to the ocean. All went fine until they reached a deep valley. Babe, marching along in front, started up the far side of the valley before the rest of the team had finished coming down. As a result, all the normal-sized oxen were quickly and fatally strung across the valley like laundry drying on a clothesline.

By the time Paul discovered what had happened, there was not much to do but tell the men back at camp that there would be plenty of beef for breakfast, lunch, and dinner.

After that, Babe continued to do the hauling alone. But Paul could see the blue ox was slowing down a bit. And, to tell the truth, he felt himself slowing down some.

To Babe, he said, "All these logging trucks and chain saws and sawmills full of fancy gadgets are making me feel a little useless—

even if I invented half the stuff myself."

Babe made a soft sound as if to say, "I agree."

Not long after, they took themselves up to Alaska, where they enjoyed some old-fashioned logging. When they had had their fill of the Arctic, they came back. In a deep woods—in Oregon or Minnesota or Maine, depending on who tells the story—Paul built a cabin for himself and a barn for Babe.

There he keeps two big iron kettles bubbling all the time: one full of pea soup for himself, and one full of moose moss soup for Babe.

In the evenings, Paul sits on his porch and Babe rests nearby, and they listen to the trees growing, which is a joy they had never shared before. And that green, growing power fills them so that they know they will be around as long as a single tree endures.

Think About It

1 How can you tell this story is a tall tale? Give some examples.

2 Which part of the story do you think is the funniest?

3 Do you think Paul Bunyan learns anything from his travels and adventures? Explain.

Meet the Author

Robert D. San Souci

Robert D. San Souci likes to travel, and his writing includes many folktales from around the world. Some of his ideas have come to him in interesting ways. Once, on a cross-country trip, his car broke down in Pecos, Texas, and he decided to visit the towns nearby. There he learned Native American legends that he later used in a book!

In addition to retelling folktales and writing novels, Mr. San Souci has worked as a story consultant for Walt Disney Feature Animation. When asked how long he plans to keep writing, he says, "as long as I have stories to tell—and an audience that is willing to listen."

Robert D. San Souci

Visit *The Learning Site!*
www.harcourtschool.com

573

Geography

by Donald Graves
illustrated by Joe Cepeda

We play the geography game.
Miss Adams pulls down a map,
any map in the world.
She says, "Find Ethiopia."
My hand is up first;
I whiz to the front
of the room and put
my finger on Ethiopia.

At home I shut my bedroom door,
pull out the bottom drawer
to my desk, and slowly turn
the Atlas pages.

Hour after hour I trace
rivers from source to sea,
hike through mountain passes,
green Amazon jungles,
visit capital cities,
and ride ocean liners
across the Atlantic
to England or France.

I beg for free road maps
at the corner Texaco station
and plot auto trips
to the White Mountains,
find the best way to a ballgame
at Fenway Park,
or imagine traveling
to Grandmother's house
for Christmas.

Paul Bunyan's Past

GIVE AN ORAL REPORT

Different stories about Paul Bunyan and Babe have been told by different storytellers. Look up Paul Bunyan in an encyclopedia or a book about American folklore. Find out how the stories got started and when the first ones were published. Take notes, and share your findings with your classmates.

Good Wood

RESEARCH THE LUMBER INDUSTRY

Wood is one of our most valuable natural resources. Read an encyclopedia article, on-line or printed, about the lumber industry. Then write a short report about how lumber workers bring down trees and cut them into boards. Tell what reforestation is.

Response

Here's How It Happened

WRITE A TALL TALE

The story says that Paul Bunyan made the Great Lakes and the Dakota plains. Think of a natural or human-made landmark in the area where you live. Write a tall tale about how it came to be. You can use Paul Bunyan and Babe as the characters or make up new characters.

Making Connections

MAP A ROUTE

The speaker in "Geography" looks at maps and imagines going places. With a partner, find a map of North America in an atlas and trace the outline on a sheet of paper. Next, list all the places the characters in "Paul Bunyan" went. Mark and label each place on your map. Draw a line connecting the places to show a possible route for Paul Bunyan's travels.

Activities

TWO LANDS, ONE HEART

Award-Winning
Illustrator

BY JEREMY SCHMIDT
AND TED WOOD

PHOTOGRAPHS BY
TED WOOD

Two Lands, One Heart

An American Boy's Journey to His Mother's Vietnam

Jeremy Schmidt and Ted Wood

PHOTOGRAPHS BY Ted Wood

An American Boy's Journey to His Mother's Vietnam

TJ's mother, Heather, is from Vietnam. She
and TJ's Uncle Jason and Aunt Jenny were
separated from the rest of their family during
the Vietnam War and grew up in an adoptive
family in America. Many years later they have
learned that their parents are alive and well.

TJ's mother and his Uncle Jason have already
made one visit to Vietnam. This time TJ, his
mother, his Aunt Jenny, and his American
grandmother have made the long plane trip
from Denver, Colorado, to Ho Chi Minh City.
They still have two more days to travel before
they reach TJ's grandparents' farm.

The countryside along the coast is bright green with rice fields
that spread as far as the eye can see.

The flight to Vietnam, a country in Southeast Asia, is a long one.

*A*fter two days in Saigon[1], it's time for TJ and his family to journey to the family farm. At seven in the morning, a chartered van picks them up at the hotel, and an hour later the city lies behind them. The brilliant green landscape of rice paddies, coconut palms, and tall clumps of bamboo looks like the country TJ has seen in pictures. But even out here, the road is busy with bicycles, scooters, horse-wagons, cars, trucks, and heavy carts pulled by water buffalo—the traditional tractors of Vietnam. With over seventy million people in this small country, the roads are always crowded.

Around noon, they stop in a small town for lunch. This restaurant seems just like an American one with tables and waiters and glasses of water. But what a menu! Grilled

[1]Saigon was renamed Ho Chi Minh City [hoh chee mihn], but many people still call it Saigon.

581

TJ lives in the Rocky Mountains, and he has never seen the ocean before. Playing with his mother on the beach, TJ delights in his first feel of warm saltwater.

Small villages dot the Vietnam coast, and colorful fishing boats fill the calm bays.

sparrows, eel soup, fried frog legs, bird's nest soup. Maybe if his brother Bradley were here, TJ would order him an eel just to see if he would eat it. But for himself, he orders something familiar—fried chicken.

Then it's back on the road, which soon begins to climb into the mountains bordering the sea. TJ has never seen the ocean, and as the van tops the last ridge he spots the clear, blue South China Sea stretching forever before him. All he can think of is jumping into that big blue pool, but he has to wait until they stop in Nha Trang [nä däng] that evening, where a sandy beach stretches for miles in front of their hotel. When he finally hits the beach, TJ can't believe his eyes. The beach is swarming with thousands of kids about his age. They try to play and talk with him, but TJ doesn't understand their language, and they walk away confused by his silence. Finally, he wades into the warm, gentle water and giggles as he bobs up and down. He wants to stay forever, but in the end, his mother drags him back to their hotel room.

The next day they start early. It's still a long drive to the farm. The mountains are steeper now, and looking down, TJ can see fishing villages in sandy coves hundreds of feet below. As the afternoon heats up and they leave the mountains, the landscape begins to blur into same-ness until the driver slows and turns off the highway. Pavement is left behind as they enter a shady tunnel on a narrow red-dirt road that winds between rice fields. Suddenly everyone is awake, both eager and nervous. After six days of traveling, they are moments from the farm.

TJ can barely control his excitement as the van nears the family farm.

The house stands back from the road, barely visible behind a dense stand of trees and bamboo. The driver honks the horn. Led by TJ's grandparents, a crowd of people runs out to greet them. They are weeping hysterically as they overwhelm Jenny and Heather. TJ is swallowed by a mass of arms touching and pulling him close. He doesn't know what to do. The crying and commotion scare him, but he sees the love streaming from his grandparents' faces with their tears.

With his arms wrapped around Heather and Jenny, TJ's grandfather leads the way back to the house. Set beneath big shade trees, the house is made of brick with a tile roof. The family crowds into a small dining room to talk over some cool coconut juice.

Although TJ already knows how to say "grandfather" (*ông*) in Vietnamese, all the talk is through an interpreter. After twenty years of living in America and speaking English, his mother has forgotten her Vietnamese. TJ would like to learn a few words, but it's a hard language to pronounce. For instance, the word *dau* [dou]: If you pronounce it with an upward tone, like asking a question (*dau?*), it means "headache." If you say it with a downward tone, it means "peanut." TJ might ask for a bowl of headaches, and what would that get him?

TJ's grandparents throw a traditional feast to welcome them to Vietnam, with dozens of dishes TJ has never eaten before.

584

The next day relatives and friends come from miles around for a family feast. It's like a big Thanksgiving dinner with dozens of relatives crammed into one house. Even with tables in every room, people have to take turns eating. The American visitors are the main attraction. So many people are looking at them through the windows and doors that TJ can't see outside. From the kitchen comes an endless parade of dishes, some of them very weird to TJ. Who would think of putting spicy meat with fruit? Or of dipping sugary rice cakes in salty hot sauce? Or of frying a salad?

TJ likes some of the food, especially the fried rice. "*Ông!* Watch this," he says, and expertly lifts rice from his bowl with chopsticks. TJ wishes he could talk Vietnamese with his grandfather, but he's proud to show him that he can at least eat like a Vietnamese boy.

There are no microwaves or stoves in this house. TJ helps his aunts cook dinner over wood fires.

When he finishes, TJ wanders toward the kitchen. Of all the rooms, this one is the most different from houses in America. The only furniture is a table. TJ's aunts cook on the dirt floor in fireplaces with no chimneys, and the walls are black from the wood smoke that hangs in the air. Big kettles of soup bubble beside sizzling woks. There is no microwave oven, no electric stove, no blenders or mixers, not even a refrigerator. It's amazing to see a kitchen without any modern tools, but TJ loves it. It reminds him of his family camping trips in the Rockies. He takes charge of feeding sticks into the fireplace while the women of the family sit on the floor chopping and slicing.

Taking a shower on the farm means
dumping a bucket of water over your
head. TJ helps his younger cousin
steady the bucket.

There is no running water
in the house. TJ's grand-
father shows him how to
get water from the well.

Out the side door is the washing area. Instead of a sink there are several huge clay pots filled with water. The water comes from a well that his great-grandfather dug—a deep shaft about three feet across and lined with bricks. Leaning over the rim, TJ can make out a faint glimmer of water thirty feet below. His grandfather tells him how they used to pull water up with a bucket, but just this year they added an electric pump and a hose. *Ông* is proud of the pump. It's the only electric machine on the farm, and it makes life much easier. Nevertheless, he wants to show TJ how they drew water in the old days. He throws a bucket down; there is a deep splash; then he pulls it up by a rope, hand over hand. It seems like a lot of work for a bit of water to wash your hands in.

As the day ends, TJ spies the nose and warm brown eyes of an ox peering out of a small thatch barn. But it's time for his family to return to the hotel where they're staying, so he'll have to wait till tomorrow to discover the mysteries of the farm.

The next morning, TJ can't wait to explore the farm and neighborhood. Only a few acres, the farm would be considered small in America. But not in Vietnam. It's the perfect size for TJ, and every few yards he discovers something new. In the fields grow rice, soybeans, corn, and mulberry leaves to feed silkworms. There is a vegetable garden in front of the house. Lining the footpaths, trees grow coconuts, guavas, papayas, avocados, bananas, and mangoes. Bamboo and eucalyptus provide wood and shade. The biggest trees have strange green fruits that grow right out of their trunks. Bigger than footballs and covered with spiny knobs, they are called jackfruit. They don't look

Although harmless, the big silkworms are a little too creepy for TJ.

very appetizing, but the insides are yellow and sweet. Now TJ knows why he hasn't seen any supermarkets; everyone has a supermarket right in their backyard.

One thing TJ is learning about Vietnam: It's a hot place, and May is the hottest time of year. Every day, the temperature rises to nearly 100 degrees. People work in the morning when it's cool and rest in the shade at midday. At home, TJ's mom would turn on the air conditioner. Here, people use old-fashioned ways to keep cool. His grandfather lies on a bamboo bed beneath a shady guava tree. The chickens climb into the rafters of the barn. TJ prefers the hammock. By pushing off the wall with one foot, he can keep the air circulating as if he's in a rocking bed under a fan.

When it cools in late afternoon, people start moving again. Women wearing straw hats work in the rice paddies, and Uncle Thao [tou] grabs TJ for a walk along the dirt road. TJ is eager to go. He likes Thao, maybe because his goofy joking reminds him of Uncle Jason, Thao's older brother. Thao looks like Jason and even laughs like Jason. At supper yesterday, Thao reached over to TJ's plate, snatched a whole rice cake, and ate it in one bite with a big grin—just like Jason showing off to TJ.

On the road, people pass them on bicycles carrying loads TJ would never see in Denver. One bicycle carries a pig as big as the bike in a basket. Another comes by with about 100 quacking ducks tied upside down by their feet to a big wooden frame. Down the road, a water buffalo has had the equivalent of a flat tire. One shoe has worn out, and three men are nailing on a new one. They are metal like horseshoes except that because a buffalo has split

TJ finds a jackfruit almost as big as he is, growing on a nearby tree.

hooves he needs two shoes for each foot. When the men finish, the big animal lumbers into the irrigation ditch and lies in the water with only his head showing. Naturally, a water buffalo's favorite place is in the water.

Although his neighbors use buffalo instead of tractors, Thao is proud of his family's oxen, which are more valuable than buffalo and easier to command. TJ loves these gentle animals and is thrilled when Thao asks him to help plow a new cornfield. From the barn, Thao brings the oxen, the yoke, and the plow, and they head for the field. The oxen follow like dogs, as if they know what to do. At the field, they even stand together, making it easy for Thao to hitch up the plow.

Then, as simple as starting a car, Thao says one word and off they go around the edge of the field. It looks so easy, Thao just walking along, occasionally tapping one of the oxen with a bamboo switch to give directions, the plow digging straight, deep grooves. TJ wants to try but sees right away that even though the oxen are doing all the pulling, it's hard work at the back end, too. He tries to keep the plow upright, and angled so it cuts to the right depth. But it's heavy, and TJ falls sideways

The water buffalo is Vietnam's hardest-working farm animal.

Uncle Thao has a good laugh as TJ attempts to stay aboard one of the oxen.

TJ tries to tell the difference between a weed and a rice plant as he helps his aunt weed the rice field.

Getting coconuts from the palm tree is a tough job. TJ uses a long bamboo stick to shake the coconuts loose.

Uncle Thao and TJ explore the river that flows by the farm.

into the dirt while the oxen keep pulling. After making two passes, TJ turns around. His furrows look like snakes next to Thao's straight lines. He glances at Thao, and his uncle is laughing.

TJ tries another job with his aunt Phieu (pyoo), helping her in the rice paddy. At this time of year, the rice plants are only a foot high, and the main job is to pull weeds. Because rice needs lots of water, the paddy is flooded. TJ steps barefoot into squishy mud, careful to put his feet between the stalks so he won't crush any of the delicate plants. Phieu shows him how to tell weeds from rice, and once he starts pulling, weeds are everywhere. It's hard work, bending over in the hot sun with only a bamboo hat for shade. At home, TJ's main chore is to keep his room clean, a job that looks pretty good to him right now.

TJ is dying of thirst after all this hot work. At home he could open the refrigerator and grab a soda. But here you have to harvest your drink. *Ông* hands TJ a special stick and takes him to a coconut tree in the front yard. Using the stick, TJ knocks down one of the heavy green coconuts, ducking so it doesn't land on his head. Then Uncle Thao cuts it open with a big knife and pours the sweet, clear coconut milk into a glass. TJ's not used to seeing water come out of a fruit, and although it tastes pretty good, he'd really rather have a Coke.

Wandering back to the ox barn, TJ spots a bamboo canoe in the rafters. "Uncle Thao," he yells. "Can we take it to the river?" The canoe is not usually for fun. Its main purpose is to carry farm produce down the river to sell in town. But Thao can't pass up a chance to show off to TJ. With TJ's help, he carries the boat down to the water, where he drops it in with a splash.

The river is perfect for learning to canoe. Thao and TJ paddle past farm fields and under big overhanging trees. A neighboring farmer walks along the bank with a herd of ducks. Around the bend they drift past two boys washing their oxen, and later a man crosses the river in a cart pulled by two water buffalo. The river hasn't changed since TJ's grandfather was a boy. It's a quiet place with no motors and nothing moving faster than a drifting canoe.

Time to abandon ship as TJ's cousins playfully attack the canoe.

As they paddle back to the landing, TJ's four girl cousins are waiting with mischief written all over their faces. "Oh no!" he says, with a big smile. The water is so shallow the girls can walk out to the canoe, and without warning, they start a water fight. In seconds TJ is soaked. Thao jumps out laughing and leaves him to his cousins' mercy. Before long they are all in the river together, splashing and laughing. Cousins are the same everywhere.

Think About It

 Why does TJ travel to Vietnam, and what does he learn there?

 What parts of TJ's journey do you think you would have liked? What parts wouldn't you have liked?

3 Why do you think the authors chose the title "Two Lands, One Heart"?

PAR AVION

CHỢ ĐƯƠNG
19599
70756

Bửu chính
Việt Nam
1000đ

Meet the Authors
Jeremy Schmidt and Ted Wood

Dear Readers,

Hello from Vietnam — the mosquitoes send their greetings! It is hot and humid here. We are not used to this, because we are from the Mountain States, just like TJ. The scenery is beautiful, though.

Traveling to new places is one of the fun parts of our work. Jeremy has been to Asia many times before, and we went to India for the first book we did together. We have worked on magazines, books, travel guides, and photo essays. We think working on books like *Two Lands, One Heart* is the most fun — as long as you bring some insect repellent!

Happy trails,

Schmidt

Ted Wood

Visit *The Learning Site!*
www.harcourtschool.com

593

Stateside Smarts

WRITE A SURVIVAL GUIDE
With a group, create a survival guide to help one of TJ's cousins from Vietnam get used to day-to-day life in America. You might include tips on transportation, money, and food. Look at some guidebooks first to see what topics they include.

RESPONSE

Explain a Grain

WRITE A REPORT
TJ helps his aunt weed a rice field. Learn more about rice, one of the world's most important foods. Use reference sources such as a world almanac to find out where rice is grown, how it is grown, and what it is used for besides food. Write a report to share your findings.

Thumbs Up!

COMMUNICATE THROUGH MOVEMENT

How might TJ have communicated in Vietnam if there had been no interpreter? In a group, make a list of signals that communicate messages about getting around, eating, and other important topics. For example, nodding your head means "yes." Make a video showing and explaining the movements, or act them out for classmates.

ACTIVITIES

Small World

MAKE A POSTER

After a wonderful water fight, TJ decides that "cousins are the same everywhere." Make a list of other things that are the same, no matter where you go. Then make a poster. Draw a picture of the earth in the middle. Around it, write sentences describing some ways life everywhere is the same.

Graphic Sources

"**T**wo Lands, One Heart" contains maps and pictures that give readers more information about Vietnam. Some kinds of information can be communicated best in pictures. In books and magazines, and on-line, information is shown in many ways, including photographs, maps, drawings, charts, graphs, tables, time lines, and diagrams. These are called **graphic sources**, or just **graphics**.

Maps can give a lot of information. Here are some things you can learn from maps:

- distances between places
- names of cities and countries
- size and location of countries
- names of bodies of water

The word *graph* comes from the ancient Greek word for *write*.

Here is another map of Vietnam. It shows Vietnam's agricultural areas, or zones.

VIETNAM

Ho Chi Minh City

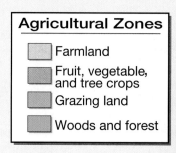

Agricultural Zones

Farmland

Fruit, vegetable, and tree crops

Grazing land

Woods and forest

Graphs show information about numbers or amounts of things. Here are two bar graphs that give facts about temperature and rainfall in Ho Chi Minh City. What information do they give you about the climate of southern Vietnam? Do you think you would rather visit Vietnam in January or in July?

HO CHI MINH CITY

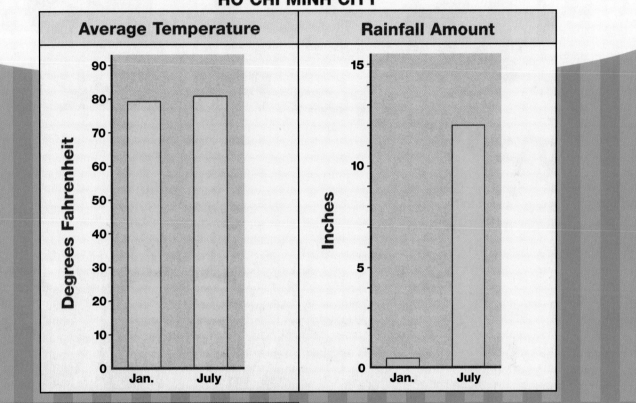

Fly Traps!
Plants That Bite Back

by Martin Jenkins • illustrated by David Parkins

Children's Choice

People do all sorts of things in their spare time. There are people who collect yogurt containers and people who make models out of bottle tops. There are beetle hunters and giant-leek growers. Me, I like watching plants that eat animals.

Plants that eat animals are called carnivorous plants. There are hundreds of different kinds and they grow all around the world.

It all started with a plant I found in a pond. It had little yellow flowers sticking out of the water. Under the water there were tangled stems with hundreds of tiny bubbles on them. A friend told me it was called a bladderwort.

There are over 200 different kinds of bladderworts. Most of them grow in ponds and rivers. They are usually very small, with narrow leaves and stems.

She said the bubbles on the stems were the bladders. Each one had a trap door shut tight, with little trigger hairs around it.

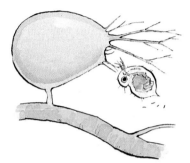

To set its traps, a bladderwort sucks the water out of its bladders.

Whenever a water flea or other bug touched a hair, the trap door swung back and in the bug went.

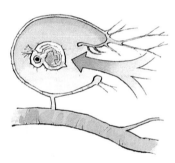

When a trap door opens, water rushes in, dragging the bug in with it.

Then the trap door slammed shut and there was no way out. And it all happened in the blink of an eye.

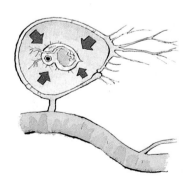

The bladderwort oozes special chemicals into the bladder. These dissolve the bug and the plant sucks it up.

Wow, that's neat, I thought. The trouble was, the traps on my plant were so small and so quick that I couldn't really see them work.

Well, I decided, I'll just have to find a bigger carnivorous plant.

So I did.

I had to climb a mountain, mind you, and walk through all its boggiest, mossiest places.

But there in the moss were little red plants, shining in the sun. I thought they were covered in dewdrops, but they weren't. They were sundews, and the shiny parts were sticky like honey. I'm sure you can guess what they were for.

When a bug gets stuck on a sundew, the leaf slowly curls up around it.

Then the soft parts of the bug are dissolved by chemicals and eaten.

I had to leave the sundews when the clouds rolled in. But as soon as I got home, I sent away for some sundew seeds of my own.

Afterward, the leaf opens up again and the leftover bug parts fall off.

Butterworts are carnivorous plants, too, and often grow in the same places as sundews. They have flat leaves like flypaper. Little bugs stick to the leaves and slowly dissolve.

The seeds weren't just for ordinary sundews, though. They were for Giant African sundews. I sowed them in a pot of moss and covered it with glass.

I watered the pot every day with rainwater straight from the water tank. Soon the seeds started to sprout and I had dozens of baby sundews.

They grew and grew, until they were almost big enough to start catching things.

Then one day I watered them with the wrong kind of water—and every single one died.

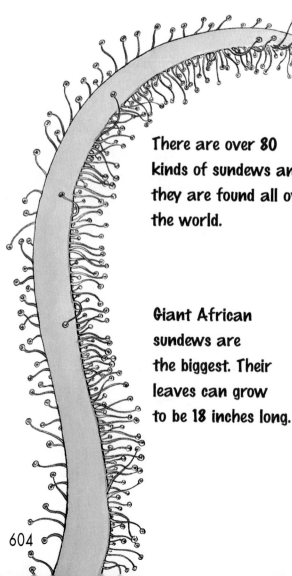

There are over 80 kinds of sundews and they are found all over the world.

Giant African sundews are the biggest. Their leaves can grow to be 18 inches long.

My sundews died because I accidentally put fertilizer in the water. All carnivorous plants hate fertilizer.

I gave up on sundews after that, but I did grow a Venus flytrap. It lived on the windowsill and caught insects. Each of its leaves had a hinge down the center, several little trigger hairs, and a spiky rim.

When a fly or a wasp walked over a leaf, it was perfectly safe if it didn't touch any of the hairs. It was even safe if it touched just one of the hairs. But if it touched two of the hairs, then . . .

Venus flytraps grow in only one small part of the southeastern United States. They are rare now because people have drained many of the marshes where they once lived.

Small insects such as ants can escape from a Venus flytrap — they're not big enough to be worth eating.

But flies and wasps are a different story. Once caught, the more they struggle the tighter the leaf presses together.

When the leaf is fully closed, it begins to dissolve its victim.

My Venus flytrap seemed quite happy, so I thought I'd try growing something even bigger.

The next plant I got was a cobra lily.

This one caught insects, too, but it didn't actually do very much. It had leaves like funnels, with a slippery rim and a little pool at the bottom.

Cobra lilies get their name because their leaves look like cobras, not because they eat them!

Cobra lilies grow along the western coast of the United States. Their leaves can be up to 18 inches long.

When insects crawled inside, they fell into the pool and couldn't climb out. So they stayed there and became bug soup for the lily.

I was very happy with my cobra lily. Surely it was the biggest carnivorous plant of all. But then my friend told me about pitcher plants.

Pitchers are even bigger, she said, but they are very difficult to grow. In that case, I thought, I'll just go and find some wild ones.

So I went—all the way to Malaysia.

And there, growing up the trees at the edge of the jungle, were hundreds of pitcher plants. Fat red ones, thin yellow ones, curly green ones, all waiting for flies.

I didn't see the biggest pitcher plant of all, though. It's called the Rajah pitcher plant and it grows on the tallest mountain in Borneo.

The pitchers' leaves look like vases, and they catch insects in the same way that cobra lilies do.

There are some
kinds of spiders, and
even some small tree
frogs, that are able
to live inside the
pitchers. They cling to
the slippery sides
and grab the insects
that fall in.

It has pitchers the size of footballs. People say it can even catch some kinds of squirrels, but I'm not convinced. One day I'll go and see for myself . . .

Think About It

1 How are the plants described in the selection different from each other? How are they alike?

2 How does the author make the topic of carnivorous plants interesting?

3 Suppose you could go anywhere in the world to learn about a plant or an animal. Where would you go and what would you study?

Meet the Author
Martin Jenkins

Martin Jenkins is a biologist who spends most of his time writing "serious things." But in his children's books he takes a light-hearted look at his travels. In *Chameleons Are Cool*, readers experience a trip to Madagascar, where a wild chameleon bit him on the thumb! "I still think they are wonderful," he says, "but tend to leave them alone." Mr. Jenkins calls *Fly Traps!* "absolutely autobiographical."

Meet the Illustrator
David Parkins

David Parkins' amusing people and animals have appeared in many books. Working on *Fly Traps!* brought back memories: "When I first started out as an illustrator, I did a book on wildlife and spent a year tramping around fields drawing berries and birds. So, in a way, this takes me back to my beginnings." Mr. Parkins lives in Lincolnshire, England. His main hobby is singing.

Visit *The Learning Site!* www.harcourtschool.com

My Visit to a Dreamy Place

Betsy Mizell

There are few places on Earth that are as special as the Galápagos Islands. As a member of the Young Explorers Club, I was lucky enough to visit these beautiful islands on the equator, about 600 miles west of the coast of South America, this past summer.

Here are some questions that *Dolphin Log* magazine asked Betsy about her trip:

Dolphin Log: What was the best part of the trip?

Betsy: Snorkeling was really fun. At first I was scared, but there were lots of beautiful fish in the water.

Dolphin Log: What was your favorite Galápagos Islands creature?

Betsy: I loved the sea lions, manta rays and sharks, but the sea lions were my favorite.

Dolphin Log: In one of the photos you sent us, you stood right next to the sea lions! Were they friendly?

Betsy: No, not at all. In fact . . . they weren't very nice. They growled at me when I got too close to them. But sea lion pups were cute.

Dolphin Log: Did it rain at all on your trip to the equator?

Betsy: Sometimes it would rain . . . for about one minute. Then it was as hot and sunny as before.

Dolphin Log: Did you know anything about the Galápagos Islands before your trip?

Betsy: My mom told me a little bit about them, and where they were. I knew that they were formed by volcanoes . . . but I didn't know they were underwater volcanoes! That was a surprise.

Dolphin Log: Tell us something else you learned on your trip.

Betsy: I learned a lot of stuff! But the most interesting, I think, was about Galápagos tortoises. I didn't know they were threatened. It's important that people take care of them.

Dolphin Log: Did you eat anything new and different on your trip?

Betsy: One night they served something called gazpacho . . .

Dolphin Log: That's a cold soup . . .

Betsy: With little shrimp in it . . .

Dolphin Log: How was it?

Betsy: Eeew. I wouldn't try it. My mom did, though. She said it was okay.

Think About It

What new things did the author learn on her trip?

Galápagos Islands

South America

Pacific Ocean

Response

Plant Alert

MAKE A WARNING SIGN

Carnivorous plants are a danger to insects! Choose one of the plants described in "Fly Traps," and make a bug-to-bug warning sign that explains what will happen if fellow insects stray too close to the plant. Think about caution signs and other traffic signs to get ideas for eye-catching symbols, shapes, and colors.

Insect-Eater

CREATE A DIAGRAM

Design your own carnivorous plant. You might invent a plant that eats pests such as fleas and mosquitoes. Draw a diagram of your plant. Show exactly how it catches its prey. Use the diagrams in the selection as models.

Activities

Plant Talk

PERFORM A SKIT

With a group, find information about a carnivorous plant. Plan a skit in which characters find the plant and talk about it. Act out the skit for classmates.

Making Connections

CREATE A BROCHURE

"Fly Traps" and "My Visit to a Dreamy Place" describe places with interesting animal and plant life. What interesting plants and animals can be found in your region? Make a travel brochure for your region that would make nature lovers want to come and visit.

Bolivia Raab is staying with her
aunt and uncle, the Goldings, for six
months while her parents are working in
Turkey. One afternoon her friends —Rory,
Derek, DeDe, and Aldo — come over to see her
parrot, Lucette. They say she should take the bird
to the "rain forest" that the school nature club
has set up in a classroom. Bolivia thinks this
may be too much excitement for her pet,
but she agrees to think about it.

The Down &

by **Johanna Hurwitz**

illustrated by
Jenny Tylden-Wright

Up Fall

The Down & Up Fall

Johanna Hurwitz

Award-Winning
Author

On Monday, as soon as they finished eating their lunches, Aldo took Bolivia to peek inside the room that the nature club had transformed into its rain forest. Even though neither the humidifier nor the heater was turned on when she arrived, Bolivia could still feel the dampness and smell the earthy odor in the air. There was a soft cushion of soil underfoot as she walked inside the room.

Mr. Peters, the adviser to the club, was there, busily watering the rubber plants.

"Hello," he said to them. "Have you come to investigate another corner of the world?"

"This is a girl from my homeroom named Bolivia Raab," said Aldo, introducing his classmate to the teacher. "She's got a real live parrot at home. I asked her to bring it to our club tomorrow."

"A parrot? That's fantastic!" exclaimed Mr. Peters. "What type is it?"

"She's a green Amazon parrot from South America,"

Bolivia explained. "I've had her since I was very young, and I've taught her to speak a little."

"Wonderful!" said Mr. Peters enthusiastically. "I bet she'd feel right at home here in our rain forest. Will you bring her to school tomorrow?"

Bolivia really was intrigued by the idea of Lucette visiting the rain forest. It seemed only fair that the bird should be given the experience. She had lived for so many years away from the tropical environment that was a parrot's natural habitat. Nevertheless, Bolivia worried that a whole day at school was more than Lucette needed. It was stressful enough for a student. Imagine how it would be for a bird!

Bolivia thought about all the students who would try to touch Lucette during the day when she wasn't around to protect her. There was bound to be some wise guy who would poke the parrot and possibly hurt her.

Mr. Peters seemed to guess what she was thinking. "We'd be very careful that no harm comes to your bird," he reassured her.

"Let me see if my uncle can drive her over to school in the afternoon in time for your club meeting," Bolivia offered. That seemed the perfect compromise. An hour and a half in the afternoon should be enough rain forest adventure for Lucette.

"Wonderful!" Mr. Peters exclaimed again. "I'll tell Kenny to bring his snakes to school tomorrow too. And I'll announce over the public address system that the rain forest will be open to the entire school."

Bolivia knew that most of the time no one paid any attention to the announcements. Otherwise she would have been worried about a thousand students trying to squeeze into the rain forest.

"Neat," said Aldo as a bell interrupted the conversation.

He turned to Bolivia. "We'd better go," he said. "Our lunch period is over."

"Okay," Bolivia said. "See you tomorrow," she called to the science teacher.

Mr. Golding was perfectly willing to deliver Lucette to the middle school the next day. "It's been a long time since I was inside a school," he commented. "Do you think they'll let me take some pictures of that rain forest?"

"Why not?" asked Bolivia. "I bet they'll be thrilled. And then I could send a picture to my parents too."

The next afternoon, just at the time when school was being dismissed, Bolivia's uncle Lou arrived there with Lucette. It was a day as warm as summer, so Bolivia hadn't worried about the outdoor temperature being too cold for her parrot. But her uncle was the cautious type. He had Lucette's traveling cage wrapped in a big blanket when he met Bolivia in the school lobby.

Rory and Derek were waiting with Bolivia.

"Poor Lucette," Rory said. "Having to go to school at her age."

"What is her age?" asked Derek.

"She's older than we are," Bolivia responded. "She's about twenty years old."

"What's in there?" asked a boy passing by in the hall. In a moment they were surrounded by a group of students curious about the large bundle in Mr. Golding's arms.

"Stand back. Stand back," Bolivia shouted. "This is my parrot, Lucette, and she's going to make a visit to the rain forest upstairs. If you want to see her, you'll have to wait in line outside the science room. Too many people at once will scare her."

Luckily at that very moment Mr. Peters joined them, and he too announced to the students that the only way to see the parrot was to visit the rain forest.

Then Bolivia, Rory, Derek, Mr. Golding (holding the parrot in the wrapped cage), and Mr. Peters (holding back the crowd) made their way up the flight of stairs and toward the room that housed the rain forest. Outside the doorway of the forest stood Aldo, DeDe, and several students Bolivia didn't know.

Mr. Peters unlocked the door, and they all went inside. The science teacher turned on both the humidifier and the electric heater.

"This is amazing," gasped Mr. Golding, marveling at the room's decor. "Look at that." He pointed to some pieces of rope that had been painted green and hung from the ceiling. "They look just like wild vines."

"It even smells like a rain forest, doesn't it?" Bolivia asked her uncle.

"How do you know?" asked Rory. "Have you ever been in a real rain forest?"

"No. But I've been in hot-houses in botanical gardens where they grow tropical plants. They always smell just like this room."

"Let me get my snakes," said one of the boys who was standing nearby. "They've been waiting in here all day." He went over to a cardboard box that had holes punched in it and removed the lid.

Mr. Golding put Lucette's cage down on the floor and removed the blanket. Everyone gathered around to stare at the parrot.

"Tell them my name," Rory demanded of the bird. "Say Rory. Go on. Rory. Say Rory," he repeated.

The parrot blinked her black eyes but didn't say a word.

Bolivia bent down and opened the cage. She carefully removed Lucette and let the parrot stand on her arm.

"I could put her on one of the rubber plants," she offered to Mr. Peters.

"Hello there. Happy New Year," Lucette suddenly squawked. Apparently she now felt ready to show off.

"There are so many people here she probably thinks it's a party," Bolivia said, laughing. She rubbed her hand across her face. It was warm in the rain forest, and her face was damp with sweat.

"Happy New Year to you," DeDe called out. "I've got to go," she told Bolivia. "They're expecting me at the band rehearsal. I'll call you tonight to find out how Lucette liked the rain forest."

"So long," Aldo said to DeDe.

"Who's in charge of the sound effects?" asked Mr. Peters.

"It's my turn," one of the girls told him. She went over to a corner where there was a cassette player half-hidden behind a rubber plant. She turned on a switch, and at once the room was filled with tropical noises. There was the sound of dripping water. And there were many birdcalls. In fact, it seemed as if the room was filled with tropical birds.

"Hello there," squawked Lucette.

"She must think she's listening to real birds," said Derek.

"Watch out," warned Kenny, the owner of the two grass snakes. "You almost stepped on Jefferson."

Bolivia looked down. There was a green snake moving in front of her just as if she were walking in a real rain forest.

Mr. Golding took the blanket and the birdcage and placed them in the hallway outside the room. They didn't belong inside a rain forest. Then he took his camera out of the case around his neck and began to take pictures of one of the more realistic toy monkeys climbing on a plant. "I wish people could smell these pictures when they're developed," he told the science teacher. "You've done a fantastic job here."

Bolivia noticed Rory turning the dial on the electric heater. She hoped he was lowering the heat. She was really feeling uncomfortably warm.

"Hello. Can I come in or do I need a passport?" a woman's voice called out at the doorway.

Bolivia turned to see who had entered the room. It was Dr. Osborne, the assistant principal of the school.

"Come in. Come in," called Mr. Peters. "We have everything here except mosquitoes."

"This is lovely. Just lovely," Dr. Osborne told the teacher.

"The nature club has done a lot of hard work to create all this," Mr. Peters informed her proudly.

"Happy New Year!" Lucette squawked from her perch on a rubber plant.

"Happy New Year?" Dr. Osborne walked toward the corner where Bolivia and Lucette were stationed.

"Watch your step!" shouted Kenny as the assistant principal narrowly missed trampling on one of his snakes.

Dr. Osborne looked down and gave an amazingly loud shriek. It was much louder than the one that Bolivia's aunt Sophie had given when she'd seen the mouse in the kitchen.

At that moment Bolivia felt a few drops of rain on her face. Then it started raining harder. She looked up at the ceiling. How in the world had Mr. Peters and his students arranged that?

Some of the students in the room began to rush out the door, but others remained, lifting their faces toward the water and enjoying the unexpected shower.

"It's just a little grass snake. He won't hurt you," said Kenny, but the assistant principal was already out the door. Bolivia wondered if she was looking to get out of the rain or to put more distance between herself and Kenny's snake.

"Get the blanket," she shouted to her uncle. The cool water felt good on her skin, but she thought she'd better protect Lucette.

"Where's this water coming from?" Aldo asked Mr. Peters. Apparently he was just as surprised as Bolivia by the rain.

"It's the sprinkler system," Mr. Peters answered. "The heat in the room seems to have triggered it." He had unplugged the electric heater. Now he was busily opening the windows, which were hidden behind painted backdrops.

"I never heard of having windows in a rain forest," Rory said. His eyeglasses were spattered with water drops, and his hair looked as if he'd been interrupted in the middle of a shower.

"Go and get the custodian," Mr. Peters instructed Aldo. "He'll know how to shut off the sprinklers."

Dr. Osborne returned to the classroom, holding an umbrella over her head. "Where's that snake?" she asked nervously.

"Here," called out Kenny, holding up his grass snake. "This is Jefferson. You scared him."

"I scared him? He scared *me*," the assistant principal said.

"Then you'd better watch out for Washington, my other snake. He's hiding under one of the plants."

"You mean, there are *two* snakes in this room? Snakes are not in my job description." Dr. Osborne looked anxiously down toward her feet.

"Happy New Year, RoryDerek!" squawked Lucette from under the blanket that Bolivia had thrown over her. This was very unusual. Generally Lucette was silent when she was covered up.

The entrance to the science room was jammed with students and teachers from the other clubs that had been meeting along the corridor. Everyone was curious about the screams and the water puddles that had oozed out of the science room.

The custodian arrived, shaking his head in dismay. "First it was dirt," he mumbled. "Now this." He carried a ladder, which he climbed on to reach a switch near the ceiling. The rain stopped as suddenly as it had begun, but the air was more humid than ever. Just the way the air should be in a rain forest, Bolivia realized as she pulled at her wet T-shirt. She looked down at her jeans, which were spattered with mud.

Dr. Osborne closed her umbrella. Mr. Peters smiled at her. "This is how we keep education alive and exciting," he explained. "These students will always remember about rain forests now."

"You can say that again," said the assistant principal. "I'll never forget this afternoon or the snakes."

"Jefferson is harmless," Kenny reassured her. "And so is Washington. Nothing bad could have happened to you." He broke into a grin. "But I am saving up for a boa constrictor."

"If you get one, don't ever bring it to school," Dr. Osborne said firmly.

"They don't eat people. Just mice," Kenny said.

The assistant principal turned to the science teacher. "This was a wonderful display," she said. "I'm sure everyone has learned a great deal from this. But perhaps it's time for you to move on to another area of study."

"Good idea," said the custodian. "I can't wait to get the dirt out of this school."

"Oh, I have plenty of other plans," Mr. Peters told Dr. Osborne. "I thought we'd turn this room into a moonscape. There are no snakes on the moon," he added.

Think About It

1 How and why does Dr. Osborne's opinion of the nature club's rain forest change during the selection?

2 Do you agree with Mr. Peters that projects like the rain forest display are a good way to "keep education alive and exciting"? Explain.

3 How would the story be different if the snakes and the parrot were not in it?

Meet the Author
Johanna Hurwitz

As a child, Johanna Frank loved books so much that by the age of ten, she had decided to become a librarian someday and to write books of her own. After graduating from college, she did become a librarian. She also married and had two children. During this time, she wrote hundreds of letters to friends and relatives. She feels that these letters were good training for her book writing.

Johanna Hurwitz has published more than forty books for children. She is especially interested in childhood and remembers her own very well. She says that everything in her books comes from real life. For example, Derek and Rory are based on her son and his friend. She really met someone who had a daughter named Bolivia and decided to use the name for one of her characters. Some of her friends' pets have appeared in her books, too.

Johanna Hurwitz

**Visit *The Learning Site!*
www.harcourtschool.com**

631

Amazon River

SOUTH AMERICA

Amazon Adventure

FROM *RANGER RICK* MAGAZINE
BY SUSAN GOODMAN

Cruising down the Mighty Amazon, exploring deep in the rainforest.

How lucky can some kids get?

"Check it out!" Kevin shouted, pointing to something swimming in the world's largest river, the Amazon.

From the deck of a river boat, Kevin and his friends watched rare river dolphins flash past.

Then the kids looked toward shore—at the houses on stilts, the banana plants, and the palm trees. This place was so different from home!

Who were these lucky kids, and what were they doing in the Amazon rainforest? They were junior high students from Michigan. And they were taking part in a Children's Rainforest Workshop.

All through the school year they had studied rainforests. They also worked hard earning money to help pay for the trip. Now all their learning would come to life as they spent a week in a small corner of the world's largest rainforest.

Life in the Forest

After flying to the city of Iquitos, Peru, the kids cruised 50 miles (80 km) down the Amazon. The boat finally docked at a jungle hideaway called Explorama Lodge. Right away the kids could see that life here would take getting used to!

Lots of rain made the air very humid, so wet clothes took days to dry. Kerosene lamps took the place of electric lights. (No videos or hair dryers here!) Mosquito netting kept creepy-crawlies out of their beds.

Look, but don't touch! This tree's long spines keep hungry animals away.

633

And to go to the bathroom, the kids had to walk down a long path to an outside toilet.

"I miss hamburgers and pizza," said April, "but I've tried some neat new foods—like fried bananas, black beans, and manioc root."

The kids didn't have to go far for animal-watching. While swinging on hammocks, they watched hummingbirds sip nectar from flowers. They shared their showers with huge moths and weird katydids. Once they even had to step over a column of marching army ants to get to the dining room.

A Living Lab

All week, the kids explored the river and the rainforest. While paddling down the Amazon in canoes, they learned that the river contains more species (kinds) of fish than the entire Atlantic Ocean.

Near their camp, one of the kids spotted a two-toed sloth crawling along a thin tree branch.

The most exciting part of the trip was a walk through the treetops.

By catching some of those fish in a net, Jake made another discovery. "These are the same kinds of tropical fish I have in my aquarium at home!" he said.

By hunting for tarantulas, butterflies, and foot-long walking sticks, the kids learned a lot about nature. But exploring the canopy walkway was the trip's high point— in more ways than one.

Getting Above It

The canopy walkway is like a narrow trail through the treetops. It starts at the top of a tower and zigzags through the rainforest canopy. (That's the top level of the forest.) It ends 1600 feet (480 m) away at another tower.

The kids knew the walkway was safe. But that first step onto it was still a little scary. Sarah said it was "fun, exciting, wonderful, frightening, and every other word that describes my mixed feelings!"

Scientists have known for a long time that tropical rainforests have more species than any other place on Earth. But, until a few years ago, they had no idea *how* many. Now they're sure that *millions* of un-known species live overhead with-out ever coming near the ground.

Discovering an unknown species would have been neat. But the kids were happy just seeing what they did. Some creatures that were hard to spot from the jungle floor were now right before their eyes.

Instead of seeing just a flash of bright feathers, the kids stood eye to eye with some incredible birds. Instead of just hearing a weird howl, they nearly shared the same branch with a howler monkey.

The sights were amazing, but what Emily liked best was her second trip on the walkway—in the black of night. "We got to see glow-in-the-dark mushrooms up there. It was *so* neat!"

Good-Bye—For Now, Anyway

By week's end, all the kids were ready to see their families—and modern toilets! Still, the kids were sorry to leave. Tim said he was going to be "rainforest sick" instead of homesick. Erica said that although she hoped the forest would always be the same, "I know I'll never be."

Colorful birds, such as this macaw, came so close that the kids could almost touch them.

Think About It

What did the students learn in the Amazon rainforest that they couldn't have learned in school?

Response

Attention, Please!

MAKE AN ANNOUNCEMENT

Mr. Peters announces over the public address system that the science club's "rain forest" is open to visitors. Write an announcement that explains what visitors should expect when they enter the science room. Read your announcement to some classmates, or tape-record it and play it for them.

Parrot Talk

WRITE INSTRUCTIONS

Bolivia taught Lucette to talk when the parrot was young. See what you can find out about how parrots learn to talk. If possible, interview a pet-store worker or bird expert. Write a set of instructions for parrot tutors. Include a list of Do's and Don't's.

Activities

Exploring Without Airfare

LIST INFORMATION SOURCES

The students in "The Down and Up Fall" study rain forests by creating a model of one. Make a list of other ways someone could learn about a place that is far away. Post your list in the classroom.

Making Connections

CREATE A CHART

Use facts from "Amazon Adventure" to compare a real rain forest with the model one in "The Down and Up Fall." Make a chart that compares and contrasts the two. Include information about temperature, rainfall, animals, and plants.

Theme

WRAP-UP

Places to Go

WRITE PARAGRAPHS Suppose you could go on the journeys with two people or characters from this theme. Which two would you choose? Write two paragraphs explaining your choices.

Authors' Purposes

MAKE A CHART
The authors of the selections in this theme had several different purposes for writing. Make a chart showing these purposes: *to entertain, to inform, to express.* Find an example of each purpose in the theme. Write the name of the selection and its author, and explain why you chose it as an example.

Ways of Life

DISCUSS CULTURES
The selections in this theme show how people live or have lived in different times, places, and cultures. In a group, choose at least three selections to focus on. Discuss what those selections show you about how people live. Then think of a way to share your ideas with classmates. For example, you might make a poster about how several ways of life are similar as well as different, or you might read aloud passages from the selections.

To Entertain	To Inform	To Express

Using the Glossary

Like a dictionary, this glossary lists words in alphabetical order. To find a word, look it up by its first letter or letters.

To save time, use the **guide words** at the top of each page. These show you the first and last words on the page. Look at the guide words to see if your word falls between them alphabetically.

Here is an example of a glossary entry:

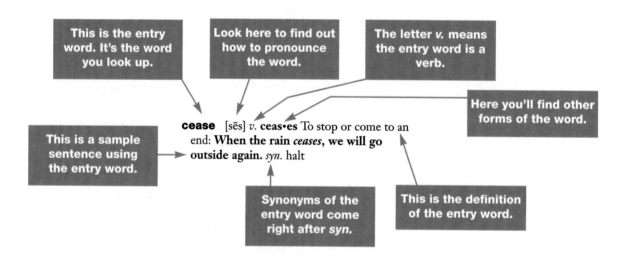

Word Origins

Throughout the glossary, you will find notes about word origins, or how words get started and change. Words often have interesting backgrounds that can help you remember what they mean.

Here is an example of a word origin note:

paddock *Paddock* comes from the Old English word *pearruc*, which means "an enclosed area." *Pearruc* is related to the word *park*.

Pronunciation

The pronunciation in brackets is a respelling that shows how the word is pronounced.

The **pronunciation key** explains what the symbols in a respelling mean. A shortened pronunciation key appears on every other page of the glossary.

PRONUNCIATION KEY*

a	add, map	m	move, seem	u	up, done
ā	ace, rate	n	nice, tin	û(r)	burn, term
â(r)	care, air	ng	ring, song	yōō	fuse, few
ä	palm, father	o	odd, hot	v	vain, eve
b	bat, rub	ō	open, so	w	win, away
ch	check, catch	ô	order, jaw	y	yet, yearn
d	dog, rod	oi	oil, boy	z	zest, muse
e	end, pet	ou	pout, now	zh	vision, pleasure
ē	equal, tree	ŏŏ	took, full	ə	the schwa, an unstressed vowel representing the sound spelled
f	fit, half	ōō	pool, food		*a* in *above*
g	go, log	p	pit, stop		*e* in *sicken*
h	hope, hate	r	run, poor		*i* in *possible*
i	it, give	s	see, pass		*o* in *melon*
ī	ice, write	sh	sure, rush		*u* in *circus*
j	joy, ledge	t	talk, sit		
k	cool, take	th	thin, both		
l	look, rule	th	this, bathe		

Other symbols
- • separates words into syllables
- ′ indicates heavier stress on a syllable
- ′ indicates light stress on a syllable

Abbreviations: *adj.* adjective, *adv.* adverb, *conj.* conjunction, *interj.* interjection, *n.* noun, *prep.* preposition, *pron.* pronoun, *syn.* synonym, *v.* verb

a·bun·dant [ə•bun′dənt] *adj.* More than enough: **The garage has *abundant* room for the many boxes we store there.** *syn.* plentiful

ac·cept·a·ble [ak•sep′tə•bəl] *adj.* Permitted, as an action that is allowed: **Blue jeans are not *acceptable* clothes for a wedding.**

ac·ci·den·tal·ly [ak•sə•dent′lē] *adv.* By mistake; without meaning to: **I *accidentally* let Josh know about his surprise party.** *syn.* mistakenly

ac·cor·di·on [ə•kôr′dē•ən] *n.* A musical instrument that sounds like a small organ: **Kaitlyn plays tunes on the *accordion* without looking at the keyboard.**

accordion

> **Fact File**
> **accordion** The word *accordion* came into use in the 1820s. It comes from the Italian word *accordare*, which means "to be in tune." A related word is *accord*, which means "to agree" or "to harmonize." *Accord* comes from the Latin word *cordis*, which means "heart." The harmony of music and feeling is related to the heart.

ac·quaint·ance [ə•kwānt′əns] *n.* Knowing someone or something: **I made the *acquaintance* of Mikaila's mother on the class trip.**

ac·ro·bat [ak′rə•bat′] *n.* A performer of physical feats such as walking a tightrope: **The circus *acrobat* did a back flip on the tightrope.** *syn.* gymnast

a·dore [ə•dôr′] *v.* To love something or someone dearly: **The puppies *adore* their owner.**

a·larm [ə•lärm′] *v.* **a·larmed** To frighten suddenly: **The noise *alarmed* the ducks and they flew away.** *syn.* startle

> **Word Origins**
> **alarm** The word *alarm* comes from the Italian word *all'arme*, which means "to arm" as in battle. This call to arms is a call to defend oneself.

al·i·bi [al′ə•bī′] *n.* A reason or an excuse for not doing something or not being in a certain place: **Dan's *alibi* was that he was in his room when the window was broken.** *syns.* explanation, defense

an·tic·i·pa·tion [an•tis′ə•pā′shən] *n.* The feeling of looking forward to something: **George's *anticipation* about his birthday was so great that he could not sleep.** *syn.* expectation

anx·ious [angk′shəs] *adj.* Eager: **Dan was *anxious* to find out if he had been chosen for the school play.**

a·pol·o·gize [ə•päl′ə•jīz] *v.* **a·pol·o·gized** To express regret over doing something wrong; to say one is sorry: **Ann *apologized* to her mother for coming home late.**

ap·par·ent·ly [ə•pâr′ənt•lē] *adv.* Seemingly easy to observe and understand: **You are *apparently* too big to ride a tricycle anymore.** *syn.* clearly

ap·pe·tiz·ing [ap′ə•tī′zing] *adj.* Delicious looking: **The fresh fruit salad plate looked *appetizing*.** *syn.* appealing

ap·pre·ci·a·tion [ə•prē′shē•ā′shən] *n.* Recognition for good qualities; gratitude for something good: **He received an award in *appreciation* of his work.** *syn.* gratefulness

ar·bor [är′bər] *n.* A place that is shaded by trees or shrubs: **We rested on a bench in the cool, shady *arbor*.**

at·ten·tive·ly [ə•ten′tiv•lē′] *adv.* With great interest and with careful attention: **Juan listened *attentively* to the directions.** *syn.* intently

at·tic [at′ik] *n.* The area or room just below the roof of a house, often used to store things: **At the end of the season, Sal put his baseball equipment away in the *attic*.** *syn.* loft

bar·be·cue [bär′bə•kyoō] *n.* A party or picnic where meat is cooked outdoors over coals: **Our family's *barbecue* is held every July 4.** *syn.* cookout

barbecue

bel·low·ing [bel′ō•ing] *n.* A loud sound made by an animal; an animal call: **The farm was full of the animals'** *bellowing* **as feeding time drew near.** *syn.* roar

bic·ker [bik′ər] *v.* To have a minor argument: **Phillip and his sister often** *bicker* **over where to sit at the dinner table.** *syn.* squabble

bil·low [bil′ō] *v.* **bil·low·ing** To rise like a wave and push outward: **The sound of the orchestra was** *billowing* **through the halls and out into the street.** *syn.* swell

bliz·zard [bliz′ərd] *n.* A winter storm with strong winds and a large amount of snow: **After the** *blizzard* **ended, our car was buried under snowdrifts for two days.** *syn.* snowstorm

bog·gy [bäg′ē] *adj.* **bog·gi·est** Soggy or swampy: **We wore boots to hike through the** *boggiest* **part of the trail.** *syn.* marshy

┌─ **Word Origins**
bog *Bog* is an old Gaelic word meaning "soft and moist," like the wet spongy ground in a bog or swamp. To get bogged down in something is to become stuck in it, as one's feet would become stuck in mud.

bond [bänd] *v.* **bond·ing** To connect well and hold together tightly: **The mother and baby are** *bonding* **whenever they spend time together.** *syn.* link

bri·gade [bri•gād′] *n.* A group of people who work together to accomplish a task: **The volunteers formed a window-cleaning** *brigade* **and got the job done quickly.** *syn.* squad

brush [brush] *n.* Low bushes and shrubs that grow close together: **The young deer leaped over rocks and** *brush* **as it ran.** *syn.* undergrowth

bur·rows [bûr′ōz] *n.* Holes or tunnels that an animal digs in the ground to live in: **Snakes shelter in their** *burrows* **to protect themselves from the hot sun.** *syn.* nests

bus·tle [bus′əl] *v.* **bus·tled** To hurry about while doing a task: **Jane** *bustled* **around the kitchen, cooking and setting the table.**

car·niv·o·rous [kär•niv′ə•rəs] *adj.* Meat-eating, or, in the case of certain plants, insect-eating: **To survive,** *carnivorous* **plants need insects.**

cease [sēs] *v.* **ceas·es** To stop or come to an end: **When the rain** *ceases*, **we will go outside again.** *syn.* halt

cer·tain·ty [sûr′tən•tē] *n.* The state of being sure about something: **I know with** *certainty* **that the book is good.**

cer·tif·i·cate [sûr•tif′ə•kit] *n.* An official piece of paper that shows one has met certain requirements: **Arthur got a** *certificate* **showing that he had completed a first-aid course.** *syn.* document

chem·i·cal [kem′i•kəl] *n.* **chem·i·cals** A substance that has certain properties: **The students wear safety glasses when mixing** *chemicals* **in science class.**

chil·e [chil′ē] *n.* A kind of stew that includes beans, chile peppers, and other ingredients: *Chile* **and salad make a tasty meal.**

chor·tle [chôr′təl] *v.* To laugh heartily: **Grandpa would grin and** *chortle* **whenever Connie told a joke.** *syn.* chuckle

┌─ **Fact File**
chortle The word *chortle* was coined in the 1800s by Lewis Carroll, the author of *Alice's Adventures in Wonderland* and *Through the Looking Glass*. *Chortle* is probably a combination of the words *chuckle* and *snort*.

cir·cu·lar [sûr′kyə•lər] *adj.* In the shape of a circle: **The wheel turned with a** *circular* **motion.** *syn.* round

cir·cum·stance [sûr′kəm•stans] *n.* **cir·cum·stanc·es** Any fact or event, especially as it relates to a larger event: **The** *circumstances* **of the accident were very unusual.**

clear·ing [klir′ing] *n.* A place where trees and shrubs have been cut away: **The campers pitched their tents in the** *clearing*.

com·pro·mise [käm′prə•mīz′] *v.* To settle a disagreement by having each party give in on certain points: **Sam and Bob agreed to** *compromise* **on how much they would spend.**

conch [känk] *n.* A sea animal of the mollusk family and the shell in which it lives: **We found a large pink** *conch* **during our vacation at the beach.**

conch

a add	e end	o odd	ōō pool	oi oil	t̶h̶ this		*a* in *above*
ā ace	ē equal	ō open	u up	ou pout	zh vision		*e* in *sicken*
â care	i it	ô order	û burn	ng ring		ə =	*i* in *possible*
ä palm	ī ice	o͝o took	yōō fuse	th thin			*o* in *melon*
							u in *circus*

con·fet·ti [kən·fet′ē] *n.* Bits of colorful paper that are thrown during celebrations to make them more festive: **The guests tossed** *confetti* **as the bride and groom passed by.**

> **Fact File**
> **confetti** The first *confetti* was actually small candies, which people would throw during carnivals and other celebrations. Then plaster candies were used. Finally, bits of paper took the place of plaster. The word *confetti* comes from the Italian word *confetto*, which means "candy." The English word *confection* also means "candy."

con·spir·a·cy [kən·spir′ə·sē] *n.* A plan in which a group acts together, often in secret, to do something harmful: **Detectives uncovered a** *conspiracy* **to steal pets.** *syn.* plot

co·or·di·na·tion [kō·ôr′də·nā′shən] *n.* The act of working together smoothly for a purpose: **The movements of the dancer's arms and legs showed graceful** *coordination.*

cor·ri·dor [kôr′ə·dər] *n.* A long passageway or hall: **Our classroom door opens onto the** *corridor.* *syn.* hallway

cou·ra·geous [kə·rā′jəs] *adj.* Brave: **The** *courageous* **firefighter saved a child from the smoky room.** *syn.* fearless

cul·ture [kul′chər] *n.* The customs and way of life of a group of people: **Music, food, and literature are some of the ways a** *culture* **expresses itself.** *syn.* civilization

cur·few [kûr′fyoo] *n.* A time, usually in the evening or at night, after which people must be home or may not gather publicly: **During the emergency, no one was allowed outside after** *curfew.*

de·com·pose [dē′kəm·pōz′] *v.* **de·com·pos·es** To decay: **A pile of fallen leaves** *decomposes* **and becomes part of the soil.** *syn.* rot

de·cor [dā·kôr′] *n.* The way a room is decorated: **The room was done in Early American** *decor.* *syn.* design

de·cree [di·krē′] *v.* **de·creed** To make an official order, such as from a ruler or a government: **The queen** *decreed* **a holiday in honor of her birthday.**

ded·i·ca·tion [ded′ə·kā′shən] *n.* Great loyalty or devotion: **The cellist feels great** *dedication* **to his music, so he practices four hours every day.** *syn.* commitment

des·per·ate·ly [des′pər·ət·lē] *adv.* With great need for help; with almost no hope: **The swimmer held on** *desperately* **to his rescuer.**

de·vice [di·vīs′] *n.* A piece of equipment that was designed to do a certain task: **The telephone is a communication** *device.* *syn.* tool

dis·a·bil·i·ty [dis′ə·bil′ə·tē] *n.* **dis·a·bil·i·ties** A condition, such as an illness or injury, that interferes with normal activity: **The Special Olympics is a sports event for athletes with** *disabilities.* *syn.* handicap

dis·ap·point·ment [dis′ə·point′mənt] *n.* The feeling that something did not meet expectations: **After I had seen the toy again and again in ads, actually owning it was a** *disappointment.* *syn.* letdown

dis·card [dis·kärd′] *v.* **dis·cards** To toss away as something without value: **Valerie** *discards* **the gift wrap after she opens a present, but Kayla saves it.**

dis·pleas·ure [dis·plezh′ər] *n.* The feeling of being annoyed: **The librarian showed his** *displeasure* **when he saw that the book cover was torn.** *syn.* irritation

dis·po·si·tion [dis′pə·zish′ən] *n.* The character of a person; the way an individual usually acts: **He has a pleasant** *disposition.* *syn.* nature

dis·solve [di·zälv′] *v.* To break up into tiny parts and become part of a liquid: *Dissolve* **some sugar into the lemonade so it will taste sweet.** *syn.* melt

doc·u·ment [däk′yə·mənt] *n.* A printed or written record that contains information: **A passport is a** *document* **that allows you to travel from one country to another.**

ear·nest·ly [ûr′nist·lē] *adv.* With honest effort; taking something seriously: **Maya tried** *earnestly* **to improve her grades.** *syn.* sincerely

eaves·drop [ēvz′dräp] *v.* **eaves·drop·ping** To listen secretly to someone else's private conversation: **Shana was** *eavesdropping* **to find out what her birthday present would be.**

> **Word Origins**
> **eavesdrop** *Eavesdrop* is an old term for the water that drips from the eaves, which are the edges of a roof. An eavesdropper may have been a person who would sit under the eaves of a roof in order to listen to someone else's conversation.

en·cour·age [in·kûr′ij] *v.* To give confidence, praise, or emotional support to: **A coach will** *encourage* **players to do their best.** *syn.* inspire

en·dan·gered [in·dān′jərd] *adj.* Being in danger of no longer existing as a species: **The bald eagle is no longer an** *endangered* **species, as its numbers have increased.**

en·rich [in·rich′] *v.* To improve something by increasing its value, importance, or effectiveness: **Marsha will** *enrich* **her vocabulary if she looks up the words she doesn't know.** *syn.* enhance

en·thu·si·as·ti·cal·ly [in·thoo′zē·as′tik·lē] *adv.* In a way that shows intense or eager interest: **The audience clapped** *enthusiastically* **when the conductor walked onstage.** *syn.* spiritedly

e·quiv·a·lent [i·kwiv′ə·lənt] *n.* Having the same meaning or worth: **One hundred pennies is the** *equivalent* **of a dollar.** *syn.* counterpart

ex·am·in·er [ig·zam′ə·nər] *n.* Someone whose job is to give official tests: **The** *examiner* **gave Sarah her driver's test.**

ex·cit·a·ble [ik·sīt′ə·bəl] *adj.* Easily stirred up or provoked: **Paul has an** *excitable* **nature, so break the bad news gently.**

ex·haus·ting [ig·zôs′ting] *adj.* Causing something to be used up or tired out: **The 10-mile hike was** *exhausting***, so we slept well that night.** *syn.* tiring

fa·cial [fā′shəl] *n.* Having to do with the face: **Her** *facial* **features are almost the same as her mother's.**

fa·mine [fam′ən] *n.* A period of time when there is not enough food, such as during a crop failure: **The lack of rain caused many crops to die, which resulted in a** *famine***.** *syn.* hunger

fas·ci·nate [fas′ə·nāt′] *v.* **fas·ci·nat·ed** To interest very much: **The baby was** *fascinated* **by bright colors.** *syns.* captivate, attract

fate·ful [fāt′fəl] *adj.* Leading to an important outcome, often by chance: **Marta's** *fateful* **meeting with the program director led to a career change.**

fer·tile [fûr′təl] *adj.* Able to support growth of plants: **Crops grew well in the** *fertile* **soil.** *syn.* fruitful

fer·til·iz·er [fûr′təl·ī′zər] *n.* Something spread on the soil, such as chemicals, to make it richer and able to produce better crops: **After we added** *fertilizer***, the plants grew better.**

flam·ma·ble [flam′ə·bəl] *adj.* Able to catch on fire: **Tamara made sure there were no** *flammable* **objects near the stove before she turned it on.** *syn.* burnable

flammable

fra·gile [fraj′əl] *adj.* Easily broken or damaged: **Noam handled the tiny,** *fragile* **glass giraffe very carefully.** *syn.* delicate

fran·ti·cal·ly [fran′tik·lē] *adv.* Excitedly, with an intense level of worry: **Lila worked** *frantically* **to finish the test before the end of class.** *syns.* anxiously, desperately

gadg·et [gaj′it] **gadg·ets** *n.* A small instrument or tool: **The** *gadgets* **Sue took camping included a hand-held can opener.**

gadget

gen·er·ous [jen′ər·əs] *adj.* Large, more than enough: **The restaurant gives** *generous* **portions of dessert.** *syn.* plentiful

⌐ Word Origins

generous *Generous* is related to the Latin word *genus*, meaning "origin" or "birth" and refers to people born into the aristocracy. Such people were expected to have a high standard of behavior. Being *generous* was one of the character traits they were expected to display.

a	add	e	end	o	odd	o͞o	pool	oi	oil	th	this
ā	ace	ē	equal	ō	open	u	up	ou	pout	zh	vision
â	care	i	it	ô	order	û	burn	ng	ring		
ä	palm	ī	ice	o͝o	took	yo͞o	fuse	th	thin		

ə = { a in *above* / e in *sicken* / i in *possible* / o in *melon* / u in *circus* }

glum·ly [glum′lē] *adv.* With a gloomy feeling or expression: **The cat gazed *glumly* at its empty bowl.** *syn.* sadly

grudge [gruj] *n.* Long-lasting bitterness or anger that one feels as a result of another's action: **Carlos held a *grudge* against Neil because Neil had never chosen him for the team.** *syn.* resentment

gym·na·si·um [jim·nā′zē·əm] *n.* A large room or building used for indoor sports and for training athletes: **The school received new sports equipment for the *gymnasium*.**

hab·i·tat [hab′ə·tat′] *n.* The place where something or someone lives: **A pond is a *habitat* for many kinds of plants, animals, and insects.** *syn.* environment

har·mo·ny [här′mə·nē] *n.* Two or more musical tones sung or played at the same time as a chord; pleasant musical sounds: **The choir sang in *harmony*.**

haze [hāz] *n.* Air that appears foggy because it contains small particles of dust, water, or pollutants: **This morning you can barely see the skyline through the *haze*.** *syn.* mist

haze

heart·i·ly [härt′əl·ē] *adv.* With much enthusiasm and energy: **The food was delicious and we were hungry, so we ate *heartily*.**

hys·ter·i·cal·ly [his·ter′ik·lē] *adv.* With uncontrolled emotion: **The sad news caused the children to weep *hysterically*.** *syn.* wildly

im·mi·grant [im′ə·grənt] *n.* **im·mi·grants** A person who comes to live in a new country: **In our school are *immigrants* from Spain, Russia, and Haiti.** *syn.* newcomer

im·plore [im·plôr′] *v.* **im·plored** To ask in a pleading way: **Joan *implored* Coach Ames to let her run the race.** *syn.* beg

im·pose [im·pōz′] *v.* To force on someone: **We don't want to *impose* our opinions on you.** *syn.* force

in·dif·fer·ent [in·dif′ə·rənt] *adj.* Showing no interest: **Simon walked calmly, *indifferent* to the activity around him.**

in·hale [in·hāl′] *v.* **in·haled** To take a deep breath in order to smell something: **Madison *inhaled* the fresh morning air.**

in·jus·tice [in·jus′tis] *n.* An unfair act: **It was an *injustice* when the innocent man was punished.**

in·stall [in·stôl′] *v.* **in·stalled** To set something into place, ready for use: **The plumber *installed* a new sink in Mrs. Johnson's kitchen.**

in·stinc·tive·ly [in·stingk′tiv·lē] *adv.* With an action that is automatic and not thought out in advance: **While training, the athlete knew *instinctively* when to run and when to rest.** *syn.* naturally

in·ter·pret·er [in·tûr′prə·tər] *n.* A person whose job it is to translate spoken words from one language to another: **Someone who enjoys learning languages may choose a career as an *interpreter*.** *syn.* translator

in·ves·ti·gate [in·ves′tə·gāt′] *v.* To search out and study the facts in order to find the truth about something: **Joel's doctor had to *investigate* the cause of his rash.** *syn.* examine

ir·ri·ga·tion [ir′ə·gā′shən] *n.* An artificial or man-made way to water the soil so that plants will grow: ***Irrigation* allows farmers to grow crops when there isn't enough rain.**

irrigation

ir·ri·ta·bly [ir′i·tə·blē] *adv.* With annoyance or anger: **The boy answered his friend *irritably* but later was sorry.** *syn.* crossly

jeal·ous [jel′əs] *adj.* Resentful of someone's relationship with another person: **Lloyd was *jealous* of his brother for having so many friends.** *syn.* envious

lav·en·der [lav′ən·dər] *n.* A pale shade of purple: **The sunset colored the sky orange, pink, and *lavender*.** *syn.* orchid

lavender

lei·sure [lē′zhər] *n.* Time free from work or other duties: **Summer vacation is a time of *leisure*.** *syn.* relaxation

> **Word Origins**
>
> **leisure** The word *leisure* comes from an Old French word meaning "something that is permitted, or freedom to do something." Now its meaning has changed to "having free time."

loathe [lōth] *v.* To dislike very much: **On the playing field, the teams act as if they *loathe* each other.** *syn.* despise

lo·cal [lō′kəl] *adj.* Having to do with a certain neighborhood or community: **The *local* newspaper printed a story about the town's oldest resident.**

log·i·cal [läj′i·kəl] *adj.* Naturally expected based on what has already happened: **A good math grade is the *logical* result of studying.** *syn.* reasonable

loy·al·ty [loi′əl·tē] *n.* Faithfulness to a person or thing: **The citizens showed their *loyalty* to the mayor by reelecting her.**

man·age·a·ble [man′ij·ə·bəl] *adj.* Able to be controlled, handled, or directed: **Homework is *manageable* if you don't leave it for the last minute.** *syn.* workable

mes·quite [mes·kēt′] *n.* A thorny tree or shrub common in the southwestern United States and in Mexico: **The ranch was surrounded by *mesquite* bushes.**

> **Fact File:**
>
> **mesquite** *Mesquite* wood has a pleasant aroma that is used to add flavor to barbecued meat. Some commercially made barbecue sauces use it.

mesquite

mod·est [mäd′ist] *adj.* Not showy; proper and quiet in manner: **Pat is *modest* about his art ability, but he is actually very talented.** *syns.* unassuming, humble

mod·i·fy [mäd′ə·fī] *v.* To change slightly: **Since it is raining, we will have to *modify* our plans for the class picnic.** *syn.* alter

mu·ral [myŏŏr′əl] *n.* A large picture painted on a wall: **The artist painted a *mural* in the lobby of the office building.**

mural

mut·ter [mut′ər] *v.* **mut·tered** To speak in an unclear way and in a low voice, usually in anger: **Debbie *muttered* a complaint that her sister did not hear.** *syn.* grumble

a add	e end	o odd	o͞o pool	oi oil	th this	a in *above*
ā ace	ē equal	ō open	u up	ou pout	zh vision	e in *sicken*
â care	i it	ô order	û burn	ng ring		ə = i in *possible*
ä palm	ī ice	o͝o took	yo͞o fuse	th thin		o in *melon*
						u in *circus*

nar·ra·tor [nar′ā·tər] *n.* A person who tells what is going on in a play or performance: **The *narrator* read his lines from the script.** *syn.* announcer

nes·tle [nes′əl] *v.* **nes·tles** To hug or pull close to give affection: **The child *nestles* her puppy in her arms.** *syn.* snuggle

o·blige [ə·blīj′] *v.* **o·bliged** To do a favor for someone: **Sal *obliged* his fans and played another song.**

oc·ca·sion·al·ly [ə·kā′zhən·əl·ē] *adv.* Happening now and then: **Walter *occasionally* plays ball after school, but usually he practices chess.** *syn.* sometimes

off·stage [ôf′stāj′] *adv.* At the part of the stage the audience can't see; behind the curtain or in the wings: **The actor practiced her lines *offstage* before the play started.**

o·ver·whelm [ō′vər·hwelm′] *v.* To overpower: **Don't *overwhelm* a new puppy with too many commands or you will confuse it.** *syn.* overburden

offstage

pad·dock [pad′ək] *n.* A small, fenced field next to a stable, where horses can exercise: **The horse and the pony grazed together in the *paddock*.**

— **Word Origins:**
paddock *Paddock* comes from the Old English word *pearruc*, which means "an enclosed area." *Pearruc* is related to the word *park*.

paddock

pag·eant [paj′ənt] *n.* A performance in honor of an important event or holiday: **Sasha played the part of a general in the town's history *pageant*.** *syn.* show

pas·time [pas′tīm′] *n.* **pas·times** An enjoyable activity one does in one's free time: **Reading and hiking are Raul's favorite *pastimes*.** *syn.* entertainment

per·se·ver·ance [pûr′sə·vir′əns] *n.* Trying to do something no matter what difficulties arise: **Through his *perseverance*, he earned a place on the baseball team.** *syns.* steadfastness, determination

pe·ti·tion·er [pə·tish′ən·ər] *n.* **pe·ti·tion·ers** One who makes a written request of those who are in charge: **The *petitioners* asked the king to lower their taxes.**

pi·o·neer [pī′ə·nir′] *n.* A person who explores and settles new land in a faraway area: **A *pioneer* had to struggle to survive on the frontier.**

— **Fact File**
pioneer The idea of a *pioneer* has come to mean someone who explores the unknown, not only on land. We refer to *pioneers* as leading the way in fields such as science, medicine, and space.

pit·e·ous·ly [pit′ē·əs·lē] *adv.* Causing feelings of sadness: **The puppy howled *piteously* the first night, so Sheila sat up with it.** *syn.* touchingly

plen·ti·ful·ly [plen′ti·fəl·ē] *adv.* With nothing lacking; with more than enough: **The art supplies closet was *plentifully* stocked with brushes, paper, paints, and clay.** *syn.* abundantly

pos·si·bil·i·ty [päs′ə·bil′ə·tē] *n.* **pos·si·bil·i·ties** Something that has a chance of happening: **There are many job *possibilities* for an educated person.** *syn.* likelihood

pros·thet·ic [präs·thet′ik] *adj.* Having to do with a replacement body part, such as a tooth, an eye, or a limb: **With her *prosthetic* hand, Hilda could draw.**

pro·trude [prō·trōōd′] *v.* **pro·trud·ed** To stick out: **The dock *protruded* thirty yards into the water.** *syns.* extend, bulge

ras·cal·ly [ras′kəl·ē] *adj.* With mischief, with dishonesty: **The *rascally* hamster escaped from its cage and hid in the house for two days.** *syn.* impish

ra·tion [rash′ən] *n.* A limited amount; a part of the whole: **Each soldier got a small daily *ration* of food and water.** *syns.* measure, share

rec·og·nize [rek′əg·nīz′] *v.* **rec·og·niz·ing** To know someone or something by details such as appearance or sound: **My dog is capable of** *recognizing* **the sound of my footsteps.** *syn.* identify

re·hears·al [ri·hûr′səl] **re·hears·als** *n.* Preparation and practice before an actual performance: **The actors read their lines during** *rehearsals.* *syn.* drill

re·pent·ant [ri·pent′ənt] *adj.* Showing sorrow and regret for past actions: **Noreen's** *repentant* **letter about the broken window led her neighbor to forgive her.** *syn.* remorseful

re·sound [ri·zound′] *v.* **re·sound·ed** To echo or to fill a place with sound: **The last notes of the symphony** *resounded* **in the hall.**

rest·less [rest′ləs] *adj.* Unable to rest or relax: **The cattle were** *restless* **as they sensed the coming storm.** *syns.* nervous, uneasy

re·tire [ri·tīr′] *v.* To leave a job because one has reached one's goals or has reached an advanced age: **The star athlete's decision to** *retire* **from basketball shocked his fans.** *syn.* withdraw

re·tort [ri·tôrt′] *v.* **re·tort·ed** To answer in an arguing way: **Jane** *retorted* **angrily when I said the mistake was her fault.**

ro·guish [rō′gish] *adj.* Full of mischief; likely to stir up trouble: **The child's** *roguish* **smile led his mother to suspect that he had made the mess.** *syn.* sneaky

rus·tle [rus′əl] *n.* A swishing sound: **The** *rustle* **of leaves in the trees means the wind is getting stronger.** *syn.* whisper

(S)

sal·a·ry [sal′ə·rē] *n.* The amount of money that a person gets for doing a job: **Josh receives his** *salary* **every Friday.** *syn.* pay

—**Fact File**
Salt is necessary for life. Because it keeps food from spoiling, it was considered very valuable in times and places where there was no refrigeration. In ancient Rome, soldiers were paid in salt! The Latin word *salarium* means "salt money" and is the root of the word *salary* that we use today.

schol·ar·ship [skäl′ər·ship] *n.* The quality and character of a serious student: **Ray's high grades showed good** *scholarship.* *syn.* studiousness

scour [skour] *v.* **scoured** To scrub hard with a rough material: **The desert sandstorm sculpted and** *scoured* **the rock formations.** *syn.* scrape

script [skript] *n.* The words of a play, including stage directions: **Each actor got a copy of the** *script.*

scrounge [skrounj] *v.* **scroung·ing** To hunt around for what is needed: **We saw a raccoon** *scrounging* **around in the trash.** *syn.* search

sculp·tor [skəlp′tər] *n.* An artist who carves wood or stone or who shapes clay: **The** *sculptor* **makes drawings before she carves.**

sculptor

skid [skid] *v.* **skid·ded** To slide in an unexpected direction: **The car** *skidded* **on the icy road before it stopped.**

smug·gle [smug′əl] *v.* **smug·gled** To take something secretly: **The diamond was** *smuggled* **out in an empty soda can.** *syn.* sneak

soft·heart·ed [sôft′härt′id] *adj.* Kind; full of mercy: **Paul is so** *softhearted* **that he kept the stray kittens.**

spin·y [spī′nē] *adj.* Covered with thorns or needles: **A porcupine's** *spiny* **quills keep enemies away.** *syn.* sharp

spiny

sports·man·ship [spôrts′mən·ship′] *n.* Conduct, such as fair play, expected of an athlete: **The losing team showed good** *sportsmanship* **by cheering for the winning team.**

spruce [sprōōs] *v.* **spruc·ing** To fix something up: **The scouts are** *sprucing* **up the campsites as part of their community service.**

a	add	e	end	o	odd	ōō	pool	oi	oil	<s>th</s>	this		*a* in *above*
ā	ace	ē	equal	ō	open	u	up	ou	pout	zh	vision		*e* in *sicken*
â	care	i	it	ô	order	û	burn	ng	ring			ə =	*i* in *possible*
ä	palm	ī	ice	ōō	took	yōō	fuse	th	thin				*o* in *melon*
													u in *circus*

stag·ger [stag′ər] *v.* To walk unsteadily: **The wounded bear could only *stagger* forward.**

straight·a·way [strāt′ə•wā′] *adv.* Without delay: **The ambulance came *straightaway*.** *syn.* immediately

strand [strand] *v.* **strand·ed** To leave behind without help: **The tourist was *stranded* when his plane took off without him.** *syn.* abandon

strength·en·ing [streng(k)th′ən•ing] *adj.* Adding more force and growing in power: **The darkening skies and *strengthening* wind meant a storm was on the way.** *syn.* increasing

sulk·i·ly [sulk′ə•lē] *adv.* With a withdrawn, unpleasant attitude: **The small child sat *sulkily* on the rug after her crayons were taken away.** *syn.* gloomily

sur·ren·der [sə•ren′dər] *n.* The act of giving up: **Generals from both sides met to work out the terms of the *surrender*.**

sus·te·nance [sus′ti•nəns] *n.* Something that supports one's basic needs: **Nutritious meals are a form of *sustenance*.** *syn.* food

swel·ter·ing [swel′tər•ing] *adj.* Extremely hot and humid: **The summer days were *sweltering*, and the swimming pool was always crowded.**

sym·pa·thet·i·cal·ly [sim′pə•thet′ik•lē] *adv.* With the same feelings as another person has: **The coach talked *sympathetically* after the player sprained his ankle.** *syn.* understandingly

teem [tēm] *v.* **teem·ing** To be very full: **The rain forest is *teeming* with animals.** *syn.* overflowing

thick·et [thik′ət] *n.* Bushes and trees that grow very close together: **We could not hike through the *thicket*, so we had to go around it.** *syn.* undergrowth

thicket

thrift·y [thrift′ē] *adj.* Careful about saving money, or doing things to make it last longer: **The *thrifty* family found ways to use all the leftovers from meals.**

top·ple [täp′əl] *v.* To make fall over: **Rahaili liked to make a big block pile and then *topple* it with the tiniest push.** *syn.* collapse

trag·e·dy [traj′ə•dē] *n.* A very sad event that brings suffering: **The fire was a *tragedy* for the families who lost their homes.** *syn.* disaster

trans·form [trans•fôrm′] *v.* **trans·formed** To undergo a change, either in appearance or in character: **The schoolyard was *transformed* into fairgrounds for Family Appreciation Day.**

tre·men·dous [tri•men′dəs] *adj.* Very large: **The diver in the shark cage saw only the shark's *tremendous* open mouth.** *syn.* enormous

trick·le [trik′əl] *n.* A thin, slow stream of something, such as water or sand: **A *trickle* of raindrops slid down the windowpane.**

tri·um·phant·ly [trī′um′fənt•lē] *adv.* In a way that indicates success or victory: **We sang *triumphantly* all the way home after winning the championship game.**

trol·ley [tro′lē] *n.* A public transportation vehicle that runs on tracks and is powered by overhead electric cables: **Troy did not like the long bus trip to San Francisco, but he enjoyed the *trolley* ride through the city.** *syn.* streetcar

trolley

trop·i·cal [träp′i•kəl] *adj.* Having to do with the hot area of the earth: **A *tropical* storm can develop into a hurricane.**

> **Fact File**
> **tropical** The area known as the *Tropics* extends from 23.5 degrees north latitude to 23.5 degrees south latitude. Within these boundaries, the sun's rays shine directly on earth. Because the area receives so much direct light, it is warm all year.

tropical

trou·ble·some [trub′əl·səm] *adj.* Causing difficulty and worry: **Carl's odd behavior was *troublesome* to his parents.** *syn.* bothersome

tun·dra [tun′drə] *n.* A flat, treeless region near the Arctic Circle: **Summer in the *tundra* is brief and cool.**

tu·tor [tōō′tər] *v.* To teach privately: **Luis is home with his leg in a cast, so his mother and father *tutor* him every day.** *syn.* instruct

un·doubt·ed·ly [un·dout′id·lē] *adv.* Surely; proven beyond question: **Science was *undoubtedly* her best subject.** *syn.* definitely

un·eas·y [un·ē′zē] *adj.* Nervous or troubled: **Jan was *uneasy* every time she had to go down into the dark basement.** *syn.* worried

un·fa·mil·iar [un′fə·mil′yər] *adj.* Not known: **Your name is *unfamiliar* to me, I recognize your face.** *syn.* strange

un·in·hab·it·ed [un′in·hab′it·id] *adj.* Unoccupied; empty: **The old cottage stood *uninhabited* for years.**

u·ni·ty [yōō′nə·tē] *n.* The feeling of acting as one; togetherness: **The people showed *unity* as they cleaned the park.** *syn.* oneness

va·cant [vā′kənt] *adj.* Empty, having nothing in it: **A new family has rented the *vacant* apartment.**

val·u·a·ble [val′yōō·ə·bəl] *adj.* Having great worth and meaning, either in terms of money or in personal terms: **A good education is a *valuable* tool for reaching one's goals.** *syn.* precious

ven·ti·late [ven′təl·āt′] *v.* To bring fresh air into a place: **In order to *ventilate* the house, open all the windows.** *syn.* freshen

> ### Word Origins
> **ventilate** The word *ventilate* comes from the Latin word *ventus*, meaning "wind." Another related meaning of *ventilate* has to do with "airing" feelings or points of view — discussing things in an open way.

ven·ture [ven′chər] *v.* To risk moving from a safe place: **The mouse sniffs the air before it will *venture* from its nest.**

vic·tim [vik′təm] *n.* A living thing that is harmed: **The mouse was the *victim* that became the snake's lunch.**

wind·break [wind′brāk] *n.* A fence or line of trees that breaks the force of the wind: **The farmer planted a *windbreak* to protect his crops.** *syn.* barrier

wist·ful·ly [wist′fəl·lē] *adv.* With a thoughtful, wishful feeling for something: **Papa sighed *wistfully* as he shared his childhood memories.** *syn.* longingly

a add	e end	o odd	o͞o pool	oi oil	th this	*a in above*
ā ace	ē equal	ō open	u up	ou pout	zh vision	*e in sicken*
â care	i it	ô order	û burn	ng ring		ə = *i in possible*
ä palm	ī ice	o͝o took	yo͞o fuse	th thin		*o in melon*
						u in circus

651

Page numbers in color refer to biographical information.

Printed in the United States of America

Acknowledgments

For permission to reprint copyrighted material, grateful acknowledgment is made to the following sources:

Atheneum Books for Young Readers, an imprint of Simon & Schuster Children's Publishing Division: From *My Name Is María Isabel* by Alma Flor Ada, cover illustration by K. Dyble Thompson. Text copyright © 1993 by Alma Flor Ada; cover illustration copyright © 1993 by K. Dyble Thompson.

Rowan Barnes-Murphy: Cover illustration by Rowan Barnes-Murphy from *Cricket* Magazine, September 1996.

Boyds Mills Press, Inc.: "Geography" and cover illustration from *Baseball, Snakes, and Summer Squash: Poems About Growing Up* by Donald Graves, illustrated by Paul Birling. Text copyright © 1996 by Donald Graves; cover illustration © 1996 by Paul Birling. "My Village" and cover illustration from *The Distant Talking Drum* by Isaac Olaleye, illustrated by Frané Lessac. Text copyright © 1995 by Issac Olaleye; illustrations copyright © 1995 by Frané Lessac.

Candlewick Press Inc., Cambridge, MA: Fly Traps! Plants That Bite Back by Martin Jenkins, illustrated by David Parkins. Text © 1996 by Martin Jenkins; illustrations © 1996 by David Parkins.

Carolrhoda Books, Inc.: Cover illustration by Karen Ritz from *Kate Shelley and the Midnight Express* by Margaret K. Wetterer. Copyright © 1990 by Carolrhoda Books, Inc.

Marshall Cavendish Corp., Tarrytown, NY: From *House, House* by Jane Yolen, photographs by The Howes Brothers and Jason Stemple. Text copyright © 1998 by Jane Yolen; color photographs copyright © 1998 by Jason Stemple.

Charlesbridge Publishing: Cover illustration by Marshall Peck III from *Can We Be Friends? Nature's Partners* by Alexandra Wright. Copyright © 1994 by Charlesbridge Publishing.

Children's Better Health Institute, Indianapolis, IN: "Wings of Hope" by Marianne J. Dyson from *U. S. Kids, a Weekly Reader* Magazine, April/May 1998. Text copyright © 1998 by Children's Better Health Institute, Benjamin Franklin Literary & Medical Society, Inc.

Children's Book Press, San Francisco, CA: In My Family/En mi familia by Carmen Lomas Garza. Copyright © 1996 by Carman Lomas Garza.

Children's Press, Inc.: Saguaro Cactus by Paul and Shirley Berquist. Text copyright © 1997 by Children's Press®, a division of Grolier Publishing Co., Inc.

Cinco Puntos Press: From "In the Days of King Adobe" in *Watch Out for Clever Women!*, folktales told by Joe Hayes, cover illustration by Vicki Trego Hill. Published by Cinco Puntos Press.

The Cousteau Society, Inc.: From "My Visit to a Dreamy Place" in *Dolphin Log* Magazine, January 1998. Text © 1999 by The Cousteau Society, Inc.

Crabtree Publishing Company: Cover photograph by Marc Crabtree from *Celebrating the Powwow* by Bobbie Kalman. Photograph copyright © 1997 by Crabtree Publishing Company.

CRICKET Magazine: From "It's Math-Not Magic" (Retitled: "It's Just Math") by Linda O. George in *CRICKET* Magazine, September 1996. Text © 1996 by Linda Olsen George.

Crown Publishers, Inc.: Cover illustration by Jon Goodell from *A Mouse Called Wolf* by Dick King-Smith. Illustration copyright © 1997 by Jon Goodell.

Dial Books for Young Readers, a division of Penguin Putnam Inc.: "I Love the Look of Words" by Maya Angelou and illustrations by Tom Feelings from *Soul Looks Back in Wonder* by Tom Feelings. Text copyright © 1993 by Maya Angelou; illustrations copyright © 1993 by Tom Feelings.

DK Publishing, Inc.: Cover illustration by Holly Meade from *Boss of the Plains: The Hat That Won the West* by Laurie Carlson. Illustration copyright © 1998 by Holly Meade.

Dramatic Publishing: From *Charlotte's Web*, dramatized by Joseph Robinette, adapted from the book by E. B. White. Text copyright MCMLXXXIII by Joseph Robinette. The play printed in this anthology is not to be used as an acting script. All inquiries regarding performance rights should be addressed to Dramatic Publishing, 311 Washington Street, Woodstock, IL 60098. Phone: (815) 338-7170, fax: (815) 338-8981.

Barbara Emmons: Illustrations by Barbara Emmons from "It's Math-Not Magic" (Retitled: "It's Just Math") by Linda O. George in *CRICKET* Magazine, September 1996.

Farrar, Straus & Giroux, Inc.: Cover illustration by Garth Williams from *Chester Cricket's Pigeon Ride* by George Selden. Illustration copyright © 1981 by Garth Williams. "Chester" and "Harry Cat" from *The Cricket in Times Square* by George Selden, illustrated by Garth Williams. Copyright © 1960 by George Selden Thompson and Garth Williams; copyright renewed © 1988 by George Selden Thompson. *The Gardener* by Sarah Stewart, illustrated by David Small. Text copyright © 1997 by Sarah Stewart; illustrations copyright © 1997 by David Small.

Susan Goodman: From "Amazon Adventure" by Susan Goodman in *Ranger Rick* Magazine, October 1994. Published by the National Wildlife Federation.

Hampton-Brown Books: Cover illustration by Raphaelle Goethais from *A Chorus of Cultures: Developing Literacy Through Multicultural Poetry* by Alma Flor Ada, Violet J. Harris, and Lee Bennett Hopkins. Illustration copyright © 1993 by Hampton-Brown Books.

Harcourt, Inc.: Lou Gehrig, The Luckiest Man by David A. Adler, illustrated by Terry Widener. Text copyright © 1997 by David A. Adler; illustrations copyright © 1997 by Terry Widener. Cover illustration by Will Hillenbrand from *Andy and Tamika* by David A. Adler. Illustration copyright © 1999 by Will Hillenbrand. "Saguaro" from *Cactus Poems* by Frank Asch, photographs by Ted Levin. Text copyright © 1998 by Frank Asch; photographs copyright © 1998 by Ted Levin. Cover illustration from *Flute's Journey: The Life of a Wood Thrush* by Lynne Cherry. Copyright © 1997 by Lynne Cherry. Text and illustration from "Berries and Birds" by Lynne Cherry and cover illustration by Greg Shed from *Down to Earth*, compiled by Michael J. Rosen. Text and illustration copyright © 1998 by Lynne Cherry; cover illustration copyright © 1998 by Greg Shed; compilation copyright © 1998 by Michael J. Rosen. Cover illustration from *Insectlopedia* by Douglas Florian. Copyright © 1998 by Douglas Florian. Cover illustration by Ellen Beier from *The Blue Hill Meadows* by Cynthia Rylant. Illustration copyright © 1997 by Ellen Beier. *The Garden Of Happiness* by Erika Tamar, illustrated by Barbara Lambase. Text copyright © 1996 by Erika Tamar; illustrations copyright © 1996 by Barbara Lambase.

HarperCollins Publishers: Cover illustration by David Diaz from *Going Home* by Eve Bunting. Illustration copyright © 1996 by David Diaz. From *Donovan's Word Jar* by Monalisa DeGross, cover illustration by Michael Hayes. Text copyright © 1994 by Monalisa DeGross; cover illustration © 1998 by Michael Hayes. *Look to the North: A Wolf Pup Diary* by Jean Craighead George, illustrated by Lucia Washburn. Text copyright © 1997 by Julie Productions, Inc.; illustrations copyright © 1997 by Lucia Washburn. "The Hen and the Apple Tree" from *Fables* by Arnold Lobel. Copyright © 1980 by Arnold Lobel. From *Sarah, Plain & Tall* by Patricia MacLachlan, cover illustration by Marcia Sewall. Text copyright © 1985 by Patricia MacLachlan; cover illustration copyright © 1985 by Marcia Sewall. Cover illustration by Marcia Sewall from *Skylark* by Patricia MacLachlan. Illustration copyright © 1994 by Marcia Sewall. From *Stealing Home* by Mary Stolz, cover illustration by Pat Cummings. Text copyright © 1992 by Mary Stolz; cover illustration copyright © 1992 by Pat Cummings. *I Have Heard of a Land* by Joyce Carol Thomas, illustrated by Floyd Cooper. Text copyright © 1998 by Joyce Carol Thomas; illustrations copyright © 1998 by Floyd Cooper. From *Charlotte's Web* by E. B. White, illustrated by Garth Williams. Copyright 1952 by E. B. White; text copyright renewed © 1980 by E. B. White; illustrations copyright renewed © 1980 by Garth Williams. From *On the Banks of Plum Creek* by Laura Ingalls Wilder, illustrated by Garth Williams. Text copyright 1937 by Laura Ingalls Wilder, renewed © 1965 by Roger Lea MacBride; illustrations copyright 1953 by Garth Williams, renewed © 1981 by Garth Williams.

Houghton Mifflin Company: Nights of the Pufflings by Bruce McMillan. Copyright © 1995 by Bruce McMillan.

Hyperion Books for Children: Cover illustration by Floyd Cooper from *Granddaddy's Street Songs* by Monalisa DeGross.Illustration copyright © 1999 by Floyd Cooper.

Laredo Publishing Company Inc.: Cover illustration by Kerry Townsend Smith from *Lucita Comes Home to Oaxaca/Regresa a Oaxaca* by Robin B. Cano, translated by Rafael E. Ricárdez. Copyright © 1998 by Robin B. Cano and Rafael E. Ricárdez.

Lee & Low Books Inc., 95 Madison Avenue, New York, NY 10016: Cover illustration by René King Moreno from *Under the Lemon Moon* by Edith Hope Fine. Illustration copyright © 1999 by René King Moreno.

Lerner Publications Company: From *The Kids' Invention Book* by Arlene Erlbach. Copyright © 1997 by Arlene Erlbach.

William Morrow & Company, Inc.: A Very Important Day by Maggie Rugg Herold, illustrated by Catherine Stock. Text copyright © 1995 by Maggie Rugg Herold; illustrations copyright © 1995 by Catherine Stock. From *The Down & Up Fall* by Johanna Hurwitz, cover illustration by Gail Owens. Text copyright © 1996 by Johanna Hurwitz; cover illustration © 1996 by Gail Owens. Cover illustration by Eric Velasquez from *Baseball Fever* by Johanna Hurwitz. Illustration copyright © 1991 by Eric Velasquez. Cover illustration by Jerry Pinkney from *Rikki-Tikki-Tavi* by Rudyard Kipling, adapted by Jerry Pinkney. Illustration copyright © 1997 by Jerry Pinkney. Cover illustration from *Fair!* by Ted Lewin. Copyright © 1997 by Ted Lewin. Cover illustration by Gail Owens from *Encyclopedia Brown and the Case of the Disgusting Sneakers* by Donald J. Sobol. Illustration copyright © 1990 by Gail Owens.

Northland Publishing Company: Cover illustration by Jeanne Arnold from *Carlos and the Skunk/Carlos y el zorrillo* by Jan Romero Stevens. Illustration copyright © 1997 by Jeanne Arnold.

Orchard Books, New York: Cover illustration by Kyrsten Brooker from *Nothing Ever Happens on 90th Street* by Roni Schotter. Illustration copyright © 1997 by Kyrsten Brooker.

Suni Paz: "The Candles of Hanukkah" by Suni Paz. Copyright © 1990 by Suni Paz (ASCAP).

Philomel Books, a division of Penguin Putnam Inc.: "Moon of Falling Leaves" and cover illustration by Thomas Locker from *Thirteen Moons on Turtle's Back* by Joseph Bruchac and Jonathan London. Text copyright © 1992 by Joseph Bruchac and Jonathan London; cover illustration copyright © 1992 by Thomas Locker. "The First Day"("The Seven Children") and cover illustration by Floyd Cooper from *It's Kwanzaa Time!* by Linda and Clay Goss. Text copyright © 1994, 1995 by Linda and Clay Goss; cover illustration © 1995 by Floyd Cooper.

Plays, Inc.: Red Writing Hood by Jane Tesh from *Plays: The Drama Magazine for Young People*, November 1997. Text copyright © 1997 by Plays, Inc. This play is for reading purposes only; for permission to produce, write to Plays, Inc., 120 Boylston St., Boston, MA 02116.

Puffin Books, a division of Penguin Putnam Inc.: Cover illustration by Robert Barrett from *Blue Willow* by Doris Gates. Illustration copyright © 1990 by Robert Barrett.

Random House Children's Books, a division of Random House, Inc.: "Paul Bunyan and Babe the Blue Ox" from *Larger Than Life: The Adventures of American Legendary Heroes* by Robert D. San Souci, illustrated by Andrew Glass. Text copyright © 1991 by Robert D. San Souci; illustrations copyright © 1991 by Andrew Glass. From *Encyclopedia Brown and the Case of Pablo's Nose* by Donald J. Sobol, cover illustration by Eric Velasquez. Text copyright © 1996 by Donald J. Sobol; cover illustration © 1996 by Eric Velasquez.

Scholastic Inc.: Cover illustration from *The Greatest Treasure* by Demi. Copyright © 1998 by Demi. Published by Scholastic Press, a division of Scholastic Inc. *One Grain of Rice: A Mathematical Folktale* by Demi. Copyright © 1997 by Demi. Published by Scholastic Press, a division of Scholastic Inc. Cover illustration by Ted Rand from *My Father's Boat* by Sherry Garland. Illustration copyright © 1998 by Ted Rand. Published by Scholastic Press, a division of Scholastic Inc. Cover illustration by Jody Wheeler from *Wild Weather: Blizzards!* by Lorraine Jean Hopping. Illustration copyright © 1998 by Jody Wheeler. *A Hello Reader!* Book published by Cartwheel Books, a division of Scholastic Inc. Hello Reader! and Cartwheel Books are registered trademarks of Scholastic Inc. From *Fire!* by Joy Masoff, principal photography by Jack Resnicki and Barry D. Smith. Copyright © 1998 by Joy Masoff. "Horned Lizard" from *This Big Sky* by Pat Mora, illustrated by Steve Jenkins. Text copyright © 1998 by Pat Mora; illustrations copyright © 1998 by Steve Jenkins. Published by Scholastic Press, a division of Scholastic Inc.

Simon & Schuster Books for Young Readers, an imprint of Simon & Schuster Children's Publishing Division: Cover illustration by Floyd Cooper from *Pulling the Lion's Tail* by Jane Kurtz. Illustration copyright © 1995 by Floyd Cooper. Cover illustration by E. B. Lewis from *Fire on the Mountain* by Jane Kurtz. Illustration copyright © 1994 by E. B. Lewis. From *Searching for Laura Ingalls: A Reader's Journey* by Kathryn Lasky and Meribah Knight, photographs by Christopher G. Knight. Text copyright © 1993 by Kathryn Lasky and Meribah Knight; photographs copyright © 1993 by Christopher G. Knight.

University Press of New England: "If flowers want to grow" (originally titled: "The City") from *Poems 1934-1969* by David Ignatow. Text © 1970 by David Ignatow, Wesleyan University Press.

Viking Penguin, a division of Penguin Putnam Inc.: From *Blue Willow* by Doris Gates. Text copyright 1940 by Doris Gates, renewed © 1968 by Doris Gates.

Walker and Company, 435 Hudson Street, New York, NY 10014: From *How to Babysit an Orangutan* by Tara Darling and Kathy Darling. Copyright © 1996 by Tara Darling and Kathy Darling. Cover photograph by William Muñoz from *Homesteading: Settling America's Heartland* by Dorothy Hinshaw Patent. Photograph copyright © 1998 by William Muñoz. From *Two Lands, One Heart: An American Boy's Journey to His Mother's Vietnam* by Jeremy Schmidt and Ted Wood. Text copyright © 1995 by Jeremy Schmidt and Ted Wood; photographs copyright © 1995 by Ted Wood.

Zheng Xu: "Grandfather Is a Chinese Pine" by Zheng Xu.

Every effort has been made to locate the copyright holders for the selections in this work. The publisher would be pleased to receive information that would allow the correction of any omissions in future printings.

Photo Credits

Key: (t), top; (b), bottom; (c), center; (l), left; (r), right

44, 45, Jim Riegel; 90, Dale Higgins; 110-111(background), Superstock; 110-111(all), courtesy, Justin Meyer/Challenge Air; 114, 116, 122, 125, Laura Ingalls Wilder Home Association; 149(l), KD Lawson/Black Star; 149(r), Sal DiMarco/Black Star; 165, Todd Bigelow/Black Star; 170-179, Bruce McMillan; 180, Benner McGee; 182-183, Bruce McMIllan; 212-229, Tara & Kathy Darling; 271, courtesy, Mary Stolz; 293, courtesy, Farrar Strauss & Giroux; 320-321, Ellis Nature Photography; 322-332, Paul Berquist; 333(t), Paul Berquist; 333(b), Ellis Nature Photography; 334(all), Paul Berquist; 336-337 (all), Ted Levin; 346-349, Photographs from the Kids Invention Book. ® 1998 by Lerner Publications. Used by permission of the publisher. All rights reserved.; 350, courtesy, Josh Parsons; 352-353, Photodisc; 353, courtesy, Reeba Daniel; 354, 355, courtesy, Larry Villella; 356-360, Photographs from the Kids Invention Book. ® 1998 by Lerner Publications. Used by permission of the publisher. All rights reserved.; 361, Larry Evans/Black Star; 362-363, Photographs from the Kids Invention Book. ® 1998 by Lerner Publications. Used by permission of the publisher. All rights reserved.; 448, Jason Semple; 449, The Howes Brothers; 468(l), (r), Lisa Quinones/Black Star; 520-521, Dale Higgins; 538(t) Ellis Nature Photograph; 538-539, Paul Berquist; 572, Dale Higgins; 594-595, Ted Wood; 613(t), David Levensen/Black Star; 613(b), courtesy, Walker Books; 614 (t), Sam Fried/Photo Researchers; 614 (b), Patti Murray/Animals Animals; 632, Minden Pictures; 632(inset), Jim Cronk; 633, Jim Cronk; 634(l), Gail Shumway; 634 (r), Jim Cronk; 635, Brian Kenney.

Illustration Credits

Guy Porfirio, Cover Art; Margaret Kasahara, 4-5, 18-21, 132-133; Fabian Negrin, 6-7, 134-137, 230-231; Mary GrandPré, 8-9, 232-235, 340-341; Gerard Dubois, 10-11, 342-345, 430-431; Margaret Chodos-Irvine, 12-13, 432-435, 526-527; Frank Ybarra, 14-15, 528-531, 638-639; Ethan Long, 16-17, 150-151, 364-365, 558-559; Mary Lynn Blasutta, 48-49; Antonio Cangemi, 50-69, 72-73; Jose Ortega, 74-93; Cathy Bennett, 94-95, 252-253; Tom Leonard, 96-109, 112-113; Nancy Freeman, 114-125, 130-131; Alexandra Wallner, 126-129; Greg Tucker, 138-149; Erika LeBarre, 167; John Hovell, 180-181; Stephen Schudlich, 184-185, 390-391, 452-453; Tom Saecker, 186-203, 210-211; Craig Spearing, 236-251; Cedric Lucas, 254-271, 274-275; Kunio Hagio, 272-273; Laura Coyle, 296-297; Steve Johnson and Lou Fancher, 316-317; Matthew Archambault, 366-373, 376-377; Gerardo Suzan, 378-389; Bethann Thornburgh, 392-405; Kelly Kennedy, 490-491; Robert Crawford, 492-505, 508-509; Jane Dill, 506-507; Stéphan Daigle, 522-523; Joe Cepeda, 574-575; Tom Leonard, 581, 592-593, 615; Map Quest.com/Laura Hartwig, 596-597; Jenny Tylden-Wright, 618-631, 636-637; Bradley Clark, 632-635.